ETHICAL ISSUES FOR A NEW MILLENNIUM

The Wayne Leys Memorial Lectures

Also of interest

Ethical Issues in Contemporary Society
Edited by John Howie and George Schedler

Ethical Principles for Social Policy
Edited by John Howie

Ethical Principles and Practice
Edited by John Howie

Ethical Issues for a New Millennium

Edited by John Howie

Southern Illinois University Press
Carbondale and Edwardsville

Publication partially funded by a subvention grant from the
Department of Philosophy, Southern Illinois University Carbondale.

Library of Congress Cataloging-in-Publication Data
Ethical issues for a new millennium / edited by John Howie.
p. cm. — (The Wayne Leys memorial lectures)
Includes bibliographical references and index.
1. Ethical problems. I. Howie, John. II. Series.
BJ1031 .E825 2002
170—dc21
                                                2001049882
ISBN 0-8093-2442-3 (cloth : alk. paper)

Printed on recycled paper. ♻

The paper used in this publication meets the minimum requirements of American
National Standard for Information Sciences—Permanence of Paper for Printed Library
Materials, ANSI Z39.48-1992. ⊚

For Mark, Philip, and Stephen

Contents

Contributors

Beth J. Singer is a professor emerita at Brooklyn College. She is the author of *Pragmatism, Rights, and Democracy* (1999), *Operative Rights* (1993), *Ordinal Naturalism: An Introduction to the Philosophy of Justus Buchler* (1983), and *The Rational Society: A Critical Study of Santayana's Social Thought* (1970); and the coeditor of *Antifoundationalism, Old and New* (1992). A member of Phi Beta Kappa, she served as president of the Society for the Advancement of American Philosophy (1986–1988) and received its Herbert W. Schneider Award for outstanding contributions to the field.

Nancy Fraser is the Henry A. and Louise Loeb Professor of Politics and Philosophy in the Graduate School of the New School of Social Research and the coeditor of the journal *Constellations*. She is the author of *Justice Interruptus: Critical Reflections on the 'Postsocialist' Condition* (1997) and *Unruly Practices: Power, Discourse, and Gender in Contemporary Social Theory* (1989); the coauthor of *Feminist Contentions: A Philosophical Exchange* (1994); and the coeditor of *Revaluing French Feminism: Critical Essays on Difference, Agency, and Culture* (1992).

Mary B. Mahowald is a professor in the Pritzker School of Medicine at the University of Chicago. She is the author of *Genes, Women, Equality* (2000), *Women and Children in Health Care: An Unequal Majority* (1996), and *An Idealistic Pragmatism* (1972); the coauthor of *Disability, Difference, Discrimination: Perspectives on Justice in Bioethics and Public Policy* (1998); the editor of *Philosophy of Women: Classical to Current Concepts* (3d ed., 1994); and the coeditor of *Genetics in the Clinic: Ethical and Social Implications for Primary Care* (2001).

Max Oelschlaeger is the Frances B. McAllister Chair in Community, Culture, and Environment at Northern Arizona University (Flagstaff). He is the author of *Postmodern Environmental Ethics* (1995), *Caring for Creation* (1994), and *The Idea of Wilderness* (1991), which was nominated for the Pulitzer Prize; and the coauthor of *Texas Land Ethics* (1997). Among his recent honors are the William C. Everhart Award for Conservation from Clemson University and the Outstanding Alumni Award from Southern Illinois University.

Richard M. Zaner is the Ann Geddes Stahlman Professor of Medical Ethics, a professor of philosophy in the Department of Medicine, a professor of ethics in the Divinity School, and the director of the Center for Clinical and Research Ethics at Vanderbilt University. He is the author of *Troubled Voices: Stories of Ethics and Illness* (1994), *Ethics and the Clinical Encounter* (1988), *The Context of Self: A Phenomenological Inquiry Using Medicine as a Clue* (1981), *The Problem of Embodiment: Some Contributions to a Phenomenology of the Body* (2d ed., 1971), and *The Way of Phenomenology* (1970). He has edited numerous other books and published many articles in professional journals and interdisciplinary studies.

Carl B. Becker is a professor of philosophy at Kyoto University in Japan. He is the author of *Breaking the Circle: Death and the Afterlife in Buddhism* (1993) and *Paranormal Experience and the Survival of Death* (1993); the editor of *Asian and Jungian Views of Ethics* (1999); and the translator of Eiji Uehiro's *Practical Ethics for Our Time* (1998). His other books on death and terminal care are published in Japanese and Chinese. In Japan, he has also served as a Fulbright lecturer at Osaka University and as a visiting professor of religions at Tsukuba University.

Leonard Harris served as director of African-American Studies at Purdue University. His numerous publications reflect his central interest in social justice. Among these are *Racism* (1999), *A Justification of Revolutionary Violence* (1970), *Children in Chaos: A "Philosophy for Children's Experience"* (with Thomas Harper and Matthew Lipman, 1991), *Philosophy Born of Struggle: An Anthology of Afro-American Philosophy from 1917* (2000), *Exploitation and Exclusion: The Question of Race and Modern Capitalism* (with Julia Maxted and Abebe Zegeye, 1991), and *The Philosophy of Alain Locke: Harlem Renaissance and Beyond* (with Alain LeRoy Locke, 1989). He is also an editor of the newsletter "Philosophy and the Black Experience" and a frequent contributor to philosophical journals.

Acknowledgments

It is indeed a pleasure to thank many persons who have assisted me and encouraged me, in difficult times, to collect and edit this group of Leys Lectures.

The Wayne Leys Memorial Lecture Fund, under the management of the Southern Illinois University Foundation, with the help of the philosophy department, makes possible these lectures by outstanding philosophers. This is the fourth group of such lectures. They focus on the relation of ethical issues to contemporary and future social relations and environmental concerns. To the extent that these philosophers invite further reflection upon their chosen themes and prompt action from their readers, they provide a living memorial to our former colleague and friend, Wayne A. R. Leys.

Heartfelt thanks go to Stephen Bagwell, an outstanding student in our graduate philosophy program. In spite of illness, he managed to bring the text into a format suitable for publication. Thanks are also due Loretta Koch, who enabled me to understand and to bring into order an especially troublesome batch of footnotes and references. To Kenneth Stikkers, chair of the philosophy department at Southern Illinois University, I must say that his encouragement came at a crucial moment in the project.

Introduction

The new millennium brings in its wake a new and more complex array of ethical issues for philosophers to ponder. These include ever-present conceptual problems underlying human rights, genetic equality, and genetic equity, a host of unforeseen issues almost literally sprouting from advances in genetics and newly formulated conceptions of death and its relevance to medical technology. Many of these are born of the biological revolution and the new possibilities of choice grounded in the expanding medical knowledge. But there are still wise ethicists who yet require from us an individual accounting for the choices we make lest we erode the moral sensitivity we have struggled to enliven. Still others whose prophetic voices cannot be overlooked insist upon the human right to rebel against governments or societies that would crush such a right or seek to deny its importance as a key to the self-governance indispensable for the moral character of humankind.

For Beth J. Singer, to have a right means to have an "operative right" for which there is a correlative obligation of respect within the community. Operative rights are not limited to what the law will allow. Singer applies her operative rights to three current and continuing issues: abortion, hate speech, and language rights. *Roe v Wade* assures women of their constitutional right to abortion. But this constitutional right cannot be called an operative right, because too few physicians are adequately trained to perform abortions, and because antiabortion activist groups have fostered believable threats to doctors who perform abortions, to abortion clinic workers, and even to those who seek the services of such physicians and clinics. Singer asks: Can citizens have a right that they are afraid to exercise? The religious objection to abortion, widely proclaimed and likely to gain new life in the years ahead, is unconvincing in two regards. It is based on an effort to make the religious view prevail while at the same time denying the constitutional right of religious freedom to one's opponents; and its criticism of the constitutional right is misplaced, because the laws in the United States only allow a woman to make her own decision and do not legally require her to abort. Doubtless, the lively discussion of the right to abortion as a right of personal autonomy will continue in the ensuing years. If the right of personal autonomy is taken seriously, then controversies such as those concerning abortion can be handled with mutual respect and careful discussion without overt conflict or violence. Such an approach would not leave the outcome to sheer political power.

Nancy Fraser underscores the collapse of the "old gender order" and the correlative nuclear family in our postindustrial age. This order required the male to work for wages to support financially the wife and children, with the wife providing "free" domestic service and the featured father as the moneymaker for the entire nuclear family. The postindustrial society must meet the needs of women and children as well as the interests of gays and lesbians who often exemplify new familial arrangements. Gender equity, for Fraser, is the standard or norm to which any adequate view of a postindustrial welfare state must comply. Neither the "Universal Breadwinner model" nor the "Caregiver Parity model" completely fulfills the seven requirements of gender equity she outlines. Notable among these requirements are the dismantling of the gender division of labor, the elimination of poverty, exploitation, and unequal pay, and the end of androcentrism as the social norm. Her postindustrial thought experiment results in an acceptance of the welfare state that provides most completely for gender equity by most nearly complying with the seven "norms" of such a society.

Mary B. Mahowald argues that while equity entails equal value or the same value, it does not require that two things be the same. Unequal capabilities of individuals and groups to achieve their goals arise from different characteristics of human beings, including sex but also socioeconomic status and physical ability as well. To eliminate or reduce inequalities requires that we give attention to different capabilities, their advantages, and their disadvantages. While class differences in the access to genetic services, for example, may be traced in part to differences in "purchasing power," other differences may arise simply because poor people tend to be less aware of the benefits that might accrue to them from having certain medical tests, or because they are not able to reschedule their work so as to keep doctors' appointments. Matters so basic as these may introduce or increase class-based inequality. To avoid unjust distribution, one must (by law, if possible) allocate genetic services on the basis of needs, burdens, and benefits procured through them. What "egalitarian" perspective is rationally defensible? Mahowald seeks to answer this question. She notes that the feminist perspective includes all marginalized or nondominant groups whether by ability, gender, race, or class. Such individuals or groups must participate efficaciously in the democratic process and in all decision making to avoid nearsightedness and arrogance.

Max Oelschlaeger cautions that we have too long ignored the obvious indices of the ecocrisis: the loss of species, the thinning of atmospheric ozone, the accelerated growth of human population, the destruction of rain forests, and the increase in carbon dioxide levels. A wiser approach would be a reconstructive and linguistic or postmodern perspective. It would avoid a "commodity fetishism" and a "greedy pig" approach. Language is necessarily the means of adaptation or the way to plan for a "sustainable universe," because it is only through language that the fissure between nature and culture can be healed. What is needed is the creation of a sustainable culture that is ecologically healthy, socially just, and economically sufficient. This is tantamount to a closing of the gap between mainstream philosophy and environmental ethics.

Richard M. Zaner underscores the impact of the new genetic knowledge upon our self-understanding. Have we really unraveled, mapped, and sequenced the essential human structure? And what would it mean if we have done so? Has the Human Genome Initiative actually achieved its aim? While offering words of caution, Zaner does at the same time raise difficult questions. Isn't it "odd," he observes, that what makes me, me is at the same time what makes you, you? And yet, it is this same unique structure that is constitutive of each human being? Is it the same I who asserts "I am my genes" that asks "am I my genes"? An optimistic view argues that only minor changes need to be made in our usual conceptions of moral principles. Such changes are surely minimal if the horror of Tay-Sachs, Alzheimer's, and Huntington's chorea can be avoided. Others, far more critically, insist that nothing less than a restatement of basic moral foundations will be required. If we take the new genetics seriously, the changes required will run far deeper. Taking a more balanced viewpoint, Zaner asks us not to allow the new genetics to distract us from the more basic and urgent tasks found in the darker corners: poverty, inadequate nutrition, poor health care, and mounting homelessness.

Carl B. Becker considers, in his essay, two overarching problems: In view of the technical advances in medicine and the obsolete character of the traditional view of death, when ought medical treatment to be terminated, and when is organ donation appropriate? In trying to answer these questions intelligently, we have to bear in mind that the notion of "brain death" assumes (it does not prove) that without brain processes one cannot experience anything. He cautions that this is a matter of "faith," not medical fact. Is it true, Becker asks, that there is convincing scientific evidence that when a patient is "brain dead," he or she can no longer feel or experience anything? Becker invites his readers to question this claim and to assess critically its most obvious immoral outcome: We treat our dead or near-dead entirely in terms of utility and capitalism. Brain-death laws were not enacted in Japan until 1997. Even after these laws were passed, two patients with the same medical condition could be treated differently provided only that the "dead" patient had an uncontested donor card. Economic forces (e.g., the profits made possible to hospitals and organ transplant surgeons) have decisive sway in these matters. But circumstances are worse still in China, which has no brain-death laws, no infrastructure for the minimal practice of justice, and a high demand for organs to transplant.

Leonard Harris insists that an insurrectionist ethics requires from its devotee that she or he has a basic moral duty to represent, defend, or promote the right of the slave to rebel. To fail to do so is to neglect one's basic moral duty. By failing to pass this crucial test, pragmatism discloses itself to be gravely defective. A comparison of the ethical perspectives of model insurrectionists and of pragmatists during their classical and formative years shows that pragmatism lacks the moral fiber to oppose authority and violate community assent in order to create a new, slaveless society and one that honors the inherent moral right to rebel.

John Howie

Ethical Issues for a New Millennium

1

Human Rights: Some Current Issues

Beth J. Singer

In this paper, I will be talking about both legal, or "civil," rights and what we call "human," or "moral," rights, which can be respected without being established by law. However, when I speak of *rights,* I am not using this term in any of the most commonly accepted senses; so before embarking on a discussion of issues involving them, I shall have to explain what I take to be the nature and the ground of rights, and why I do so.

WHAT DOES IT MEAN TO HAVE A RIGHT?

It has long been assumed that we have rights that are either God-given or inherent in human nature—so-called natural rights. We often hear someone exclaim "But I have a right (to X, Y, or Z)!" when—and in many cases, specifically because—that right is not recognized or respected. In the pragmatist sense, a claim to have a right under these circumstances could only mean "I *ought to* have a right!"

What does it mean, then, to have what the philosopher Alan Gewirth would call an "effective" right?[1] To me, it means that the right in question is among the social norms of a human community, the principles that govern people's behavior. That is, effective rights, which for me are the only rights, are operative social institutions;

1

they only exist in communities or societies in which it is understood
that they ought to be respected. Thus my own name for them is
operative rights.[2] The communities in which they are operative need
not be geographic ones; by a *community,* I mean any collectivity of
individuals who share a common set of social norms, that is, who
have what the American pragmatist George Herbert Mead called
"the attitude of a generalized other." These individuals need not
know one another; there are what I call "extended communities"
of people among whom particular norms are operative, notably the
extended community of all those who respect and claim to have
rights. But to say that only operative rights exist must not be taken
to mean that those rights are the only ones that ought to do so. I
have argued—and will argue here—that certain rights ought to be
established and be operative in all communities. I have also argued
that groups or communities as well as individuals can and should
have rights, a principle that is applicable to one of the issues I shall
discuss, which has to do with linguistic minorities.

Having classified rights as social norms or institutions, I still have
not explained their content. Rights are often thought of as entitlements, but not every entitlement is a right. Someone may be entitled
to praise for a job well done, but I don't believe anybody would
argue that there is a right to that praise. I take the concept of a right
as an entitlement to be appropriate, but that is only half the story.
To be a right, an entitlement must be accompanied by the obligation to respect it and to actively express this respect whenever this
is appropriate and possible. As an institution, the right comprises
the entitlement together with the correlative obligation of respect:
The two are inseparable and definitive of one another. For convenience's sake, however, the entitlement can be referred to as a right,
as it is in ordinary language, and I shall speak of it as such.

But there is another qualification: For an entitlement to be a right
rather than merely a prerogative, it cannot be what Will Kymlicka
calls a "special" or "group-differentiated right," granted to some
members of the community but denied to others.[3] A given right may
not be exercisable by all individuals or under all circumstances—
for example, once we have grown up, we can no longer claim a right
to parental care. But where there is a right, it is in principle appli-

cable to all. So-called women's rights, for instance, would only be rights if they gave men in the same situation or condition the same entitlements. This is very different from an entitlement that is limited to specified individuals or groups, as was the "right" to vote at one time in the United States.

Finally, given this analysis of rights as social norms or institutions, it should be apparent that rights can be operative in a community without being written into its laws. When someone cuts ahead of a group of people waiting in line at the bank, for instance, it is appropriate to think, or even say, "she (or he) has no right to do that." According to the norms of our society, those in line have a right to their places, even if it is only an informal right. At the same time, rights can be made law and yet not be operative or be imperfectly so. A conspicuous example of this is provided by the antiabortion movement, which persists in spite of the fact that the decision of the US Supreme Court in the case of *Roe v Wade* affirmed a constitutional right to elective abortions.

In what follows, I shall discuss three topics that involve issues concerning rights and that are currently matters of dispute or active conflict: abortion, so-called hate speech, and what are referred to as language rights. Rather than explicitly arguing for a particular position, I intend to discuss and criticize some of the ways each of these issues has been treated, identify key assumptions on which they rest, and point out some of the implications of these assumptions. Then I shall try to show how each issue would be approached in terms of the concept of rights I have just outlined. In the process, I expect to develop my own view somewhat further. My hope is that the framework I suggest will point the way to a constructive solution of the problems involved.

THE DISPUTE CONCERNING ABORTION

Although the decision in *Roe v Wade* recognized a constitutional right to abortion, it is a right that is increasingly difficult to exercise. The Court had held that "the right to privacy" (defined by Justice Harry Blackmun in connection with another case as "the right to be left alone"), "founded in the Fourteenth Amendment's concept of personal liberty and restrictions upon state action, . . . is broad enough to encompass a woman's decision whether or not to terminate her pregnancy."[4] The difficulty in exercising this right is partly a consequence of the fact that fewer and fewer physicians have had the necessary training. A 1991 survey showed that first-trimester abortion techniques were routinely taught in only 12 percent of American residency programs in obstetrics and gynecology, with about 56 percent offering this training as an elective but not requiring it, and 27 percent providing no such training at all. In 1996, the Accreditation Council for Graduate Medical Education began to require obstetrics and gynecology residency programs to include both family planning and abortion training for their students, but it is too soon to judge the impact of this decision on the availability of abortion.[5] Moreover, a nationwide study of programs in family practice showed that only 12 percent offered abortion training. The net result is that, as of 1992, only 16 percent of all US counties had an abortion provider, a decline of 31 percent since 1978. Ninety-four percent of nonmetropolitan counties had no abortion services at all.[6]

Even where abortion is available, it often is so only to women of means. Some states, such as Illinois and Oregon, will cover the cost of at least some abortions for poor women with state money, but Congress has barred the use of federal Medicaid funds for abortion except in cases of rape or incest or when the woman's life would be endangered if she were forced to carry for the full term.[7] But even when money is not an issue, physical attacks on both staff and patients trying to enter or leave abortion clinics and even killings by antiabortion forces have made many women who would exercise the right to have an abortion too fearful to do so and have caused some abortion providers to leave their jobs or seek police protection.[8] In the words of Jack Hitt, writing in the *New York Times Magazine*, "Rights are meant to be exercised in a clear light, in all towns and neighborhoods and cities, without fear of ostracism or physical harm. Anti-abortion forces insist that abortion should be the exception. . . . Can people be said to possess a right if they're too afraid to exercise it?"[9]

These can be said to be practical problems, but in discussing the philosophic issues that arise concerning the abortion question, practical and historical considerations are unavoidable. Until the mid-

1800s, abortion was not illegal in England or America nor was it prohibited by most religious groups, provided it occurred before "quickening," when the mother first perceived fetal movement, because it was only then that a woman was deemed to be pregnant. Assuming that they were simply "irregular," women on their own or with the help of midwives or herbalists freely used herbal potions and purgatives, took hot baths, and engaged in strenuous exercises that often actually resulted in their aborting.[10] It was not until late in the nineteenth century that abortion became illegal in most states; but this illegality in the years before *Roe v Wade* doubtless helped to foster the subsequent growth of the antiabortion movement.

I would like to discuss the two main categories of argument against abortion, both of which have elicited responses designed to refute them. The first type appeals to religion, the other is secular. Either type may appeal to the principle that a fetus is a human being, and in each we find more than one treatment of this conception, although the religious arguments are more nearly uniform. In addition to those that attribute biological humanity to the fetus, there are secular arguments that appeal to the concept of *personhood,* or somewhat more narrowly, *moral personhood.* Personhood and moral personhood in turn are defined in diverse ways, and I shall deal with those that I take to be representative and influential.

One point that is sometimes overlooked is that those who try in the name of religion to prevent abortions from taking place fail to recognize that in trying to make their own religious views prevail, they are denying the constitutional right of freedom of religion to those of other persuasions.[11] Moreover, religious objections to laws permitting abortion are misplaced: The laws do not make them mandatory under any circumstances but leave individuals free to follow the dictates of their own religions or their own consciences.

But there are other issues concerning arguments from religion. Some antiabortion protesters, especially Protestants, make a general appeal to biblical authority, and many Christian scholars invoke religious principles in arguing against the practice of abortion. However, it has been charged that the appeal to the Scriptures is based on ignorance of what is actually said therein. Michael Gorman and Paul D. Simmons have both pointed out that the New Testa-

ment is silent about abortion.[12] Gorman nevertheless finds explicit
opposition to abortion in early Jewish documents that were excluded
from both the Old and New Testaments. Taking these into account,
he maintains that the writers of the New Testament could be silent
on the abortion issue because they simply assumed that abortion was
not an option for the people of God.[13]

Arguing against him, Simmons contends that "The outlines and
foundations for thought in the New Testament era [the first century
A.D.] are to be found in the Old Testament."[14] To begin with, he cites
two passages. Exodus 21:22–25, he points out, "makes a normative distinction between a fetus and a woman and their relative
standing before the Covenant Law."

> The context is a story of a pregnant woman who becomes in-
> volved in a brawl between two men and has a miscarriage. The
> question concerns how such a matter should be resolved at law.
> The penalty exacted for the loss of the fetus is monetary—a
> fine is imposed on the men. . . . However, if the woman is in-
> jured or dies as a result of the injuries, *lex talionis* is applied:
> "thou shalt give life for life, eye for eye, tooth for tooth, hand
> for hand, foot for foot, burning for burning, wound for wound,
> stripe for stripe."[15]

While this is certainly no argument for elective abortion, it has bearing on the issue in that it clearly illustrates the contention that a
mature woman is to be valued more highly than a fetus.

The second passage cited by Simmons, however, Numbers 5:11–
28, "*prescribes* a ritual abortion." It describes a case in which a
husband accuses his wife of infidelity and fears that the other man
is responsible for her pregnancy. As Simmons recounts it, "A priest
pronounces the oaths, and forces the woman to drink a concoction
he has prepared as he pronounces the curse." He quotes this curse
from the biblical text: "may this water that brings the curse pass into
your bowels and make your body swell and your thigh fall away."
Probably because the fetus was considered to be part of the woman's
body, the "falling away of the thigh" was a euphemism for the ex-
pulsion of the fetus.[16] Simmons makes it clear that the story is not
to be read as an argument for abortion on demand. But, he says,

"this passage illustrates the fact that abortion was not a forbidden option for God's people."[17]

Simmons, then, cites three familiar passages from the Old Testament that have direct bearing on the question that features so heavily in current writing on the abortion issue as well as in the claims of antiabortion demonstrators. This is the question that he takes to be "the central issue in abortion," namely, "whether a fetus is to be morally or legally regarded as a person." He takes the Bible to provide "definitive guidance on this question."[18]

The first text he cites is Genesis 2:7. God "formed man of dust from the ground, and breathed into his nostrils the breath of life; and man became a living soul." This, Simmons maintains, indicates that to be a person, a human being, is to have both "birth and breath," plainly in opposition to the position that because the soul enters the body at the moment of conception, even a fertilized ovum is a human being. He also cites the passage at Genesis 1:26–28, which portrays a person as "created in the image of God," construing this to mean that humans have the "spiritual, intellectual, personal and moral . . . capacities [that] make it possible for people knowingly to do the will of God." And, finally, he cites Genesis 3:22, wherein God declares that "mankind . . . is to know good and evil." It is this that enables a person to be "a moral decision-maker." Persons, he says, are "free moral agents, able to discern the will of God and responsible to do so." Possession of spiritual and intellectual capacities and the ability to discern and follow the will of God are far beyond the capacities of a fetus and even of a newborn; but in accordance with the first passage he quotes from Genesis, a newborn is "a recognized and protected subject with birth and breath."[19] Simmons has not dealt explicitly with fetal rights or the right of a woman voluntarily to terminate a pregnancy, but the passages he cites support the position that when such a question arises, the woman's interests should take priority over those of the fetus, and that if personhood is the prerequisite for having rights, a woman and even a newborn infant qualify, whereas a fetus does not.

Much of the secular debate about abortion revolves around the concept of fetal rights and the question as to whether a fetus is the kind of being that can have rights. John Noonan has argued that fetuses are human beings and have rights from the moment of conception.[20] Endeavoring to develop a humanistic substitute for the theological notion of ensoulment, he points out that the appeal to viability, which some philosophers who reject the theological concept take as the criterion for a fetus's having a right to life, is unreliable.[21] This is especially so in the light of recent developments in neonatology, which enable premature infants to survive at ever earlier points in their development, even though they could not do so independently. Instead of this or other criteria such as the ability to communicate, Noonan appeals to a genetic definition of humanity. "The positive argument for conception as the decisive moment of humanization is that at conception the new being receives the genetic code. It is this genetic information which determines his characteristics, which is the biological carrier of the possibility of human wisdom, which makes him a self-evolving being. A being with a human genetic code is a man."[22]

Noonan takes this to mean that fetuses have equal rights with other humans, and drawing a parallel with the theological view, he stresses "what a fundamental question the theologians resolved in asserting the inviolability of the fetus." For instance, in answer to the argument that sometimes a fetus should be aborted for its own good, he contends, "To say a being was human was to say it had a destiny to decide for itself which could not be taken from it by another man's decision."[23] His humanistic argument has the same consequence. Nevertheless, he points out, "To regard the fetus as possessed of equal rights with other humans [is] not . . . to decide every case where abortion might be employed." In cases involving conflicts between the rights of the pregnant woman and those of the fetus, grounds must be found for deciding whose rights should prevail. But, Noonan stresses, "cases of conflict involving the fetus are different in . . . two respects: the inability of the fetus to speak for itself and the fact that the right of the fetus regularly at stake is the right to life itself."[24]

Mary Anne Warren, arguing against Noonan (although citing a different paper than the one just quoted), takes an opposite position, contrasting the *genetic* sense of being human with the moral sense. To be human in the moral sense is to be a *person,* and only a person can be "a member of the moral community," that is, "the set of beings with full and equal moral rights."[25] Warren defines the moral community as consisting "of all and only *people*," that is, persons, "rather than all and only human beings."[26] She takes rationality to be an important criterion of personhood, but while a biological human may have "the *potential* for rational thought," she holds that this shows that it has at most "the potential for *becoming* human in the moral sense."[27]

In what does personhood in the full sense consist? What traits enable humans to constitute a moral community? Warren does not try, in a short paper, to develop a complete analysis of the concept of personhood, but she presents a brief statement of five criteria for being considered a person. Even more briefly summarized, they are these: Consciousness, and in particular, the capacity to feel pain; a developed capacity for reasoning and problem solving; self-motivated activity; the capacity to communicate in indefinitely many ways on indefinitely many topics; self-awareness and a concept of selfhood and identity. At the same time, she asserts that "it is a part of this concept that all and only people have full moral rights."[28]

Warren does not insist that a being must necessarily have all of the capacities she cites in order to count as a person. Rather, she says, "All we need to claim to demonstrate that a fetus is not a person is that any being which satisfies *none* of [them] is certainly not a person." On this basis, she concludes that a fetus "is a human being which is not yet a person, and which therefore cannot coherently be said to have full moral rights."[29]

Personhood, then, is for Warren a necessary condition for having rights. But she has not explained what it is about personhood that makes it the sufficient condition. Rather, like Noonan, she seems to take it for granted, saying that "the attributes which are relevant in determining whether or not an entity is enough like a person to be regarded as having some of the same moral rights are no different from those which are relevant to determining whether it is human."[30] But neither the capacity for moral judgment nor the ability to respect rights is included in her list of qualifications, and she indicates that of the traits on that list, it is the capacity to reason that is most important to personhood.[31]

On the question of a fetal right to life, Warren says, "I think that a rational person must conclude that . . . the right to life of a fetus is to be based upon its resemblance to a person."[32] But this resemblance is admittedly a matter of degree, and she concludes, first, "that even a fully developed fetus is not personlike enough to have any significant right to life on the basis of its personlikeness";[33] and second, that "even if a potential person does have some *prima facie* right to life . . . the rights of any actual person invariably outweigh those of any potential person whenever the two conflict." Thus the right to life of a fetus, as a potential person, "could not possibly outweigh the right of a woman to obtain an abortion."[34]

Perhaps the reason both Noonan and Warren fail to specify the particular human traits that make one eligible for rights is that, at least in the papers considered here, neither of them takes up the question what a right is. Because of this, from the point of view developed in my book *Operative Rights*, both of them would be said to fall short of justifying the attribution of rights either to fetuses or to fully developed persons. Participation in rights in general is not only a matter of a community's conferring entitlements; it requires the ability to respect them and to acknowledge the obligation to do so. Any right is a mutual relation of entitlement and obligation between every member of the community and all others. If there is to be a right to life, the obligation to respect it must be conferred by the norms upon all, together with the entitlement.

This means that the ability to respect rights is integral to having them, and this ability can only start to develop as an infant begins to interact with others and to internalize the attitudes of those around it—to acquire the perspective of Mead's "generalized other." If this is so, then the question of a right to life could not be decided on the basis of the attribution of rights to a fetus. The fetus would not be a member of what we may now call (to use another of Alan Gewirth's terms) "the community of rights."[35] Membership in this community is acquired only through enculturation, a process that begins at birth. I have argued that it is only by being treated as a participant in rights that the infant starts to become a full-fledged member of this community and therefore that it should be so treated from the moment of birth.

I have also argued that it is impossible for persons to live in a way that we would consider to be human without some system of social norms to regulate their mutual relations.[36] In this connection, I maintain that to be operative in a society, norms must be accepted by its members, which means voluntarily so, even if not always as a result of deliberation. It follows that all those who are to govern themselves by a common set of norms should be able to participate in establishing new norms, as well as in perpetuating and changing those that are already established. To ensure this, all must be granted and must respect two entitlements, which I term the *fundamental generic rights*—generic in the sense that they ought to be operative in all communities.[37] The first is a right of personal autonomy—the right to make judgments and decisions for oneself, which can also be thought of as a right to self-determination; the second is a right of personal authority—the right to have one's judgments listened to and taken seriously. For these rights to be jointly operative results in an important qualification of the right to autonomy: It imposes the obligation upon the autonomous individual to listen to the others and to evaluate their judgments in the process of forming his or her own.

To relate this to the question of abortion, a right to abortion would be an application of the generic right of personal autonomy, an application exercisable, if they so choose, by women who require it. I believe this autonomy to be what is intended in the Court's opinion in *Roe v Wade* and by other writers on the topic who refer to a right of privacy.[38] Moreover, if the fundamental generic rights were jointly operative and actually exercised, controversies such as that over abortion would be handled by mutually respectful discussion rather than by overt conflict. Persons would come to understand that while they were under the obligation to engage in such discussion and to avoid inflicting harm upon one another, they were also obligated to permit one another the freedom of autonomous choice. Nonviolent protesters would be exercising their constitutional right to freedom of expression, but they would be bound not only to grant the same freedom to others but to consider the others' views, just as the others would be obligated to listen to them and consider their opinions seriously. In the absence of this sort of dialogue, I am afraid, the deciding factor will be political power.

Hate Speech

"Hate speech, as Americans call it," says British writer Ursula Owen, "is a troubling matter for people who believe in free speech. It is abusive, insulting, intimidating and harassing. And it may lead to violence, hatred or discrimination," even killing.[39] The reason it is so troubling is stated succinctly: "In a world where the effects of speech that fosters hatred are all too visible, there are two difficult questions that must be asked about the defense of free expression: At what cost? And at the expense of whose pain?"[40] As Owen points out, the tension between the right of free speech and the need for protection is revealed in the International Covenant on Civil and Political Rights, adopted by the United Nations in 1966: Article 19, already slightly more restrictive in its formulation than the First Amendment to the US Constitution, states that "everyone shall have the right to hold opinions without interference" and "everyone shall have the right to freedom of expression" but subject to restrictions "such as are provided by law and are necessary . . . for respect of the rights or reputations of others" or "for the protection of national security or of public order, or of public health or morals." Article 20 is still more restrictive, not only prohibiting "any propaganda for war" but also stipulating that "any advocacy of national, racial or religious hatred that constitutes incitement to discrimination, hostility or violence must be prohibited."[41]

In the United States, the question is when and to what extent hate speech can be curbed without infringing the right of free speech guaranteed by the First Amendment. But some have asked the broader question: whether it should ever be curbed; whether doing so will alleviate or only exacerbate the social problems that generate it. The belief that the expression of bigotry should be curbed is not new, but it has been especially newsworthy since the 1980s, when hate speech became a serious problem on college and university campuses. Not only students have been involved. In 1992, a professor at City College of New York, Leonard Jeffries, accused Jews of financing the Atlantic slave trade and accused Jews and Italians of conspiring to denigrate African Americans in films. Other activities, such as public demonstrations, also raise the question of freedom of expression (the controversial march by a group of neo-Nazis in Skokie, Illinois, in 1977 is an illustration), but for the most part, I shall concentrate on oral speech and its expression in print.

One question regarding hate speech is whether there aren't circumstances in which it should cease to count as mere speech and instead be counted as action and as harmful in ways that mere speech would not be. The use of language for incitement of violence or for sexual harassment is now widely taken to be more than simply expression of opinion. In one sense, every use of language is itself an action: The philosopher John Searle and those who build on his work write of "speech acts"; and Justus Buchler notes that even when it serves to convey an assertion, speaking is what he calls an "active judgment." The question concerning not only hostile or bigoted speech but also speech that could provoke action that might endanger people is when we should treat it as speech, which would have to be considered eligible for First Amendment protection, and when as conduct, which would not. In a famous statement (not always attributed to him), Supreme Court Justice Oliver Wendell Holmes said, "the most stringent protection of free speech would not protect a man in falsely shouting fire in a theater and causing panic."[42] But in the opinion in which this statement occurs, Holmes provides an important principle, namely, that "the character of every act depends upon the circumstances in which it is done." An actor on stage in the theater could falsely shout "Fire!" and the issue of free speech would not arise. Holmes went on to say, enunciating a standard that remains important, "the question in every case is whether the words are used in such circumstance and are of such a nature as to create a clear and present danger that they will bring about the substantive evils that Congress has a right to prevent."[43]

In addition to international law, the laws of virtually all other nations delineate the category of prohibited speech more narrowly than the US courts have in interpreting the First Amendment. Finland, for instance, has a statute specifying that "whosoever spreads statements or other notices among the public where a certain race or national or ethnic or religious group is threatened, slandered or insulted, shall be sentenced for incitement to discrimination against a population group to a fine or imprisonment for at most two years."[44]

The Finnish statute construes all slanderous or insulting statements as well as threatening ones as cases of incitement to discrimination. There are respected scholars and educators in the United
States who would impose equally strict limits on what is permissible.
In a speech delivered at a conference on hate speech on campus some
years ago, Richard Delgado of the University of Wisconsin Law
School pointedly noted that there are "words that wound," speech
that not only interferes with the abused students' ability to study and
learn but also undermines their self-respect. Acknowledging this,
Charles Lawrence of the Stanford Law School argued that "We have
not listened to the real victims."[45] Writing in a law review, another
Stanford professor, Mari Matsuda, noted that American law pro-
tects people against defamation and libel, because "false speech
damages their standing in the community and limits their opportunities, their self-worth, their free enjoyment of life." Lawyers and
lawmakers, Matsuda says, "see this and yet fail to see that the very
same things happen to the victims of racist speech."[46] Difficult as it
may be, she insists, we need to devise measures that will protect
against offensive speech on campus, because it does "real harm to
real people," people who deserve both protection and redress.

Yet there are equally respectable scholars who view it differently.
Franklyn S. Haiman, John Evans Professor Emeritus of Communication Studies at Northwestern University, has challenged the view
that "racist, sexist or homophobic diatribes are . . . acts of harassment that are more like physical blows" than they are like expres-
sions of ideas and therefore ought to be restricted. He argues that
"there is a crucial difference between verbal communication and
physical blows. A physical blow will hurt no matter what goes on
in the victim's mind, but a verbal attack will hurt only if it is men-
tally understood. It is not the words themselves that hurt but the
meaning they convey."[47] Haiman also points out that "Placing limits on the verbal expression of group hatreds does not make the
underlying attitudes go away. Instead they go underground to fes-
ter and perhaps erupt in more violent form later."[48] Nowhere is this
better illustrated than in India: Under Indian law, promoting "dis-
harmony or feelings of enmity, hatred or ill-will between different
religious, racial, language or regional groups or castes or commu-

nities," whether through spoken or written words, is punishable by imprisonment for up to three years or a fine or both.[49] But regardless of the law, and despite India's Ghandian heritage, violent clashes between religious and ethnic groups continually erupt.

In opposition to the suppression of hate speech, Haiman cites John Stuart Mill's argument in *On Liberty:* "the peculiar evil of silencing the expression of an opinion is that it is robbing the human race, posterity as well as the existing generation—those who dissent from the opinion, still more than those who hold it. If the opinion is right, they are deprived of the opportunity of exchanging error for truth; if wrong, they lose, what is almost as great a benefit, the clearer perception and livelier impression of truth produced by its collision with error."[50]

Adopting a position similar to Mill's, Haiman lets Supreme Court Justice Louis Brandeis speak for him: "If there be time to expose through discussion the falsehood and fallacies, to avert the evil by the process of education, the remedy to be applied is more speech, not enforced silence. Only an emergency can justify repression. Such must be the rule if authority is to be reconciled with freedom. Such, in my opinion, is the command of the Constitution."[51] Echoing this view, when Leonard Jeffries, mentioned earlier, was invited by the student government of the College of Staten Island to speak there, Marlene Springer, president of the college, affirmed her belief in the First Amendment and the student government's right to invite Jeffries to talk. "There are elements of truth in what he says, but they get very distorted," she said. "I hope students will learn in college to tell these things apart, whether they are in a speech, a newspaper or somewhere else."[52]

The prescription of open discussion and the opportunity for refutation or confirmation have implications for situations such as tha in Skokie, Illinois, where neo-Nazis were marching in open opposi tion to demonstrations that had been held in Chicago calling f desegregation. Arieh Neier of the American Civil Liberties Unic who successfully defended the Nazis in a lawsuit against the tc of Skokie when it initially refused to grant a permit for the den stration, has presented an argument that is directly relevant t issue of hate speech, addressing the problem of incitement ar

"clear and present danger" argument. "Even if the deeds they advocated were unlawful," Neier claims, "everyone had an opportunity to hear contrary views before any crime was committed. Indeed, opposing points of view all but drowned out [the demonstrators]. Defending them protected freedom of speech. There was no manifest danger that the violence they might incite would follow so soon that debate could not take place. That is, the danger was neither clear nor present."[53] This was in the United States, where freedom of the press and the other media as well as free speech are protected. In contrast, in Rwanda and Yugoslavia, state radio and television were monopolies, and voicing opposition was prohibited. "Freedom of speech," Neier insists, "is ultimately the greatest protection against the kind of crimes that took place [there]."[54]

Also favoring free speech and discussion, Suzanne Rice argues that "Legalistic policies intended to proscribe hate speech on college campuses have failed to remedy the problem they address."[55] "Where communication is concerned," she points out, "the First Amendment asserts the individual's right to free speech, but not the legal right to be heard, nor the corresponding responsibility to listen."[56] What we need, she asserts, is extralegal—that is, moral—standards for communicative interaction. She endorses an approach through "virtue ethics" that would have us try to instill "specifically communicative virtues" such as patience, tolerance for alternative points of view, respect for differences, a willingness and ability to listen thoughtfully and attentively, an openness to giving and receiving criticism, and honest and sincere self-expression.[57]

Communication embodying the virtues Rice cites is consonant with John Dewey's conception of democracy as a way of life.[58] It is also consistent with the position developed in *Operative Rights,* where it is supported by the arguments for the fundamental generic rights. It is the joint exercise of these rights, for which I use the term *dialogic reciprocity,* that I hold to be requisite for maintaining a stable community and dealing effectively with conflicts.[59] In any community in which the fundamental generic rights of autonomy and authority were operative, all its members, including those who utter hate speech or advocate discriminatory practices as well as those who challenge them, would have both generic rights. The

mutuality of these rights would require them to engage in respect-ful, critical, and self-critical dialogue with one another regarding the content and motivation of what each side has to say. Both the causes and potential consequences of each position, not just those of hate speech but also those of the desire and the perceived need to elimi-nate it, would have to be examined by both parties jointly, and ei-ther or both might find it necessary to modify their position.

RIGHTS AND LINGUISTIC MINORITIES

The question of the rights of minorities to retain their traditional languages has long been of concern in many countries of the world and has been dealt with by a number of international bodies. The United Nations Declaration on the Rights of Persons Belonging to National or Ethnic, Religious and Linguistic Minorities was adopted by a resolution of the General Assembly on December 18, 1992. Article 2, section 1 provides that "Persons belonging to . . . minori-ties have the right to enjoy their own culture, to profess and prac-tice their own religion, and to use their own language, in private and in public, freely and without interference or any form of discrimi-nation." It further stipulates, in Article 4, section 3, that "States should take appropriate measures so that, wherever possible, per-sons belonging to minorities may have adequate opportunities to learn their mother tongue or to have instruction in their mother tongue."[60] In context, these provisions seem to concern long-estab-lished minority populations. The Universal Declaration of Linguis-tic Rights (the Barcelona Declaration), proposed in 1996 to the United Nations by an assembly of representatives of nongovernmen-tal organizations from close to ninety different countries, adds an important distinction that may have special relevance to the situa-tion in the United States. This is the distinction between a *language community* and a *language group*. "This Declaration considers as a *language community* any human society established historically in a particular territorial space, whether this space be recognized or not, which identifies itself as a people and has developed a common language as a natural means of communication and cultural cohe-sion among its members."[61]

Examples of a community in this sense would be the French-,

German-, and Italian-speaking peoples that comprise the nation of Switzerland. But second, "This Declaration considers as a *language group* any group of persons sharing the same language which is established in the territorial space of another language community but which does not possess historical antecedents equivalent to those of that community. Examples of such groups are immigrants, refugees, deported persons and members of diasporas."[62] Native American peoples and native Hawaiians, given these definitions, would be language communities; whereas immigrant populations, even sizable ones, in which their native languages are still in use would comprise language groups. However, the history of migrations suggests that there is a continuum, and language groups that have settled in particular locations and remained there for several generations would appear to have become language communities. Some contemporary Mexican American communities seem to fit into this category. A statement in the introductory portion of the Barcelona Declaration has special relevance for these. Under the heading "A basis for harmonious social relations," it says that "the Declaration focuses on the rights of language communities which are historically established in their own territory with a view to defining a gradation, applicable to each case, of the rights of language groups with different degrees of historicity and self-identification."

Article 3, section 1, of the Barcelona Declaration specifies the following "inalienable personal rights" as applicable to language groups as well as to language communities: the right to be recognized as a member of a language community; the right to the use of one's own language both in private and in public; the right to the use of one's own name; the right to interrelate and associate with other members of one's language community of origin; and the right to maintain and develop one's own culture. In addition, section 2 adds the following provisions for members of language groups: the right for their own language to be taught; the right of access to cultural services; the right to an equitable presence of their language and culture in the communications media; the right to receive attention in their own language from government bodies and in socioeconomic relations. Without a doubt, implementation of these rights is difficult, but most are already operative in the United States, some of them covered by law.

Nevertheless, the strong "English only" movement, reflected in repeated efforts to have Congress pass a law making English the official language of the United States, raises both practical problems and questions of rights. For instance, what would be the consequences for Hawaii, where both English and the Hawaiian dialect are recognized as official languages, if English were to become the sole official language of the nation? If Puerto Rico, where Spanish has been entrenched as the primary language ever since it was a Spanish possession, became a state, the establishment of English as the sole official language would also be especially problematic there.

One problem that would arise nationwide if English were to be the sole language in which public affairs could be conducted relates to the implementation of the right to vote for citizens with limited English. The Voting Rights Act, passed in 1965 (and amended several times since), was designed to ensure that in accordance with the Fourteenth and Fifteenth Amendments, minorities, including linguistic minorities, could exercise the right to vote. Provided certain requirements are satisfied (such as the required percentage of eligible voters belonging to a single language minority and a specified proportion of those eligible to vote having failed to register), a section of the act stipulates that registration materials, notices of elections, voting instructions, and ballots must be provided in the minority language as well as in English. To protect the right of equal treatment provided by the Fourteenth Amendment, additional legislation has been passed, including laws providing for interpreters in the courts and in certain situations in the prisons. Local ordinances have similar aims. Where I live, a summons to appear in court must be written in both English and Spanish.

In a country whose constitution and laws are written in English, where all legal procedures are conducted in English, and where generations of immigrants have learned English, it is not surprising that such laws are controversial. Yet despite the fact that so many immigrants have been assimilated, there are still communities in the United States in which traditional languages continue to be prized and perpetuated. Few residents of other states are aware that the Constitution of Louisiana requires its public schools to give instruction in the French language and culture as well as in the history of French populations.[63] Better known is the fact that the Federal Communications Commission has increasingly been compelled to grant licenses to stations that broadcast in languages other than English. Placed against the background of history, these facts do not seem out of place. The early colonists were from many countries, and the Continental Congress saw fit to publish extracts of its Votes and Proceedings (1774), the Declaration of Articles Setting Forth Causes of Taking Up Arms (1775), and Resolves of Congress (1776) in German as well as English. Even the Articles of Confederation (1777) were printed in French as well as in English.[64] And in view of the strong opposition to bilingualism in California today, we should recall its history as a Spanish possession and a part of Mexico as well as the immediate sequel to that history. On June 3, 1849, the US military governor of the territory recommended that there be a convention to write a constitution for it. The result was a bilingual constitution, adopted on October 10 and ratified on November 13, 1849. It remained in effect until 1879, more than a quarter of a century after California's admission to the Union in September 1850.[65]

There is concern today over other issues concerning language rights. One that was featured in news reports is the question whether members of linguistic minorities should have the right to communicate among themselves in their own languages while at work. Another, much debated, is the use of bilingual education in schools in minority areas. Bilingual programs typically have two aims, the first being to aid non-English-speaking students to make the transition into the standard curriculum. The second and more controversial aim, which is in line with the provisions of both the UN Declaration and the Barcelona Declaration, is to help maintain the language and culture of non-English-speaking students while at the same time seeing to it that they learn English.

In a small book in which he defends bilingual education against various attacks, Stephen D. Krashen lists the following three components of what he takes to be "good bilingual programs":

1. Comprehensible input in English, provided directly in the form of ESL [English as a Second Language, sometimes called "language immersion"] and sheltered [i.e., easily comprehensible] subject matter classes.
2. Subject matter teaching done in the first language, without translation. . . .
3. Literacy development in the first language.[66]

The second and third of these provoke controversy, but Krashen argues that teaching in the child's first language "provides background information that helps make the English that children read and hear more comprehensible," and that literacy developed in the child's first language "transfers to the second language."[67] His plan is designed to forward both of the aims just specified, while helping minority children achieve a level of education that will enable them to function successfully in American society.

Opposed to such programs, Diane Ravitch, a prominent scholar in the field of education, claims that bilingual education illustrates the "politicization" of education, reflecting the demands of interest groups. "The history of this program," she maintains, "exemplifies a campaign on behalf of social and political goals that are only tangential to education."[68] She charges that with the Bilingual Education Act of 1968 (since renewed several times), Congress was, for the first time, legislating a particular pedagogical method.[69] The Supreme Court, in the 1974 case of *Lau v Nichols*, did not endorse a particular method but did rule that "There is no equality of treatment merely by providing students with the same facilities, textbooks, teachers, and curriculum; for students who do not understand English are effectively foreclosed from any meaningful decision."[70] However, a task force subsequently appointed by the US Office of Education to implement the decision, which was composed, according to Ravitch, of bilingual educators and representatives of minority groups, established regulations mandating bilingual education and describing in detail how these regulations were to be carried out. Ravitch's own position is that educational decisions should be made by "appropriate lay and professional authorities on educational grounds." She also holds that "In a democratic society, all of us share the responsibility to protect schools, colleges, and universities against unwarranted political intrusion into educational affairs."[71]

As Ravitch and others note, research on the success of bilingual education has been contradictory. However, she cites what she takes to be "one of the few evidently unbiased, nonpolitical assessments of bilingual research," published in the *Harvard Educational Review* in 1982, in which the researcher concluded that "bilingual programs are neither better nor worse than other instructional methods."[72] Ravitch also cites "a four-year study commissioned by the United States Office of Education [that] concluded that students who learned bilingually did not achieve at a higher level in regular classes, nor were their attitudes toward school significantly different."[73]

Until more definitive studies are carried out, Krashen and other professionals will have to evaluate their own and one another's programs. But in addition, Ravitch's mandate for shared responsibility can have different implications from those she intends. The rights of autonomy and authority, if granted as they should be to all citizens, would call for an ongoing public dialogue on the subject of their children's education. Ravitch's rejection of "politicization," if this be taken in the sense of a struggle for power over educational policy and practice, is consistent with the principle of participatory democracy endorsed by Dewey and Mead. One topic for discussion is the implications for bilingual education of the United Nations and Barcelona declarations, with which the Bilingual Education Act is consistent. The second aim of bilingual education, namely, to help maintain the language and culture of non-English-speaking students, is an important part of what all three would have us promote; but the documents themselves, as well as the law, are proper subjects for consideration in a democratic forum.

Part of the debate over language rights concerns whether such a right would be a collective one or an individual right granted to the members of a minority community. But what does it mean to call it a "collective" right? Most people, and many philosophers, adhere to the traditional idea that only individuals can have rights. Those who do entertain the possibility of collective rights tend to construe such a right on the analogy of individual rights, as one that belongs to a community as an entity. The Hungarian philosopher György

Andrássy, who strongly endorses language rights, recognizes both individual and collective language rights. In speaking of "a constitutionally ensured collective language right," Andrássy takes the bearer of such a right to be a "cultural community."[74] While he is not talking about language rights, Joseph Raz also recognizes collective rights but conceives them differently. Defining rights in terms of interests, he holds a right to be an interest that is a sufficient reason for holding another or others to be under a duty. A collective right serves an interest that individuals share as, and only as, members of a group.[75]

The Canadian philosopher Denise Réaume accepts Raz's definition of a right and notes that "one might argue that groups are the appropriate holders of rights with respect to at least some collective goods."[76] (I assume that by the latter term she means goods in which there is a collective interest.) Réaume describes collective goods as "participatory goods," whose value lies in the fact that they can be enjoyed only publicly or communally.[77] On this basis, she concludes that "there can be no individual right to a collective good but only a collective right, held jointly by all who share in the collective good."[78] A right to "linguistic security" would be such a right. Réaume's usage here suggests that by "a collective right" she means one that is had by individuals jointly insofar as they share in a collective interest or collective good. But she also speaks of groups themselves as appropriate rights holders. I propose that what is needed is the distinction I have made between the rights of groups or communities as such, which I call *communal* rights, and those that I take to be more properly termed *collective*. The distinction is peculiarly applicable to language rights (and to the broader right of a cultural community to its own culture).

In *Operative Rights*, drawing an analogy to individual rights and assuming the mutuality of all rights, I argue (now using *community* in my own, broad sense) that a community that is capable of acting as a body can participate in rights within a wider community. An example would be the right of all the member countries of the UN Security Council to a vote therein—a right that must be implemented by individual representatives but which belongs to those countries as entities. A *collective* right, by comparison, would be one that can only be exercised by individuals jointly and whose exercise marks them as belonging to a particular community. Language rights are the best example I can think of.

The right to use a particular language can only be exercised by members of that linguistic community in communication with one another. Even though a community as a body can also be said to have a (communal) right to its own language, insofar as it is exercised jointly by its individual members rather than by that community in interaction or communication with others, it is a collective right. But it would be truly a right only if a comparable right were granted to the members of every linguistic community in the wider community that includes them all. The linguistic rights of minority communities, that is, would be no more "rights" than that of the majority. Were this not the case, we would be granting them special status, not establishing a right.

To give communities and their members rights to their own languages as well as to other aspects of their culture, including religion, can be justified by recognizing these rights as extensions or applications of the fundamental generic right of autonomy, the communal and collective rights analogous to the individual one. But autonomy cannot be absolute, and for a multilingual society to grant linguistic autonomy to its member communities in no way implies a right to communicate solely in a minority language. In cutting the minority off from the wider community, such a right would be self-defeating as well as impossible to exercise.

NOTES

1. See Alan Gewirth, *Reason and Morality* (Chicago: University of Chicago Press, 1978), 99–100.

2. See Beth J. Singer, *Operative Rights* (Albany: State University of New York Press, 1993).

3. See Will Kymlicka, *Liberalism, Community, and Culture* (Oxford: Clarendon Press, 1989), in which he argues for "special rights" for aboriginal peoples, and *Multicultural Citizenship* (Oxford: Clarendon Press, 1995), where "group-differentiated rights" are said to be "rights that the members of other groups do not have" (p. 34).

4. *Roe v Wade*, 410 US 113; The quoted passages are from Justice Powell's reference to *Roe v Wade* in delivering the Court's opinion in an-

other case, *Akron Center for Reproductive Health, Inc., et al. v City of Akron et al.,* 103 SCt 2481.

5. "Access to Abortion," fact sheet, Washington, DC: National Abortion Federation, March 25, 1998. See also H. T. MacKay and A. P. MacKay, "Abortion Training in Obstetrics and Gynecology Residency Programs in the United States, 1991–1992," *Family Planning Perspectives* 27, no. 3 (May–June 1995): 112–15.

6. Jody E. Steinauer, Teresa DePineres, Anne M. Robert, John Westfall, and Philip Darney, "Training Family Practice Residents in Abortion and Other Reproductive Health Care: A Nationwide Survey," *Family Planning Perspectives* 29, no. 5 (September–October 1997): 222. See also S. K. Henshaw and J. Van Vort, "Abortion Services in the United States, 1991 and 1992," *Family Planning Perspectives* 26, no. 3 (May–June 1994): 100–106.

7. *Facts in Brief* (New York: Alan Guttmacher Institute, January 1997). At the same time, as Rosalind Pollack Petchesky points out, Medicaid will pay 90 percent of the cost for sterilization of a recipient. *Abortion and Woman's Choice: The State, Sexuality, and Reproductive Freedom,* rev. ed. (Boston: Northeastern University Press, 1990), 296.

8. Reporting the death of a police officer in such an attack in Birmingham, Alabama, the *New York Times* reported on January 30, 1998, that from 1982 (when the Bureau of Alcohol, Tobacco, and Firearms first began to keep records) until the date of the article, the ATF had recorded 199 attacks on abortion clinics (pp. A1, A11). Since 1994, in the United States and Canada, two physicians who provided abortions have been murdered and four others shot ("Access to Abortion," 2). The *Times* quotes Dr. David N. Mesches as saying, "I do believe that physicians are intimidated in this country and do not wish to be trained [in performing abortions, fearing for their safety]. And there is good reason for that" ("Casualty of the Abortion Debate," *New York Times,* March 24, 1998, p. B2).

9. Jack Hitt, "Who Will Do Abortions Here?" *New York Times Magazine,* January 18, 1998, 55.

10. Petchesky, *Abortion and Woman's Choice,* 29–30. Later in the century, abortions as well as efforts at birth control were especially common among working-class women, because so many of them had to work themselves and because raising children was so expensive (pp. 53–54).

11. A case in point, which also materially affects the problem of unavailability of birth-control information as well as elective abortions, was provided by the expected merger of three hospitals in New York State, one of which is Catholic. According to the *New York Times,* "As part of the proposal, the two nonreligious hospitals have agreed not to provide elective abortions, sterilizations, or birth-control counseling, which are opposed by the Catholic Church. Opponents of the merger have contended that, while women with higher incomes could get these services through private doc-

tors, the merger would place a significant barrier to such services to the poor" ("Casualty of the Abortion Debate," B2).

12. Michael J. Gorman, "Why Is the New Testament Silent about Abortion?" *Christianity Today,* January 11, 1993, 27–29. Paul D. Simmons, "Biblical Authority and the Not-So Strange Silence of Scripture about Abortion," *Christian Bioethics* 2, no. 1 (1996): 66–82.

13. Gorman, "Why Is the New Testament Silent?"

14. Simmons, "Biblical Authority," 69.

15. Simmons, "Biblical Authority," 69.

16. Simmons, "Biblical Authority," 82, n. 2.

17. Simmons, "Biblical Authority," 70.

18. Simmons, "Biblical Authority," 70.

19. Simmons, "Biblical Authority," 71.

20. John T. Noonan Jr., "An Almost Absolute Value in History," in J. T. Noonan, ed., *The Morality of Abortion: Legal and Historical Perspectives* (Cambridge: Harvard University Press, 1970). Excerpted in Patricia H. Werhane, A. R. Gini, and David T. Ozar, eds., *Philosophical Issues in Human Rights: Theories and Applications* (New York: Random House, 1986), 29–33.

21. Concerning the Catholic doctrine of ensoulment, Petchesky points out that "Even within Catholic doctrine, the precise moment when the fetus became 'animated' with a soul was for centuries the source of some dispute; Catholic moral theologians throughout the early modern period argued for various exceptions and qualifications to the abortion prohibition. Not until 1869 was abortion at any stage of pregnancy, for any reason, declared a mortal sin punishable by excommunication" (Petchesky, *Abortion and Woman's Choice,* 333). See also Daniel Callahan, *Abortion: Law, Choice, and Morality* (New York: Macmillan, 1970); and John T. Noonan Jr., *Contraception: A History of Its Treatment by the Catholic Church* (Cambridge: Harvard University Press, 1966).

22. Noonan, "Almost Absolute," in Werhane et al., *Philosophical Issues,* 32–33.

23. Noonan, "Almost Absolute," in Werhane et al., *Philosophical Issues,* 33.

24. Noonan, "Almost Absolute," in Werhane et al., *Philosophical Issues,* 33.

25. Mary Anne Warren, "On the Moral and Legal Status of Abortion," *Monist* 57, no. 1 (January 1973): 47. (An excerpt of this article is included in Werhane et al., *Philosophical Issues.*)

26. Warren, "On the Moral and Legal Status," 54.

27. Warren, "On the Moral and Legal Status," 53.

28. Warren, "On the Moral and Legal Status," 56.

29. Warren, "On the Moral and Legal Status," 56.

30. Warren, "On the Moral and Legal Status," 57.

31. Warren, "On the Moral and Legal Status," 55.

32. Warren, "On the Moral and Legal Status," 57.

33. Warren, "On the Moral and Legal Status," 58.

34. Warren, "On the Moral and Legal Status," 59.

35. Alan Gewirth, *The Community of Rights* (Chicago: University of Chicago Press, 1996).

36. See Singer, *Operative Rights,* chap. 3. In the words of Clifford Geertz, humans "unmodified by the customs of particular places do not in fact exist, have never existed, and most important, could not in the very nature of the case exist" (*The Interpretation of Culture* [New York: Basic Books, 1973], 256).

37. The term *generic rights* is another that I adapt from Alan Gewirth, who uses it to refer to what he takes to be the fundamental, universally existent human rights. See, e.g., *Human Rights: Essays on Justification and Applications* (Chicago: University of Chicago Press, 1982).

38. See, e.g., Petchesky, *Abortion and Woman's Choice:* "While privacy, like property, has a distinctively negative connotation when applied to persons as persons—in their concrete, physical being—it also has a positive sense that roughly coincides with the notion of 'individual self-determination'" (pp. 3–4).

39. Ursula Owen, "The Speech That Kills," *Index on Censorship* 27, no. 1 (January–February 1998): 32.

40. Owen, "Speech That Kills," 33.

41. Owen, "Speech That Kills," 32–33; see also *Human Rights: A Compilation of International Instruments*, vol. 1, pt. 1, *Universal Instruments* (New York: United Nations, 1994), 28.

42. Oliver Wendell Holmes, *Schenck v United States*, 249 US 47 (1919).

43. Holmes, *Schenck v United States.*

44. Quoted in "'Hate Speech' and Freedom of Expression," Human Rights Watch Policy Paper (March 1992), 4.

45. Quoted in Jon Weiner, "Words That Wound: Free Speech for Campus Bigots?" *Nation,* February 26, 1990, 273. Mari J. Matsuda, Charles R. Lawrence III, Richard Delgado, and Kimberle Williams Crenshaw, *Words That Wound: Critical Race Theory, Assaultive Speech, and the First Amendment* (Boulder: Westview Press, 1993).

46. Quoted from the *Michigan Law Review* (1989) in Weiner, "Words That Wound," 273. See also Matsuda et al., *Words That Wound.*

47. Franklyn S. Haiman, "Why Hate Speech Must Be Heard," *Chicago Tribune,* October 30, 1991, sec. 1, p. 19.

48. Haiman, "Why Hate Speech," 19.

49. "'Hate Speech' and Freedom of Expression," 6.

50. Haiman, "Why Hate Speech," 19, quoting John Stuart Mill, *On Liberty* (1859). See *On Liberty,* ed. Elizabeth Rapaport (Indianapolis: Hackett, 1978), 16–17.

51. Haiman, "Why Hate Speech," 19, quoting Louis Brandeis, *Whitney v California* (1927).

52. For reasons that had nothing to do with the campus protests that had occurred during the previous week, Jeffries canceled his official talk but appeared anyway, planning an informal discussion. Karen W. Arenson, "Students Arrested as Jeffries Cancels Talk," *New York Times,* April 3, 1998, p. B3.

53. Arieh Neier, "Clear and Present Danger," *Index on Censorship* 27, no. 1 (January–February 1998): 59.

54. Neier, "Clear and Present Danger," 59.

55. Suzanne Rice, "'Hate Speech' and the Need for Moral Standards in Communicative Interaction," *Philosophy of Education,* Proceedings of the Fiftieth Annual Meeting of the Philosophy of Education Society, ed. Michael S. Katz, 1994, 95.

56. Rice, "'Hate Speech,'" 91.

57. Rice, "'Hate Speech,'" 92. See also Suzanne Rice and Nicholas C. Burbules, "Communicative Virtues and Educational Relations," *Philosophy of Education,* Proceedings of the Forty-Eighth Annual Meeting of the Philosophy of Education Society, ed. H. A. Alexander, 1992.

58. See, e.g., John Dewey, "Democracy and Educational Administration," *Official Report of the Convention of the Department of Superintendence of the National Education Association* (March 1937), 48–55, in John Dewey, *The Later Works,* vol. 11, ed. Jo Ann Boydston (Carbondale: Southern Illinois University Press, 1991), 217–25.

59. While I define it in my own way, the term *dialogic reciprocity* is derived from a paper by Drucilla Cornell, "In Defense of Dialogic Reciprocity," *Tennessee Law Review* 54 (1987): 335–43.

60. *Human Rights,* 1: 142.

61. Universal Declaration of Linguistic Rights (Declaration of Barcelona, June 6, 1996), article 1, preliminary title: "Concepts," sec. 1.

62. Universal Declaration, sec. 5.

63. Bill Piatt, *¿Only English? Law and Language Policy in the United States* (Albuquerque: University of New Mexico Press, 1990), 6.

64. Piatt, *¿Only English?,* 8–9.

65. *Encyclopedia of California,* vol. 1 (New York: Somerset, 1998), 80; James Brooke, "Less To Celebrate at This Gold Rush Anniversary," *New York Times,* March 22, 1998, p. 16.

66. Stephen D. Krashen, *Under Attack: The Case Against Bilingual Education* (Culver City: Language Education Associates, 1996), 4. Despite its title, this book is a strong defense of bilingual education, containing prescriptions for improving and supplementing it as well as refutation of the arguments against it.

67. Krashen, *Under Attack,* 4.

68. Diane Ravitch, "Politicization and the Schools: The Case of Bilingual Education," *Proceedings of the American Philosophical Society* 129, no. 2 (June 1985); reprinted in James W. Noll, ed., *Taking Sides: Clashing Views on Controversial Educational Issues,* 8th ed. (Guilford: Dushkin, 1995), 241.

69. Ravitch, "Politicization," 244.

70. *Lau v Nichols,* 414 US 563; Ravitch, "Politicization," 244–45.

71. Ravitch, "Politicization," 248.

72. Ravitch, "Politicization," 246. Ravitch is quoting from Iris Rotberg, "Some Legal and Research Considerations in Establishing Federal Policy in Bilingual Education," *Harvard Educational Review* 52 (May 1982): 148–68.

73. Ravitch, "Politicization," 245–46.

74. György Andrássy, "National or Ethnic Minorities and Individual Language Rights," *Studia Iuridica, Auctoritate Universitatis Pécs Publicata* 123 (1996): 37.

75. Joseph Raz, *The Morality of Freedom* (Oxford: Clarendon Press, 1986), 166, 208.

76. Denise G. Réaume, "The Group Right to Linguistic Security: Whose Right, What Duties?" in *Group Rights,* ed. Judith Baker (Toronto: University of Toronto Press, 1994), 119–20.

77. Réaume, "Group Right," 120.

78. Réaume, "Group Right," 121.

2

After the Family Wage:
A Postindustrial Thought Experiment

Nancy Fraser

The current crisis of the welfare state has many roots—global economic trends, massive movements of refugees and immigrants, popular hostility to taxes, the weakening of trade unions and labor parties, the rise of national and "racial"-ethnic antagonisms, the decline of solidaristic ideologies, and the collapse of state socialism. One absolutely crucial factor, however, is the crumbling of the old gender order. Existing welfare states are premised on assumptions about gender that are increasingly out of phase with many people's lives and self-understandings. They therefore do not provide adequate social protections, especially for women and children.

The gender order that is now disappearing descends from the industrial era of capitalism and reflects the social world of its origin. It was centered on the ideal of the family wage. In this world, people were supposed to be organized into heterosexual, male-headed nuclear families, which lived principally from the man's labor market earnings. The male head of the household would be paid a family wage, sufficient to support children and a wife-and-mother, who performed domestic labor without pay. Of course, countless lives never fit this pattern. Still, it provided the normative picture of a proper family.

The family-wage ideal was inscribed in the structure of most industrial-era welfare states.[1] That structure had three tiers, with social-insurance programs occupying the first rank. Designed to protect people from the vagaries of the labor market (and to protect the economy from shortages of demand), these programs replaced the breadwinner's wage in case of sickness, disability, unemployment, or old age. Many countries also featured a second tier of programs, providing direct support for full-time female homemaking and mothering. A third tier served the "residuum." Largely a holdover from traditional poor relief, public assistance programs provided paltry, stigmatized, means-tested aid to needy people who had no claim to honorable support because they did not fit the family-wage scenario.[2]

Today, however, the family-wage assumption is no longer tenable—either empirically or normatively. We are currently experiencing the death throes of the old, industrial gender order with the transition to a new, postindustrial phase of capitalism. The crisis of the welfare state is bound up with these epochal changes. It is rooted in part in the collapse of the world of the family wage and of its central assumptions about labor markets and families.

In the labor markets of postindustrial capitalism, few jobs pay wages sufficient to support a family single-handedly; many, in fact, are temporary or part-time and do not carry standard benefits.[3] Women's employment is increasingly common, moreover—although far less well paid than men's.[4] Postindustrial families, meanwhile, are less conventional and more diverse.[5] Heterosexuals are marrying less and later and divorcing more and sooner. And gays and lesbians are pioneering new kinds of domestic arrangements.[6] Gender norms and family forms are highly contested, finally. Thanks in part to the feminist and gay-and-lesbian liberation movements, many people no longer prefer the male breadwinner/female homemaker model. One result of these trends is a steep increase in solo-mother families: Growing numbers of women, both divorced and never married, are struggling to support themselves and their families without access to a male breadwinner's wage. Their families have high rates of poverty.

In short, a new world of economic production and social reproduction is emerging—a world of less stable employment and more diverse families. Though no one can be certain about its ultimate shape, this much seems clear: The emerging world, no less than the world of the family wage, will require a welfare state that effectively insures people against uncertainties. It is clear, too, that the old forms of welfare state, built on assumptions of male-headed families and relatively stable jobs, are no longer suited to providing this protection. We need something new, a postindustrial welfare state suited to radically new conditions of employment and reproduction.

What, then, should a postindustrial welfare state look like? Conservatives have lately had a lot to say about "restructuring the welfare state," but their vision is counterhistorical and contradictory; they seek to reinstate the male breadwinner/female homemaker family for the middle class, while demanding that poor single mothers "work." Neoliberal proposals have recently emerged in the United States, but they, too, are inadequate in the current context. Punitive, androcentric, and obsessed with employment despite the absence of good jobs, they are unable to provide security in a postindustrial world.[7] Both these approaches ignore one crucial thing: A postindustrial welfare state, like its industrial predecessor, must support a gender order. But the only kind of gender order that can be acceptable today is one premised on gender equity.

Feminists, therefore, are in a good position to generate an emancipatory vision for the coming period. They, more than anyone, appreciate the importance of gender relations to the current crisis of the industrial welfare state and the centrality of gender equity to any satisfactory resolution. Feminists also appreciate the importance of care work for human well-being and the effects of its social organization on women's standing. They are attuned, finally, to potential conflicts of interest within families and to the inadequacy of androcentric definitions of work.

To date, however, feminists have tended to shy away from systematic reconstructive thinking about the welfare state. Nor have we yet developed a satisfactory account of gender equity that can inform an emancipatory vision. We need now to undertake such thinking. We should ask: What new, postindustrial gender order should replace the family wage? And what sort of welfare state can best support such a new gender order? What account of gender equity best captures our highest aspirations? And what vision of social welfare comes closest to embodying it?

Two different sorts of answers are presently conceivable, I think, both of which qualify as feminist. The first I call the *Universal Breadwinner* model. It is the vision implicit in the current political practice of most US feminists and liberals. It aims to foster gender equity by promoting women's employment; the centerpiece of this model is state provision of employment-enabling services such as day care. The second possible answer I call the *Caregiver Parity* model. It is the vision implicit in the current political practice of most Western European feminists and social democrats. It aims to promote gender equity chiefly by supporting informal care work; the centerpiece of this model is state provision of caregiver allowances.

Which of these two approaches should command our loyalties in the coming period? Which expresses the most attractive vision of a postindustrial gender order? Which best embodies the ideal of gender equity? In this chapter, I outline a framework for thinking systematically about these questions. I analyze highly idealized versions of Universal Breadwinner and Caregiver Parity in the manner of a thought experiment. I postulate, contrary to fact, a world in which both these models are feasible in that their economic and political preconditions are in place. Assuming very favorable conditions, then, I assess the respective strengths and weaknesses of each.

The result is not a standard policy analysis, for neither Universal Breadwinner nor Caregiver Parity will in fact be realized in the near future; and my discussion is not directed primarily at policymaking elites. My intent, rather, is theoretical and political in a broader sense. I aim, first, to clarify some dilemmas surrounding *equality* and *difference* by reconsidering what is meant by *gender equity*. In so doing, I also aim to spur increased reflection on feminist strategies and goals by spelling out some assumptions that are implicit in current practice and subjecting them to critical scrutiny.

My discussion proceeds in four parts. In the first section, I propose an analysis of gender equity that generates a set of evaluative standards. Then, in the second and third sections, I apply those standards to Universal Breadwinner and Caregiver Parity, respectively. I conclude, in the fourth section, that neither of those approaches, even in an idealized form, can deliver full gender equity. To have a shot at *that*, I contend, we must develop a new vision of a postindustrial welfare state that effectively dismantles the gender division of labor.

GENDER EQUITY: A COMPLEX CONCEPTION

In order to evaluate alternative visions of a postindustrial welfare state, we need some normative criteria. Gender equity, I have said, is one indispensable standard. But in what precisely does it consist?

Feminists have so far associated gender equity with either equality or difference, where "equality" means treating women exactly like men, and where "difference" means treating women differently insofar as they differ from men. Theorists have debated the relative merits of these two approaches as if they represented two antithetical poles of an absolute dichotomy. These arguments have generally ended in stalemate. Proponents of "difference" have successfully shown that equality strategies typically presuppose "the male as norm," thereby disadvantaging women and imposing a distorted standard on everyone. Egalitarians have argued just as cogently, however, that difference approaches typically rely on essentialist notions of femininity, thereby reinforcing existing stereotypes and confining women within existing gender divisions.[8] Neither equality nor difference, then, is a workable conception of gender equity.

Feminists have responded to this stalemate in several different ways. Some have tried to resolve the dilemma by reconceiving one or another of its horns; they have reinterpreted difference or equality in what they consider a more defensible form. Others have concluded "a plague on both your houses" and sought some third, wholly other, normative principle. Still others have tried to embrace the dilemma as an enabling paradox, a resource to be treasured, not an impasse to be gotten round. Many feminists, finally, have retreated altogether from normative theorizing—into cultural positivism, piecemeal reformism, or postmodern antinomianism.

None of these responses is satisfactory. Normative theorizing remains an indispensable intellectual enterprise for feminism, indeed for all emancipatory social movements. We need a vision or picture of where we are trying to go and a set of standards for evaluating various proposals as to how we might get there. The equality/difference theoretical impasse is real, moreover; it cannot be simply sidestepped or embraced. Nor is there any "wholly other" third term that can magically catapult us beyond it. What, then, should feminist theorists do?

I propose we reconceptualize gender equity as a complex, not a simple, idea. This means breaking with the assumption that gender equity can be identified with any single value or norm, whether it be equality, difference, or something else. Instead we should treat it as a complex notion comprising a plurality of distinct normative principles. The plurality will include some notions associated with the equality side of the debate as well as some associated with the difference side. It will also encompass still other normative ideas that neither side has accorded due weight. Wherever they come from, however, the important point is this: Each of several distinct norms must be respected simultaneously in order that gender equity be achieved. Failure to satisfy any one of them means failure to realize the full meaning of gender equity.

In what follows, I assume that gender equity is complex in this way. And I propose an account of it that is designed for the specific purpose of evaluating alternative pictures of a postindustrial welfare state. For issues other than welfare, a somewhat different package of norms might be called for. Nevertheless, I believe that the general idea of treating gender equity as a complex conception is widely applicable. The analysis here may serve as a paradigm case demonstrating the usefulness of this approach.

For this particular thought experiment, in any case, I unpack the idea of gender equity as a compound of seven distinct normative principles. Let me enumerate them one by one.

The antipoverty principle. The first and most obvious objective of social-welfare provision is to prevent poverty. Preventing poverty is crucial to achieving gender equity now, after the family wage, given the high rates of poverty in solo-mother families and the vastly increased likelihood that US women and children will live in such families.[9] If it accomplishes nothing else, a welfare state should at least relieve suffering by meeting otherwise unmet basic needs. Arrangements such as those in the United States that leave women, children, and men in poverty are unacceptable according to this criterion. Any postindustrial welfare state that prevented such poverty would constitute a major advance. So far, however, this does not say enough. The antipoverty principle might be satisfied in a variety of different ways, not all of which are acceptable. Some ways, such as the provision of targeted, isolating, and stigmatized poor relief for solo-mother families, fail to respect several of the following normative principles, which are also essential to gender equity in social welfare.

The antiexploitation principle. Antipoverty measures are important not only in themselves but also as a means to another basic objective: preventing exploitation of vulnerable people.[10] This principle, too, is central to achieving gender equity after the family wage. Needy women with no other way to feed themselves and their children, for example, are liable to exploitation—by abusive husbands, by sweatshop bosses, and by pimps. In guaranteeing relief of poverty, then, welfare provision should also aim to mitigate exploitable dependency.[11] The availability of an alternative source of income enhances the bargaining position of subordinates in unequal relationships. The nonemployed wife who knows she can support herself and her children outside of her marriage has more leverage within it; her "voice" is enhanced as her possibilities of "exit" increase.[12] The same holds for the low-paid nursing home attendant in relation to her boss.[13] For welfare measures to have this effect, however, support must be provided as a matter of right. When receipt of aid is highly stigmatized or discretionary, the antiexploitation principle is not satisfied.[14] At best, the claimant would trade exploitable dependence on a husband or a boss for exploitable dependence on a caseworker's whim.[15] The goal should be to prevent at least three kinds of exploitable dependencies: exploitable dependence on an individual family member, such as a husband or an adult child; exploitable dependence on employers and supervisors; and exploitable dependence on the personal whims of state officials.

Rather than shuttle people back and forth among these exploitable dependencies, an adequate approach must prevent all three simultaneously.[16] This principle rules out arrangements that channel a homemaker's benefits through her husband. It is likewise incompatible with arrangements that provide essential goods, such as health insurance, only in forms linked conditionally to scarce employment. Any postindustrial welfare state that satisfied the antiexploitation principle would represent a major improvement over current US arrangements. But even it might not be satisfactory. Some ways of satisfying this principle would fail to respect several of the following normative principles, which are also essential to gender equity in social welfare.

A postindustrial welfare state could prevent women's poverty and exploitation and yet still tolerate severe gender inequality. Such a welfare state is not satisfactory. A further dimension of gender equity in social provision is redistribution, reducing inequality between women and men. Equality, as we saw, has been criticized by some feminists. They have argued that it entails treating women exactly like men according to male-defined standards, and that this necessarily disadvantages women. That argument expresses a legitimate worry, which I shall address under another rubric below. But it does not undermine the ideal of equality per se. The worry pertains only to certain inadequate ways of conceiving equality, which I do not presuppose here. At least three distinct conceptions of equality escape the objection. These are essential to gender equity in social welfare.

Income equality. One form of equality that is crucial to gender equity concerns the distribution of real per capita income. This sort of equality is highly pressing now, after the family wage, when US women's earnings are approximately 70 percent of men's, when much of women's labor is not compensated at all, and when many women suffer from "hidden poverty" due to unequal distribution within families.[17] As I interpret it, the principle of income equality does not require absolute leveling. But it does rule out arrangements that reduce women's incomes after divorce by nearly half, while men's incomes nearly double.[18] It likewise rules out unequal pay for equal work and the wholesale undervaluation of women's labor and skills. The income-equality principle requires a substantial reduction in the vast discrepancy between men's and women's incomes. In so doing, it tends, as well, to help equalize the life chances of children, as a majority of US children are currently likely to live at some point in solo-mother families.[19]

Leisure-time equality. Another kind of equality that is crucial to gender equity concerns the distribution of leisure time. This sort of equality is highly pressing now, after the family wage, when many women, but only a few men, do both paid work and unpaid primary care work and when women suffer disproportionately from "time poverty."[20] One recent British study found that 52 percent of women surveyed, compared to 21 percent of men, said they "felt tired most of the time."[21] The leisure-time equality principle rules out welfare arrangements that would equalize incomes while requiring a double shift of work from women but only a single shift from men. It likewise rules out arrangements that would require women, but not men, to do either the "work of claiming" or the time-consuming "patchwork" of piecing together income from several sources and of coordinating services from different agencies and associations.[22]

Equality of respect. Equality of respect is also crucial to gender equity. This kind of equality is especially pressing now, after the family wage, when postindustrial culture routinely represents women as sexual objects for the pleasure of male subjects. The principle of equal respect rules out social arrangements that objectify and deprecate women—even if those arrangements prevent poverty and exploitation, and even if in addition they equalize income and leisure time. It is incompatible with welfare programs that trivialize women's activities and ignore women's contributions—such as "welfare reforms" in the United States that assume single mother claimants do not "work." Equality of respect requires recognition of women's personhood and recognition of women's work.

A postindustrial welfare state should promote equality in all three of these dimensions. Such a state would constitute an enormous advance over present arrangements, but even it might not go far enough. Some ways of satisfying the equality principles would fail to respect the following principle, which is also essential to gender equity in social welfare.

The antimarginalization principle. A welfare state could satisfy all the preceding principles and still function to marginalize women. By limiting support to generous mothers' pensions, for example, it could render women independent, well provided for, well rested, and respected but enclaved in a separate domestic sphere, removed from the life of the larger society. Such a welfare state would be unacceptable. Social policy should promote women's full participation on a par with men in all areas of social life—in employment, in politics, in the associational life of civil society. The antimarginalization principle requires provision of the necessary conditions for women's participation, including day care, elder care, and provision for breast-feeding in public. It also requires the dismantling of masculinist work cultures and woman-hostile political environments. Any postindustrial welfare state that provided these things would represent a great improvement over current arrangements. Yet even it might leave something to be desired. Some ways of satisfying the antimarginalization principle would fail to respect the last principle, which is also essential to gender equity in social welfare.

The antiandrocentrism principle. A welfare state that satisfied many of the foregoing principles could still entrench some obnoxious gender norms. It could assume the androcentric view that men's current life patterns represent the human norm and that women ought to assimilate to them. (This is the real issue behind the previously noted worry about equality.) Such a welfare state is unacceptable. Social policy should not require women to become like men nor to fit into institutions designed for men in order to enjoy comparable levels of well-being. Policy should aim instead to restructure androcentric institutions so as to welcome human beings who can give birth and who often care for relatives and friends, treating them not as exceptions but as ideal-typical participants. The antiandrocentrism principle requires decentering masculinist norms—in part by revaluing practices and traits that are currently undervalued because they are associated with women. It entails changing men as well as changing women.

Here, then, is an account of gender equity in social welfare. On this account, gender equity is a complex idea comprising seven distinct normative principles, each of which is necessary and essential.

No postindustrial welfare state can realize gender equity unless it satisfies them all.

How, then, do the principles interrelate? Here everything depends on context. Some institutional arrangements permit simultaneous satisfaction of several principles with a minimum of mutual interference; other arrangements, in contrast, set up zero-sum situations in which attempts to satisfy one principle interfere with attempts to satisfy another. Promoting gender equity after the family wage, therefore, means attending to multiple aims that are potentially in conflict. The goal should be to find approaches that avoid trade-offs and maximize prospects for satisfying all—or at least most—of the seven principles.

In the next sections, I use this approach to assess two alternative models of a postindustrial welfare state. First, however, I want to flag four sets of relevant issues. One concerns the social organization of care work. Precisely how this work is organized is crucial to human well-being in general and to the social standing of women in particular. In the era of the family wage, care work was treated as the private responsibility of individual women. Today, however, it can no longer be treated in that way. Some other way of organizing it is required, but a number of different scenarios are conceivable. In evaluating postindustrial welfare state models, then, we must ask: How is responsibility for care work allocated between such institutions as the family, the market, civil society, and the state? And how is responsibility for this work assigned within such institutions: by gender? by class? by "race"-ethnicity? by age?

A second set of issues concerns the bases of entitlement to provision. Every welfare state assigns its benefits according to a specific mix of distributive principles, which defines its basic moral quality. That mix, in each case, needs to be scrutinized. Usually it contains varying proportions of three basic principles of entitlement: need, desert, and citizenship. Need-based provision is the most redistributive, but it risks isolating and stigmatizing the needy; it has been the basis of traditional poor relief and of modern public assistance, the least honorable forms of provision. The most honorable, in contrast, is entitlement based on desert, but it tends to be antiegalitarian and exclusionary. Here one receives benefits according to one's "contributions," usually tax payments, work, and service—where *tax payments* means wage deductions paid into a special fund, *work* means primary labor-force employment, and *service* means the military, all interpretations of those terms that disadvantage women. Desert has usually been seen as the primary basis of earnings-linked social insurance in the industrial welfare state.[23] The third principle, citizenship, allocates provision on the basis of membership in society. It is honorable, egalitarian, and universalist but also expensive, hence hard to sustain at high levels of quality and generosity; some theorists worry, too, that it encourages free riding, which they define, however, androcentrically.[24] Citizenship-based entitlements are most often found in social-democratic countries, where they may include single-payer universal health insurance systems and universal family or child allowances; they are virtually unknown in the United States—except for public education. In examining models of postindustrial welfare states, then, one must look closely at the construction of entitlement. It makes considerable difference to women's and children's well-being, for example, whether day care places are distributed as citizenship entitlements or as desert-based entitlements, that is, whether or not they are conditional on prior employment. It likewise matters, to take another example, whether care work is supported on the basis of need, in the form of a means-tested benefit for the poor, or whether it is supported on the basis of desert, as return for "work" or "service," now interpreted nonandrocentrically, or whether, finally, it is supported on the basis of citizenship under a universal Basic Income scheme.

A third set of issues concerns differences among women. Gender is the principal focus of this chapter, to be sure, but it cannot be treated en bloc. The lives of women and men are crosscut by several other salient social divisions, including class, "race"-ethnicity, sexuality, and age. Models of postindustrial welfare states, then, will not affect all women—nor all men—in the same way; they will generate different outcomes for differently situated people. For example, some policies will affect women who have children differently from those who do not; some, likewise, will affect women who have access to a second income differently from those who do not; and some, finally, will affect women employed full-time differently from those employed part-time and differently yet again from those who are not employed. For each model, then, we must ask: Which groups of women would be advantaged and which groups disadvantaged?

A fourth set of issues concerns desiderata for postindustrial welfare states other than gender equity. Gender equity, after all, is not the only goal of social welfare. Also important are nonequity goals, such as efficiency, community, and individual liberty. In addition there remain other equity goals, such as "racial"-ethnic equity, generational equity, class equity, and equity among nations. All of these issues are necessarily backgrounded here. Some of them, however, such as "racial"-ethnic equity, could be handled via parallel thought experiments: One might define "racial"-ethnic equity as a complex idea, analogous to the way gender equity is treated here, and then use it, too, to assess competing visions of a postindustrial welfare state.

With these considerations in mind, let us now examine two strikingly different feminist visions of a postindustrial welfare state. And let us ask: Which comes closest to achieving gender equity in the sense I have elaborated here?

THE UNIVERSAL BREADWINNER MODEL

In one vision of postindustrial society, the age of the family wage would give way to the age of the Universal Breadwinner. This is the vision implicit in the current political practice of most US feminists and liberals. (It was also assumed in the former communist countries!) It aims to achieve gender equity principally by promoting women's employment. The point is to enable women to support themselves and their families through their own wage earning. The breadwinner role is to be universalized, in sum, so that women, too, can be citizen-workers.

Universal Breadwinner is a very ambitious postindustrial scenario, requiring major new programs and policies. One crucial element is a set of employment-enabling services, such as day care and elder care, aimed at freeing women from unpaid responsibilities so they could take full-time employment on terms comparable to men.[25] Another essential element is a set of workplace reforms aimed at removing equal-opportunity obstacles, such as sex discrimination and sexual harassment. Reforming the workplace requires reforming the culture, however—eliminating sexist stereotypes and breaking the cultural association of breadwinning with masculinity. Also required are policies to help change socialization so as, first, to reorient women's aspirations toward employment and away from domesticity, and second, to reorient men's expectations toward acceptance of women's new role. None of this would work, however, without one additional ingredient: macroeconomic policies to create full-time, high-paying, permanent jobs for women.[26] These would have to be true breadwinner jobs in the primary labor force, carrying full, first-class social-insurance entitlements. Social insurance, finally, is central to Universal Breadwinner. The aim here is to bring women up to parity with men in an institution that has traditionally disadvantaged them.

How would this model organize care work? The bulk of such work would be shifted from the family to the market and the state, where it would be performed by employees for pay.[27] Who, then, are these employees likely to be? In many countries today, including the United States, paid institutional care work is poorly remunerated, feminized, and largely racialized and/or performed by immigrants.[28] But such arrangements are precluded in this model. If the model is to succeed in enabling *all* women to be breadwinners, it must upgrade the status and pay attached to care work employment, making it, too, into primary labor-force work. Universal Breadwinner, then, is necessarily committed to a policy of "comparable worth"; it must redress the widespread undervaluation of skills and jobs currently coded as feminine and/or "nonwhite," and it must remunerate such jobs with breadwinner-level pay.

Universal Breadwinner would link many benefits to employment and distribute them through social insurance, with levels varying according to earnings. In this respect, the model resembles the industrial-era welfare state.[29] The difference is that many more women would be covered on the basis of their own employment records. And many more women's employment records would look considerably more like men's.

Not all adults can be employed, however. Some will be unable to work for medical reasons, including some not previously employed. Others will be unable to get jobs. Some, finally, will have care work responsibilities that they are unable or unwilling to shift elsewhere. Most of these last will be women. To provide for these people, Universal Breadwinner must include a residual tier of social welfare that provides need-based, means-tested wage replacements.[30]

Universal Breadwinner is far removed from present realities. It requires massive creation of primary labor-force jobs—jobs sufficient to support a family single-handedly. That, of course, is wildly askew of current postindustrial trends, which generate jobs not for bread-winners but for "disposable workers."[31] Let us assume for the sake of the thought experiment, however, that its conditions of possibility could be met. And let us consider whether the resulting postindustrial welfare state could claim title to gender equity.

Antipoverty. We can acknowledge straight off that Universal Breadwinner would do a good job of preventing poverty. A policy that created secure breadwinner-quality jobs for all employable women and men—while providing the services that would enable women to take such jobs—would keep most families out of poverty. And generous levels of residual support would keep the rest out of poverty through transfers.[32]

Antiexploitation. The model should also succeed in preventing exploitable dependency for most women. Women with secure bread-winner jobs are able to exit unsatisfactory relations with men. And those who do not have such jobs but know they can get them will also be less vulnerable to exploitation. Failing that, the residual system of income support provides backup protection against exploitable dependency—assuming that it is generous, nondiscretionary, and honorable.[33]

Income equality. Universal Breadwinner is only fair, however, at achieving income equality. Granted, secure breadwinner jobs for women—plus the services that would enable women to take them—would narrow the gender wage gap.[34] Reduced inequality in earnings, moreover, translates into reduced inequality in social-insurance benefits. And the availability of exit options from marriage should encourage a more equitable distribution of resources within it. But the model is not otherwise egalitarian. It contains a basic social fault-line dividing breadwinners from others, to the considerable disadvantage of the others—most of whom would be women. Apart from comparable worth, moreover, it does not reduce pay inequality among breadwinner jobs. To be sure, the model reduces the weight of gender in assigning individuals to unequally compensated bread-winner jobs; but it thereby increases the weight of other variables, presumably class, education, "race"-ethnicity, and age. Women—and men—who are disadvantaged in relation to those axes of social differentiation will earn less than those who are not.

Leisure-time equality. The model is quite poor, moreover, with respect to equality of leisure time, as we know from the Communist experience. It assumes that all of women's current domestic and care work responsibilities can be shifted to the market or the state. But that assumption is patently unrealistic. Some things, such as childbearing, attending to family emergencies, and much parenting work, cannot be shifted—short of universal surrogacy and other presumably undesirable arrangements. Other things, such as cooking and (some) housekeeping, could—provided we were prepared to accept collective living arrangements or high levels of commodification. Even those tasks that are shifted, finally, do not disappear without a trace but give rise to burdensome new tasks of coordination. Women's chances for equal leisure, then, depend on whether men can be induced to do their fair share of this work. On this, the model does not inspire confidence. Not only does it offer no disincentives to free riding, but in valorizing paid work, it implicitly denigrates unpaid work, thereby fueling the motivation to shirk.[35] Women without partners would in any case be on their own. And those in lower-income households would be less able to purchase replacement services. Employed women would have a second shift on this model, then, albeit a less burdensome one than some have now; and there would be many more women employed full-time. Universal Breadwinner, in sum, is not likely to deliver equal leisure. Anyone who does not free ride in this possible postindustrial world is likely to be harried and tired.

Equality of respect. The model is only fair, moreover, at delivering equality of respect. Because it holds men and women to the single standard of the citizen-worker, its only chance of eliminating the gender respect gap is to admit women to that status on the same terms as men. This, however, is unlikely to occur. A more likely outcome is that women would retain more connection to reproduction and domesticity than men, thus appearing as breadwinners manqué. In addition, the model is likely to generate another kind of respect gap. By putting a high premium on breadwinner status, it invites disrespect for others. Participants in the means-tested residual system will be liable to stigmatization; and most of these will be women. Any employment-centered model, even a feminist one, has a hard time constructing an honorable status for those it defines as "nonworkers."

Antimarginalization. This model is also only fair at combating women's marginalization. Granted, it promotes women's participation in employment, but its definition of participation is narrow. Expecting full-time employment of all who are able, the model may actually impede participation in politics and civil society. Certainly, it does nothing to promote women's participation in those arenas. It fights women's marginalization, then, in a one-sided, "workerist" way.

Antiandrocentrism. Lastly, the model performs poorly in overcoming androcentrism. It valorizes men's traditional sphere—employment—and simply tries to help women fit in. Traditionally female care work, in contrast, is treated instrumentally; it is what must be sloughed off in order to become a breadwinner. It is not itself accorded social value. The ideal-typical citizen here is the breadwinner, now nominally gender-neutral. But the content of the status is implicitly masculine; it is the male half of the old breadwinner/homemaker couple, now universalized and required of everyone. The female half of the couple has simply disappeared. None of her distinctive virtues and capacities has been preserved for women, let alone universalized to men. The model is androcentric.

We can summarize the merits of Universal Breadwinner as follows:

Antipoverty	good
Antiexploitation	good
Income equality	fair
Leisure-time equality	poor
Equality of respect	fair
Antimarginalization	fair
Antiandrocentrism	poor

Not surprisingly, Universal Breadwinner delivers the best outcomes to women whose lives most closely resemble the male half of the old family-wage ideal couple. It is especially good to childless women and to women without other major domestic responsibilities that cannot easily be shifted to social services. But for those women, as well as for others, it falls short of full gender equity.

THE CAREGIVER PARITY MODEL

In a second vision of postindustrial society, the era of the family wage would give way to the era of Caregiver Parity. This is the picture implicit in the political practice of most Western European feminists and social democrats. It aims to promote gender equity principally by supporting informal care work. The point is to enable women with significant domestic responsibilities to support themselves and their families either through care work alone or through care work plus part-time employment. (Women without significant domestic responsibilities would presumably support themselves through employment.) The aim is not to make women's lives the same as men's but rather to "make difference costless."[36] Thus, childbearing, child rearing, and informal domestic labor are to be elevated to parity with formal paid labor. The caregiver role is to be put on a par with the breadwinner role—so that women and men can enjoy equivalent levels of dignity and well-being.

Caregiver Parity is also extremely ambitious. On this model, many (though not all) women will follow the current US female practice of alternating spells of full-time employment, spells of full-time care work, and spells that combine part-time care work with part-time employment. The aim is to make such a life pattern costless. To this end, several major new programs are necessary. One is a program of caregiver allowances to compensate childbearing, child raising, housework, and other forms of socially necessary domestic labor; the allowances must be sufficiently generous at the full-time rate to support a family—hence, equivalent to a breadwinner wage.[37] Also required is a program of workplace reforms. These must facilitate the possibility of combining supported care work with part-time employment and of making transitions between different life states.

The key here is flexibility. One obvious necessity is a generous program of mandated pregnancy and family leave so that caregivers can exit and enter employment without losing security or seniority. Another is a program of retraining and job search for those not returning to old jobs. Also essential is mandated flex-time so that caregivers can shift their hours to accommodate their care work responsibilities, including shifts between full- and part-time employment. Finally, in the wake of all this flexibility, there must be programs to ensure continuity of all the basic social-welfare benefits, including health, unemployment, disability, and retirement insurance.

This model organizes care work very differently from Universal Breadwinner. Whereas that approach shifted care work to the market and the state, this one keeps the bulk of such work in the household and supports it with public funds. Caregiver Parity's social-insurance system also differs sharply. To assure continuous coverage for people alternating between care work and employment, benefits attached to both must be integrated in a single system. In this system, part-time jobs and supported care work must be covered on the same basis as full-time jobs. Thus, a woman finishing a spell of supported care work would be eligible for unemployment insurance benefits on the same basis as a recently laid off employee in the event she could not find a suitable job. And a supported care worker who became disabled would receive disability payments on the same basis as a disabled employee. Years of supported care work would count on a par with years of employment toward eligibility for retirement pensions. Benefit levels would be fixed in ways that treat care work and employment equivalently.[38]

Caregiver Parity also requires another, residual tier of social welfare. Some adults will be unable to do either care work or waged work, including some without prior work records of either type. Most of these people will probably be men. To provide for them, the model must offer means-tested wage-and-allowance replacements.[39] Caregiver Parity's residual tier should be smaller than Universal Breadwinner's, however; nearly all adults should be covered in the integrated breadwinner-caregiver system of social insurance.

Caregiver Parity, too, is far removed from current US arrangements. It requires large outlays of public funds to pay caregiver allowances, hence major structural tax reform and a sea change in political culture. Let us assume for the sake of the thought experiment, however, that its conditions of possibility could be met. And let us consider whether the resulting postindustrial welfare state could claim title to gender equity.

Antipoverty. Caregiver Parity would do a good job of preventing poverty—including for those women and children who are currently most vulnerable. Sufficiently generous allowances would keep solo-mother families out of poverty during spells of full-time care work. And a combination of allowances and wages would do the same during spells of part-time supported care work and part-time employment.[40] Since each of these options would carry the basic social-insurance package, moreover, women with "feminine" work patterns would have considerable security.[41]

Antiexploitation. Caregiver Parity should also succeed in preventing exploitation for most women, including for those who are most vulnerable today. By providing income directly to nonemployed wives, it reduces their economic dependence on husbands. It also provides economic security to single women with children, reducing their liability to exploitation by employers. Insofar as caregiver allowances are honorable and nondiscretionary, finally, recipients are not subject to caseworkers' whims.[42]

Income equality. Caregiver Parity performs quite poorly, however, with respect to income equality, as we know from the Nordic experience. Although the system of allowances-plus-wages provides the equivalent of a basic minimum breadwinner wage, it also institutes a "mommy track" in employment—a market in flexible, noncontinuous full- and/or part-time jobs. Most of these jobs will pay considerably less even at the full-time rate than comparable breadwinner-track jobs. Two-partner families will have an economic incentive to keep one partner on the breadwinner track rather than to share spells of care work between them; and given current labor markets, making the breadwinner the man will be most advantageous for heterosexual couples. Given current culture and socialization, moreover, men are generally unlikely to choose the mommy track in the same proportions as women. So the two employment tracks will carry traditional gender associations. Those associations are likely in turn to produce discrimination against women in the breadwinner track. Caregiver Parity may make difference cost less, then, but it will not make difference costless.

Leisure-time equality. Caregiver Parity does somewhat better, however, with respect to equality of leisure time. It makes it possible for all women to avoid the double shift if they choose, by opting for full- or part-time supported care work at various stages in their lives. (Currently, this choice is available only to a small percentage of privileged US women.) We just saw, however, that this choice is not truly costless. Some women with families will not want to forego the benefits of breadwinner-track employment and will try to combine it with care work. Those not partnered with someone on the caregiver track will be significantly disadvantaged with respect to leisure time and probably in their employment as well. Men, in contrast, will largely be insulated from this dilemma. On leisure time, then, the model is only fair.

Equality of respect. Caregiver Parity is also only fair at promoting equality of respect. Unlike Universal Breadwinner, it offers two different routes to that end. Theoretically, citizen-workers and citizen-caregivers are statuses of equivalent dignity. But are they really on a par with one another? Caregiving is certainly treated more respectfully in this model than in current US society, but it remains associated with femininity. Breadwinning likewise remains associated with masculinity. Given those traditional gender associations, plus the economic differential between the two lifestyles, caregiving is unlikely to attain true parity with breadwinning. In general, it is hard to imagine how "separate but equal" gender roles could provide genuine equality of respect today.

Antimarginalization. Caregiver Parity performs poorly, moreover, in preventing women's marginalization. By supporting women's informal care work, it reinforces the view of such work as women's work and consolidates the gender division of domestic labor. By consolidating dual labor markets for breadwinners and caregivers, moreover, the model marginalizes women within the employment sector. By reinforcing the association of caregiving with femininity, finally, it may also impede women's participation in other spheres of life, such as politics and civil society.

Antiandrocentrism. Yet Caregiver Parity is better than Universal Breadwinner at combating androcentrism. It treats caregiving as intrinsically valuable, not as a mere obstacle to employment, thus challenging the view that only men's traditional activities are fully human. It also accommodates "feminine" life patterns, thereby rejecting the demand that women assimilate to "masculine" patterns. But the model still leaves something to be desired. Caregiver Parity stops short of affirming the universal value of activities and life patterns associated with women. It does not value caregiving enough to demand that men do it, too; it does not ask men to change. Thus, Caregiver Parity represents only one-half of a full-scale challenge to androcentrism. Here, too, its performance is only fair.

Caregiver Parity's strengths and weaknesses are summarized below:

Antipoverty	good
Antiexploitation	good
Income equality	poor
Leisure-time equality	fair
Equality of respect	fair
Antimarginalization	poor
Antiandrocentrism	fair

In general, Caregiver Parity improves the lot of women with significant care work responsibilities. But for those women, as well as for others, it fails to deliver full gender equity.

Toward a Universal Caregiver Model

Both Universal Breadwinner and Caregiver Parity are highly utopian visions of a postindustrial welfare state. Either one of them would represent a major improvement over current US arrangements. Yet neither is likely to be realized soon. Both models assume background preconditions that are strikingly absent today. Both presuppose major political-economic restructuring, including significant public control over corporations, the capacity to direct investment to create high-quality permanent jobs, and the ability to tax profits and wealth at rates sufficient to fund expanded high-quality social programs. Both models also assume broad popular support for a postindustrial welfare state that is committed to gender equity.

If both models are utopian in this sense, neither is utopian enough. Neither Universal Breadwinner nor Caregiver Parity can actually make good on its promise of gender equity—even under very favorable conditions. Although both are good at preventing women's poverty and exploitation, both are only fair at redressing inequality of respect: Universal Breadwinner holds women to the same standard as men, while constructing arrangements that prevent them from meeting it fully; Caregiver Parity, in contrast, sets up a double standard to accommodate gender difference, while institutionalizing policies that fail to assure equivalent respect for "feminine" activities and life patterns. When we turn to the remaining principles, moreover, the two models' strengths and weaknesses diverge. Universal Breadwinner fails especially to promote equality of leisure time and to combat androcentrism, while Caregiver Parity fails especially to promote income equality and to prevent women's marginalization. Neither model, in addition, promotes women's full participation on a par with men in politics and civil society. And neither values female-associated practices enough to ask men to do them too; neither asks men to change. (The relative merits of Universal Breadwinner and Caregiver Parity are summarized below.) Neither model, in sum, provides everything feminists want. Even in a highly idealized form, neither delivers full gender equity.

	Universal Breadwinner	Caregiver Parity
Antipoverty	good	good
Antiexploitation	good	good
Income equality	fair	poor
Leisure-time equality	poor	fair
Equality of respect	fair	fair
Antimarginalization	fair	poor
Antiandrocentrism	poor	fair

If these were the only possibilities, we would face a very difficult set of trade-offs. Suppose, however, we reject this Hobson's choice and try to develop a third alternative. The trick is to envision a postindustrial welfare state that combines the best of Universal Breadwinner with the best of Caregiver Parity while jettisoning the worst features of each. What third alternative is possible?

So far we have examined—and found wanting—two initially plausible approaches: one aiming to make women more like men are now; the other leaving men and women pretty much unchanged, while aiming to make women's difference costless. A third possibility is to induce men to become more like most women are now—namely, people who do primary care work.

Consider the effects of this one change on the models we have just examined. If men were to do their fair share of care work, Universal Breadwinner would come much closer to equalizing leisure time and eliminating androcentrism, while Caregiver Parity would do a much better job of equalizing income and reducing women's marginalization. Both models, in addition, would tend to promote equality of respect. If men were to become more like women are now, in sum, both models would begin to approach gender equity.

The key to achieving gender equity in a postindustrial welfare state, then, is to make women's current life patterns the norm for everyone. Women today often combine breadwinning and caregiving, albeit with great difficulty and strain. A postindustrial welfare state must ensure that men do the same, while redesigning institutions so as to eliminate the difficulty and strain. We might call this vision *Universal Caregiver*.

What, then, might such a welfare state look like? Unlike Caregiver Parity, its employment sector would not be divided into two different tracks; all jobs would be designed for workers who are caregivers, too; all would have a shorter work week than full-time jobs have now; and all would have the support of employment-enabling services. Unlike Universal Breadwinner, however, employees would not be assumed to shift all care work to social services. Some informal care work would be publicly supported and integrated on a par with paid work in a single social-insurance system. Some would be performed in households by relatives and friends, but such households would not necessarily be heterosexual nuclear families. Other supported care work would be located outside households altogether—in civil society. In state-funded but locally organized institutions, childless adults, older people, and others without kin-based responsibilities would join parents and others in democratic, self-managed care work activities.

A Universal Caregiver welfare state would promote gender equity by effectively dismantling the gendered opposition between breadwinning and caregiving. It would integrate activities that are currently separated from one another, eliminate their gender coding, and encourage men to perform them too. This, however, is tantamount to a wholesale restructuring of the institution of gender. The construction of breadwinning and caregiving as separate roles, coded masculine and feminine respectively, is a principal undergirding of the current gender order. To dismantle those roles and their cultural coding is, in effect, to overturn that order. It means subverting the existing gender division of labor and reducing the salience of gender as a structural principle of social organization.[43] At the limit, it suggests deconstructing gender.[44] By deconstructing the opposition between breadwinning and caregiving, moreover, Universal Caregiver would simultaneously deconstruct the associated opposition between bureaucratized public institutional settings and intimate private domestic settings. Treating civil society as an additional site for care work, it would overcome both the "workerism" of Universal Breadwinner and the domestic privatism of Caregiver Parity. Thus, Universal Caregiver promises expansive new possibilities for enriching the substance of social life and for promoting equal participation.

Only by embracing the Universal Caregiver vision, moreover, can we mitigate potential conflicts among our seven component principles of gender equity and minimize the need for trade-offs. Rejecting this approach, in contrast, makes such conflicts, and hence trade-offs, more likely. Achieving gender equity in a postindustrial welfare state, then, requires deconstructing gender.

Much more work needs to be done to develop this third—Universal Caregiver—vision of a postindustrial welfare state. A key is to develop policies that discourage free riding. Contra conservatives, the real free riders in the current system are not poor solo mothers who shirk employment. Instead they are men of all classes who shirk care work and domestic labor, as well as corporations that free ride on the labor of working people, both underpaid and unpaid.

A good statement of the Universal Caregiver vision comes from the Swedish Ministry of Labor: "To make it possible for both men and women to combine parenthood and gainful employment, a new view of the male role and a radical change in the organization of working life are required."[45] The trick is to imagine a social world in which citizens' lives integrate wage earning, caregiving, community activism, political participation, and involvement in the associational life of civil society—while also leaving time for some fun. This world is not likely to come into being in the immediate future. But it is the only imaginable postindustrial world that promises true gender equity. And unless we are guided by this vision now, we will never get any closer to achieving it.

NOTES

"After the Family Wage: A Postindustrial Thought Experiment" (Copyright © Nancy Fraser) is reprinted from Nancy Fraser, *Justice Interruptus: Critical Reflections on the "Postsocialist" Condition* (New York: Routledge, 1997). Research for this essay was supported by the Center for Urban Affairs and Policy Research, Northwestern University. For helpful comments, I am indebted to Rebecca Blank, Joshua Cohen, Fay Cook, Barbara Hobson, Axel Honneth, Jenny Mansbridge, Linda Nicholson, Ann Shola Orloff, John Roemer, Ian Schapiro, Tracy Strong, Peter Taylor-Gooby, Judy Wittner, Eli Zaretsky, and the members of the Feminist Public Policy Work Group of the Center for Urban Affairs and Policy Research, Northwestern University.

1. Mimi Abramowitz, *Regulating the Lives of Women: Social Welfare Policy from Colonial Times to the Present* (Boston: South End Press, 1988); Nancy Fraser, "Women, Welfare, and the Politics of Need Interpretation," *Unruly Practices: Power, Discourse, and Gender in Contemporary Social Theory* (Minneapolis: University of Minnesota Press, 1989); Linda Gordon, "What Does Welfare Regulate?" *Social Research* 55, no. 4 (winter 1988): 609–30; Hilary Land, "Who Cares for the Family?" *Journal of Social Policy* 7, no. 3 (July 1978): 257–84. An exception to the built-in family-wage assumption is France, which from early on accepted high levels of female waged work. See Jane Jenson, "Representations of Gender: Policies to 'Protect' Women Workers and Infants in France and the United States Before 1914," in *Women, the State, and Welfare*, ed. Linda Gordon (Madison: University of Wisconsin Press, 1990).

2. This account of the tripartite structure of the welfare state represents a modification of the account I proposed in Fraser, "Women, Welfare." There, I followed Barbara Nelson in positing a two-tier structure of ideal-typically "masculine" social-insurance programs and ideal-typically "feminine" family support programs. See Nelson, "Women's Poverty and Women's Citizenship: Some Political Consequences of Economic Marginality," *Signs: Journal of Women in Culture and Society* 10, no. 2 (winter

1984): 209–31 and "The Origins of the Two-Channel Welfare State: Workmen's Compensation and Mothers' Aid," in Gordon, *Women, the State, and Welfare*. Although that view was a relatively accurate picture of the US social-welfare system, I now consider it analytically misleading. The United States is unusual in that the second and third tiers are conflated. The main program of means-tested poor relief—Aid to Families with Dependent Children (AFDC)—is also the main program that supports women's child raising. Analytically, these are best understood as two distinct tiers of social welfare. When social insurance is added, we get a three-tier welfare state.

3. David Harvey, *The Condition of Postmodernity: An Inquiry into the Origins of Cultural Change* (Oxford: Blackwell, 1989); Scott Lash and John Urry, *The End of Organized Capitalism* (Cambridge: Polity Press, 1987); Robert Reich, *The Work of Nations: Preparing Ourselves for 21st Century Capitalism* (New York: Knopf, 1991).

4. Joan Smith, "The Paradox of Women's Poverty: Wage-Earning Women and Economic Transformation," *Signs: Journal of Women in Culture and Society* 9, no. 2 (winter 1984): 291–310.

5. Judith Stacey, "Sexism by a Subtler Name? Postindustrial Conditions and Postfeminist Consciousness in the Silicon Valley," *Socialist Review*, no. 96 (1987): 7–28.

6. Kath Weston, *Families We Choose: Lesbians, Gays, Kinship*. (New York: Columbia University Press, 1991).

7. Nancy Fraser, "Clintonism, Welfare, and the Antisocial Wage: The Emergence of a Neoliberal Political Imaginary," *Rethinking Marxism* 6, no. 1 (spring 1993): 9–23.

8. Some of the most sophisticated discussions are found in *Feminist Legal Theory: Readings in Law and Gender*, ed. Katharine T. Bartlett and Rosanne Kennedy (Boulder: Westview Press, 1991).

9. David T. Ellwood, *Poor Support: Poverty in the American Family* (New York: Basic Books, 1988).

10. Robert Goodin, *Reasons for Welfare: The Political Theory of the Welfare State* (Princeton: Princeton University Press, 1988).

11. Not all dependencies are exploitable. In *Reasons for Welfare* (pp. 175–76), Goodin specifies the following four conditions that must be met if a dependency is to be exploitable: the relationship must be asymmetrical; the subordinate party must need the resource that the superordinate supplies; the subordinate must depend on some particular superordinate for the supply of needed resources; and the superordinate must enjoy discretionary control over the resources that the subordinate needs from him or her.

12. Albert O. Hirschman, *Exit, Voice, and Loyalty: Responses to Decline in Firms, Organizations, and States* (Cambridge: Harvard University Press, 1970); Susan Moller Okin, *Justice, Gender, and the Family* (New

York: Basic Books, 1989); Barbara Hobson, "No Exit, No Voice: Women's Economic Dependency and the Welfare State," *Acta Sociologica* 33, no. 3 (fall 1990): 235–50.

13. Frances Fox Piven and Richard A. Cloward, *Regulating the Poor* (New York: Random House, 1971); Gosta Esping-Andersen, *The Three Worlds of Welfare Capitalism* (Princeton: Princeton University Press, 1990).

14. Goodin, *Reasons for Welfare.*

15. Edward V. Sparer, "The Right to Welfare," in *The Rights of Americans: What They Are—What They Should Be,* ed. Norman Dorsen (New York: Pantheon, 1970).

16. Ann Shola Orloff, "Gender and the Social Rights of Citizenship: The Comparative Analysis of Gender Relations and Welfare States," *American Sociological Review* 58, no. 3 (June 1993): 303–28. The antiexploitation objective should not be confused with current US attacks on "welfare dependency," which are highly ideological. These attacks define "dependency" exclusively as receipt of public assistance. They ignore the ways in which such receipt can promote claimants' independence by preventing exploitable dependence on husbands and employers. For a critique of such views, see Nancy Fraser and Linda Gordon, "A Genealogy of 'Dependency': Tracing a Keyword of the U.S. Welfare State," *Signs: Journal of Women in Culture and Society* 19, no. 2 (winter 1994): 309–36.

17. Ruth Lister, "Women, Economic Dependency, and Citizenship," *Journal of Social Policy* 19, no. 4 (1990): 445–67; Amartya Sen, "More Than 100 Million Women Are Missing," *New York Review of Books,* December 20, 1990, 61–66.

18. Lenore Weitzman, *The Divorce Revolution: The Unexpected Social Consequences for Women and Children in America* (New York: Free Press, 1985).

19. Ellwood, *Poor Support,* 45.

20. Lois Bryson, "Citizenship, Caring, and Commodification" (paper presented at conference on "Crossing Borders: International Dialogues on Gender, Social Politics, and Citizenship," Stockholm, May 27–29, 1994); Arlie Hochschild, *The Second Shift: Working Parents and the Revolution at Home* (New York: Viking Press, 1989); Juliet Schor, *The Overworked American: The Unexpected Decline of Leisure* (New York: Basic Books, 1991).

21. Lister, "Women, Economic Dependency."

22. Laura Balbo, "Crazy Quilts," in *Women and the State,* ed. Ann Showstack Sassoon (London: Hutchinson, 1987).

23. Actually, there is a heavy ideological component in the usual view that public assistance is need-based, while social insurance is desert-based. Benefit levels in social insurance do not strictly reflect "contributions." Moreover, all government programs are financed by "contributions" in the form of taxation. Public assistance programs are financed from general

revenues, both federal and state. Welfare recipients, like others, contribute to these funds, for example, through payment of sales taxes. See Nancy Fraser and Linda Gordon, "Contract Versus Charity: Why Is There No Social Citizenship in the United States?" *Socialist Review* 22, no. 3 (July–September 1992): 45–68.

24. The free-rider worry is usually posed androcentrically as a worry about shirking paid employment. Little attention is paid, in contrast, to a far more widespread problem, namely, men's free riding on women's unpaid domestic labor. A welcome exception is Peter Taylor-Gooby, "Scrounging, Moral Hazard, and Unwaged Work: Citizenship and Human Need" (unpublished typescript, 1993).

25. Employment-enabling services could be distributed according to need, desert, or citizenship, but citizenship accords best with the spirit of the model. Means-tested day care targeted for the poor cannot help but signify a failure to achieve genuine breadwinner status; and desert-based day care sets up a catch-22: one must already be employed in order to get what is needed for employment. Citizenship-based entitlement is best, then, but it must make services available to all. This rules out Swedish-type arrangements, which fail to guarantee sufficient day care places and are plagued by long queues. For the Swedish problem, see Barbara Hobson, "Economic Dependency and Women's Social Citizenship: Some Thoughts on Esping-Andersen's Welfare State Regimes" (unpublished typescript, 1993).

26. That, incidentally, would be to break decisively with US policy, which has assumed since the New Deal that job creation is principally for men. Bill Clinton's 1992 campaign proposals for "industrial" and "infrastructural investment" policies were no exception in this regard. See Fraser, "Clintonism, Welfare."

27. Government could itself provide care work services in the form of public goods, or it could fund marketized provision through a system of vouchers. Alternatively, employers could be mandated to provide employment-enabling services for their employees, either through vouchers or in-house arrangements. The state option means higher taxes, of course, but it may be preferable nevertheless. Mandating employer responsibility creates a disincentive to hire workers with dependents, to the likely disadvantage of women.

28. Evelyn Nakano Glenn, "From Servitude to Service Work: Historical Continuities in the Racial Division of Paid Reproductive Labor," *Signs: Journal of Women in Culture and Society* 18, no. 1 (autumn 1992): 1–43.

29. The industrial-era welfare state, too, conditions entitlement on desert and defines "contribution" in traditional androcentric terms as employment and wage deductions.

30. Exactly what else must be provided inside the residual system will depend on the balance of entitlements outside it. If health insurance is provided universally as a citizen benefit, for example, then there need be no

means-tested health system for the nonemployed. If, however, mainstream health insurance is linked to employment, then a residual health care system will be necessary. The same holds for unemployment, retirement, and disability insurance. In general, the more that is provided on the basis of citizenship, instead of on the basis of desert, the less has to be provided on the basis of need. One could even say that desert-based entitlements create the necessity of need-based provision; thus, employment-linked social insurance creates the need for means-tested public assistance.

31. Peter Kilborn, "New Jobs Lack the Old Security in Time of 'Disposable Workers,'" *New York Times,* March 15, 1993, pp. A1, A6.

32. Failing that, however, several groups are especially vulnerable to poverty in this model: those who cannot work; those who cannot get secure, permanent, full-time, good-paying jobs—disproportionately women and people of color; and those with heavy, hard-to-shift, unpaid care work responsibilities—disproportionately women.

33. Failing that, however, the groups mentioned in the previous note remain especially vulnerable to exploitation—by abusive men, by unfair or predatory employers, by capricious state officials.

34. Exactly how much remains depends on the government's success in eliminating discrimination and in implementing comparable worth.

35. Universal Breadwinner presumably relies on persuasion to induce men to do their fair share of unpaid work. The chances of that working would be improved if the model succeeded in promoting cultural change and in enhancing women's voices within marriage. But it is doubtful that this alone would suffice, as the Communist experience suggests.

36. Christine A. Littleton, "Reconstructing Sexual Equality," in Bartlett and Kennedy, *Feminist Legal Theory.*

37. Caregiver allowances could be distributed on the basis of need, as a means-tested benefit for the poor—as they have always been in the United States. But that would contravene the spirit of Caregiver Parity. One cannot consistently claim that the caregiver life is equivalent in dignity to the breadwinner life, while supporting it only as a last-resort stop-gap against poverty. (This contradiction has always bedeviled mothers' pensions—and later Aid to Dependent Children—in the United States. Although these programs were intended by some advocates to exalt motherhood, they sent a contradictory message by virtue of being means-tested and morals-tested.) Means-tested allowances, moreover, would impede easy transitions between employment and care work. Since the aim is to make caregiving as deserving as breadwinning, caregiver allowances must be based on desert. Treated as compensation for socially necessary "service" or "work," they alter the standard androcentric meanings of those terms.

38. In *Justice, Gender, and the Family,* Okin has proposed an alternative way to fund care work. In her scheme, the funds would come from what are now considered to be the earnings of the caregiver's partner. A man with

a nonemployed wife, for example, would receive a paycheck for one-half of "his" salary; his employer would cut a second check in the same amount payable directly to the wife. Intriguing as this idea is, one may wonder whether it is really the best way to promote a wife's independence from her husband, as it ties her income so directly to his. In addition, Okin's proposal does not provide any care work support for women without employed partners. Caregiver Parity, in contrast, provides public support for all who perform informal care work. Who, then, are its beneficiaries likely to be? With the exception of pregnancy leave, all the model's benefits are open to everyone; so men as well as women can opt for a "feminine" life. Women, however, are considerably more likely to do so. Although the model aims to make such a life costless, it includes no positive incentives for men to change. Some men, of course, may simply prefer such a life and will choose it when offered the chance; most will not, however, given current socialization and culture. We shall see, moreover, that Caregiver Parity contains some hidden disincentives to male caregiving.

39. In this respect, it resembles the Universal Breadwinner model: Whatever additional essential goods are normally offered on the basis of desert must be offered here, too, on the basis of need.

40. Wages from full-time employment must also be sufficient to support a family with dignity.

41. Adults with neither care work nor employment records would be most vulnerable to poverty in this model; most of these would be men. Children, in contrast, would be well protected.

42. Once again, it is adults with neither care work nor employment records who are most vulnerable to exploitation in this model; and the majority of them would be men.

43. Okin, *Justice, Gender, and the Family.*

44. Joan Williams, "Deconstructing Gender," in Bartlett and Kennedy, *Feminist Legal Theory.*

45. Quoted in Lister, "Women, Economic Dependency," 463.

3

Genetic Equality? Gender, Class, and Ability Differences

Mary B. Mahowald

In common parlance, the term *equality* is often used interchangeably with *equity, fairness,* and *justice.* One thinks, for example, of the child who objects to unequal portions of dessert declaring, "That's not fair," or of discussions by adults of "equal pay for equal work" as a matter of economic equity. A just society is commonly construed as one in which all persons are treated equally, that is, without valuing some more than others on irrelevant grounds such as race, class, gender, ability, or sexual orientation.

Philosophers have distinguished among these terms. Equity, for example, has been used to refer to the unequal distribution of goods, based on an unequal need or right to them. Justice has been identified as the overarching ethical principle that requires fair procedures or equitable distribution. Justice as fairness, whether in John Rawls's or others' accounts, is described as necessitating inequality to promote equity.[1]

In both popular and philosophical accounts, equality is often identified with sameness. Equal treatment of individuals or groups is thus construed as providing them with the same treatment, neither more nor less, either quantitatively or qualitatively. For example, "preferential treatment" is viewed as unequal treatment because it treats different individuals or groups differently by putting one individual's or group's interests before those of others rather than on the same plane.

In this essay, I utilize a concept of equality that is different from sameness but accords with the popular interchangeability of equality with justice, fairness, and equity. I develop this concept in the context of a discussion of genetic differences among people, paying particular attention to differences associated with gender and disability. I also apply this concept to a set of differences, often involving gender and disability, that are applicable but not exclusively related to genetics, that is, class-based differences. I argue that this concept of equality is essential to ethically justifiable applications of genetics to all individuals. Because gender differences overlap with differences in ability and class, I argue on epistemological as well as ethical grounds for utilization of an egalitarian standpoint as a means of promoting genetic equality. Finally, I suggest a strategy for insuring that this concept is not simply supported theoretically but practically as fully as possible.

The Concept of Equality

Justice is universally accepted as a basic principle of law and ethics. Some regard it as superseding all other obligations, and some identify it with virtue in general or with the virtuous life. Most people, whether philosophers or nonphilosophers, agree with the formal principle of justice, based on Aristotle: Equals should be treated equally and unequals unequally.[2] They robustly disagree, however, with regard to the material principle of justice, which involves the meaning of equality that underlies the formal principle. Who should be considered equal and what it means to treat them equally are widely debated by scholars. In contrast, these questions are probably not debated enough by political leaders who champion equality as a fundamental social value. Clearly, the goals articulated in the name of equality are sometimes at odds with one another.

When Aristotle considers *equity* as distinct from *equality*, he refers to a situation in which like but different individuals or groups are regarded and treated justly but differently because they are equally valued.[3] The relationship between equity and equality is thus definable through the concept of *equal* value or the *same* value. Only when both terms are used as adjectives modifying *value* or modifying a synonym for value may they be appropriately interchanged. Equity deals with different individuals who are equally valued or valued to the same extent; inequity refers to a situation in which like but different individuals or groups are regarded and treated unjustly because they are not equally valued or valued to the same extent.[4] The concept of sameness relates to that of equality only when the value of different entities, as distinct from the entities themselves, is considered. In other words, while equality entails equal value or the same value for different entities, it does not imply that they are the same.

To clarify the concept further, consider how equality is expressed in arithmetical or algebraic equations such as $(2 + 3 = 5)$ and $(x = y)$. We may think of these symbol sets as applicable to the relationships between humans who are rich or poor, able or disabled, male or female. With regard to sex differences, for example, two people who are men and three people who are women equal five human beings, and one woman (x) equals one man (y), or to be chromosomally correct, $XX = XY$. In the first equation, we do not mean that two men and three women are precisely the same as any five human beings, and in the second equation we do not mean that a man is the same as a woman. In other words, the equality sign does not connote identity, because equality does not imply sameness even while it signifies the same value.

The same rationale is applicable to human beings with chromosomal arrangements other than XX or XY, some of which are associated with disabilities. Women with Turner syndrome and men with Klinefelter syndrome, for example, are not genetically identifiable as either XX or XY but as XO or XXY, respectively. Despite their differences, each equally represents a human being, to be valued to the same degree as individuals with XX or XY genotypes.

Likewise, justice demands that people from widely discrepant social or economic classes are of equal or the same value, even while they themselves (as well as their lifestyle, power, or circumstances) are quite different. Acknowledging such differences in no way implies that one class is of greater value than another. Neither does it imply that such differences should be ignored in dealing with these different people. In fact, the concept of equality, as I understand it, demands attention to these differences so as to insure that the individuals or groups who embody them are treated as equal in practice as well as in theory.

In *Inequality Reexamined*, Nobel laureate Amartya Sen provides a partial explanation for widespread confusion and ambiguity regarding the concept of equality: Most ethical theories concerning social arrangements are egalitarian in some respect; the differences among them arise from the variables identified as deserving equal attention or distribution. For Sen, even theories commonly considered antiegalitarian are egalitarian in terms of one focus while inegalitarian in terms of another. Citing Robert Nozick's libertarian theory as an example, he writes:

> A libertarian approach may give priority to extensive liberties to be *equally* guaranteed to each, and this demands rejecting equality—or any 'patterning'—of end states (e.g., the distribution of incomes or happiness). What is taken—usually by implication—to be a more central focus rules the roost, and inequalities in the variables that are, in effect, treated as peripheral must, then, be accepted in order not to violate the right arrangement (including equality) at the more central level.[5]

Sen considers it "a category mistake" to subscribe to the prevalent notion that one cannot maximize both liberty and equality. "Liberty," he says, "is among possible fields of application of equality, and equality is among the possible patterns of distribution of liberty."[6] The field and the pattern are simultaneously supportable.

For Sen, the correct question to pose regarding alternative theories of justice is not whether one is more egalitarian than another but what equality is endorsed by each theory, whether implicitly or explicitly, and how does the theorist defend that endorsement? His own answers to these questions take into account not only individual liberty and equal opportunity but the capability of individuals and groups to achieve the goals they define for themselves. "Capability," he says, "reflects a person's ability to choose between alternative lives (functioning combinations), and its valuation need not presuppose unanimity regarding some one specific set of objectives."[7] In other words, capability is determined from the standpoint of the individual agent or group. It is the power to achieve advantage over others, or at least to reduce one's disadvantage vis-à-vis others, but it is not equivalent to that power. Using Sen's concept, the ideal of genetic equality may be defined as a situation in which differences triggered or caused by genetics do not advantage an individual or group over others, despite the different capabilities with which they are associated. As a formula, this may be expressed as follows:

$$\frac{\text{Advantage of X}}{\text{Advantage of Y}} = 1$$

When differences associated with genetics lead to one individual or group having advantage over the other, there is inequality, which may be expressed as:

$$\frac{\text{Advantage of X}}{\text{Advantage of Y}} \neq 1$$

Differences associated with genetics may be virtually unchangeable, such as those due to sex or genetic endowment, while others, such as those due to gender socialization and socioeconomic status, are changeable. However, neither changeable nor unchangeable differences are necessarily associated with inequality. To the extent that differences related to genetics influence the capabilities and potential advantages of individuals and groups, genetic equality requires identification of the differences, determination of whether they are in fact associated with inequality, and efforts to eliminate or ameliorate the inequalities that occur. All of the differences added together for each individual or group would then be equal to the sum of differences in every other; in other words, a comparison of the advantages enjoyed by individuals or groups would always produce a ratio equal to 1, or as close as possible an approximation to 1.

According to Sen, capabilities of individuals and groups are influenced by factors beyond the primary goods delineated by Rawls. For Rawls, the primary goods include self-respect, rights and liberties, powers and opportunities, income and wealth, health and vigor, intelligence and imagination.[8] Such goods identify the means by which individuals may pursue their own idea of the good but fail to address the extent to which individuals are free (or unfree) to employ the means. The extent of one's freedom to employ the means is influenced by biological, social, and cultural factors that must also be considered. In other words, Rawls's account is helpful in developing a better understanding of how to promote equality of opportunity for different people to achieve different objectives, but he ignores the fact that people are not equally capable of utilizing the equal opportunities that Rawls (and Rawlsians) would set before them.

Unequal capabilities arise from many different characteristics of human beings, including but not limited to the overlapping characteristics of sex, socioeconomic status, and ability. As Sen puts it, such diverse characteristics "give us very divergent powers to build freedom in our lives even when we have the same bundle of primary goods."[9] To eliminate or reduce the inequalities associated with the "divergent powers" of individuals or groups requires attention to their different capabilities and their related advantages or disadvantages.

GENDER DIFFERENCES IN GENETICS

That genetics affects men and women differently is evident in clinical manifestations of genetic diseases, reproductive roles involving genetic testing or interventions, psychosocial factors related to genetic conditions and treatment, and caregiving of those who have genetic diseases. Having extensively documented these differences elsewhere, I but briefly consider them here.[10]

The clinical manifestations of gender differences in genetic disease may be categorized as follows:

those affecting only or primarily one sex, such as hemophilia in males and breast cancer in females;

those affecting the sexes in unequal ratios, such as fragile X syndrome (predominantly in males) and anencephaly (predominantly in females);

those determined by the sex or other characteristic of the transmitting parent, such as Down syndrome (transmitted by older mothers) and Marfan syndrome (transmitted by older fathers);

those affecting fertility in males or females, such as cystic fibrosis (males are infertile) and congenital adrenal hyperplasia (females are infertile); and

those in which pregnancy exacerbates the risk for affected women,
such as cystic fibrosis and sickle cell anemia.

All of these sex-based differences are relevant to equality to the
extent that they are associated with discrepant impact. Except for
the last, however, sex-based differences in the impact of genetic diseases entail burdens for men as well as women. In fact, because most
X-linked disorders are transmitted only to sons, men are burdened
more than women are by some genetic disorders. Still, women alone
transmit these and mitochondrial disorders to their children, and this
entails a psychological burden that men do not face.

Although mothers and fathers are equally parents of their offspring, they are not equally affected by their involvement in reproduction. Through prenatal procedures, women alone undergo tests
and treatment for the sake of their potential children. The risks,
invasiveness, cost, and effectiveness of these procedures vary considerably, from those that are routinely performed, relatively noninvasive, and highly accurate to those that are experimental, expensive,
invasive, and indefinitive in their results. For example, ultrasound is
routinely performed and noninvasive but often indefinitive, while
preimplantation genetic diagnosis is experimental and definitive but
costly and invasive because it involves in vitro fertilization. Many
genetic disorders are only identifiable late in pregnancy, when tests
and interventions are more difficult for women who undergo them.
Male partners are equally responsible for fertilization and for the
nurturance of children but do not themselves experience pregnancy
or childbirth, let alone the risks associated with prenatal tests and
interventions. Even when the male partner triggers the genetic disorder in the fetus, diagnostic and therapeutic procedures occur
through the woman's body.

As genetic tests proliferate and possibilities for fetal therapies increase, women will probably be expected, and in some cases pressured, to undergo more and greater risks for the sake of their potential offspring. Some fetal treatments, such as dietary restrictions

or supplementation, are noninvasive; others, such as fetal surgery, are radically invasive and highly experimental.[11] Moreover, as the infertility industry expands, women may increasingly feel pressured by family members or clinicians, as well as by stereotypical social expectations regarding childbearing, to accept invasive, costly, and risky treatment to solve the problem of male infertility associated with genetic disorders. Intracytoplasmic sperm injection (ICSI), for example, has been used to treat infertility in men with cystic fibrosis. The only "procedure" required of a man "undergoing" this treatment is self-administered: masturbation. In addition to gestation and childbirth, his partner experiences the risks and side effects of pain and discomfort associated with ovulation stimulation, ova retrieval, and embryo transfer.

Biological differences between men and women may trigger different psychological impacts on them. Women, for example, are more likely than men to feel guilty about genetic abnormalities in their offspring, even when these are attributable to their male partners rather than themselves. This feeling is related not only to their relatively unchangeable role in childbearing but also to their relatively changeable role in child rearing; in both cases, women's responsibilities are greater than those of men.

The connection between the impact of biological and psychological differences on men and their impact on women is also illustrated by studies showing that women place less emphasis than men on their genetic tie to children. Because modern reproductive technology allows for separation of genetics and gestation, women can be related to their offspring in one way but not the other; both relationships are biological, but gestation is more important to many women.[12] Men, of course, can only be biologically related to offspring through genetics. But many men not only prefer to have children who are genetically related to them (rather than adopted); they also consider the genetic tie between their partners and their children more important than the gestational relationship between them. Women are generally more open to adoption, placing greater emphasis on social parenthood.

Beyond the empirical sex-based differences related to biology and psychology are empirical gender-based differences in societal and economic practices. I will consider the economic impact of genetics in the next section. Its societal impact is greatly influenced by cultural and religious values and traditions, some of which are more egalitarian than others in their views about women, men, and the relationship between them. Probably the most complicated and controversial issue addressed by these traditions is abortion, which is hardly separable from prenatal decisions involving genetics. Although many traditions support abortion if it is necessary to save a woman's life, few view abortion as morally unproblematic, especially in the later stages of pregnancy, when definitive prenatal diagnosis is most likely to be performed. Whether or not women have a legal right to abortion, the autonomy of their decisions at that point may well be compromised by culturally defined and confining circumstances. Their interest in prenatal testing and intervention is surely influenced by these circumstances also.

Class Differences in Genetics

Relating gender differences to class differences is the phenomenon that Diana Pearce has characterized as "the feminization of poverty": the fact that the majority of the world's poor are women and their children.[13] In this section, however, I want to focus on class as a societal category that applies to men as well as women. Regardless of whether the poor are men or women, class differences connote inequality because they imply that one group has advantages vis-à-vis another. The advantage of one class over others is the capability afforded by their purchasing power. For the most part, poor people have none except that which the government provides, and that is not nearly equal to the capability enjoyed by others to take advantage of new genetic technologies, regardless of their cost. Technologies that have proved their cost-effectiveness to providers are typically covered by the government or by private insurance; those that have not proved their cost-effectiveness are available only to those who are able and willing to pay for them. Not only new genetic tests but advances in gene therapy are denied to those who cannot pay, including fetuses and children. The inequality engendered by this denial is exacerbated by the fact that poverty is itself an environmental factor that may influence the expression of multifactorial genetic diseases.

The impact of poverty on access to genetic services is not simply a matter of who can pay for them. Access also requires social circumstances and supports that do not interfere with their provision. Poor people, however, are less likely to be educated about the availability and usefulness of genetic tests or interventions. Those who are immigrants are less likely than others to find practitioners who can speak their language. Many poor people lack transportation or childcare costs essential for their access to genetic services. Their ability to change work schedules so as to fit appointment schedules is often limited, and required waiting times sometimes result in their being unable to obtain a legal abortion after positive genetic diagnosis.[14]

Both women and men have been denied access to jobs or insurance because of discriminatory practices associated with genetic disease or genetic susceptibility to disease. In a free-enterprise system, this will increasingly be the case as genetic tests proliferate. Such discriminatory practices introduce or exacerbate class-based inequality. The only way, I believe, by which such inequality can be avoided, or at least ameliorated, is by laws against genetic discrimination on the part of insurance companies and employers. Only bona fide occupational qualifications constitute a morally legitimate basis for excluding employees on grounds of genetic disease or genetic susceptibility. To insure against genetic discrimination, laws may require insurance companies to expand their customer base sufficiently to allow them to profit while taking all comers.

Underallocation of services to poor people is but one side of the coin of class-based differences in genetics. The other side, I think, involves two types of unjust allocation: allocation that entails a notion of equality as sameness, and overallocation, that is, distribution of resources that is in effect disadvantaging rather than equalizing to their recipients. Distribution of the same genetic services to everyone is unjust for the obvious reason that individuals have different need of them, or different burdens and benefits to be obtained through them. Equality, as I have defined it, entails distribution that takes account of these differences, following in effect the Marxist maxim of distribution based on need so as to minimize class-based inequality.

Overallocation of genetic services may occur towards those who are affluent enough to pay for them but are nonetheless disadvantaged by obtaining them because the services entail disproportionate risks or complications. Social pressures to undergo experimental or novel genetic interventions may be greater for this group as a potential but fallible means of optimizing their own or their children's health. This pressure, whether intended or not, may be exacerbated by the enthusiasm and solicitation of clinician/researchers who desire the data obtained through testing of a wide range of clients and by the advertising methods of commercial testing companies whose profits are measured by the number and type of tests they perform. Again, as tests proliferate, the class of people who can pay out of pocket may be increasingly subject to this kind of unjust overallocation of genetic services.

Class-based differences in genetics are not always associated with allocation of services. They are also apparent in the disparity of income and prestige between different providers of genetic services. In the United States, for example, genetic counseling may be offered through master's-prepared genetic counselors, the great majority of whom are women, or through doctorally prepared geneticists, who are more likely to be men.[15] Not surprisingly, the remuneration and respect accorded to the master's-level counselors are considerably less than that accorded to medical geneticists whose counseling may be neither more informative nor more helpful to their clients. The disparity between these different groups of providers is consistent with the hierarchical, usually patriarchal, structure that prevails within the health care system: Women have long outnumbered men as health caregivers, but men have typically occupied higher levels of prestige and income within the system.

Yet another class-related difference is evident in the contrast between the providers of genetic services, both master's-prepared and doctorally prepared, and many of their clients. The vast majority of counselors are white, whereas clients belong to multiple ethnic groups. In situations where genetic services are covered by private or governmental insurance, that is, where its cost-effectiveness has determined its provision, the providers typically belong to a more advantaged socioeconomic group than their clients. The class difference that arises from this socioeconomic disparity is exacerbated by the position of vulnerability or dependence that clients or patients typically experience vis-à-vis their caregivers.[16] This dependence is perhaps most manifest when it arises from a disability, whether genetic or otherwise, on the part of the patient. As we will see in the next section, class-based and gender-based inequities mingle in that context as well.

ABILITY DIFFERENCES ASSOCIATED WITH GENETICS

Differences in ability are partly determined by genetics, partly by environment, and partly by the choices we make. All three factors intermingle: Environment influences whether and how genes are expressed; our choices often determine the environmental factors that affect that expression and the goals to which our abilities are relevant. The term *inability* refers to the lack of a particular ability, but this concept does not entail *disability* unless it signifies an impairment to functioning that most other individuals enjoy. Because of their different determinants and because abilities vary not only qualitatively but quantitatively, it is impossible, at least in some instances, to determine the cutoff point at which a given limitation or impairment constitutes a disability. For example, while my nearsightedness (which has a genetic component) would be disabling if I had no corrective lenses, it hardly counts as that in my current environment. If I were a foot shorter than I am, as I might be if I had the genetic condition known as achondroplasia, I would probably experience my shortness as seriously disabling even if I were perfectly healthy. If I were moderately retarded due to a specific genetic condition but loved to work on an assembly line where my manual skills were an asset, my mental retardation might not be considered a disability.

According to Anita Silvers, the idea that "individuals with physical, sensory, and cognitive impairments together form a class of 'the disabled' is an invention of the current century."[17] In earlier times, she says, these conditions were simply viewed as "conditions." Today, however, at least in Western culture, "to be disabled is to be disadvantaged regardless of how much success one achieves individually."[18] The disadvantaging mainly occurs because those who are currently able build and maintain societal structures that facilitate the expression of their abilities, disregarding the impairments that many other people experience. Although most people become disabled at some point in their lives, those who are currently able seldom see themselves as likely to join the ranks of the disabled.

More often than not, people with disabilities are poorer than those who are currently able because their income level is compromised through the costs of treatment and of enablement and through social prejudice. Caregivers of those with disabilities are, more often than not, poorer than those who have no caregiving responsibility because caregiving involves minimal or no remuneration. Although advances in medical treatment of some genetic disorders have extended the lifespan for some of the disabled, this has also prolonged the costs of caregiving. As with class differences, gender differences clearly overlap with issues involving care for the disabled. Except for the minority of caregivers who hold positions of high social and economic status (mainly physicians), those who provide care either formally, in institutional settings, or informally, in home settings, are mainly women. Typically, neither they nor those they care for are highly esteemed by others.

Qualitative and quantitative differences in the impact of disabilities on those who are disabled, their caregivers, and others in society are influenced not only by gender and class but also by race, sexuality, and other characteristics associated with social bias. Genetic equality demands that all of these factors be taken into account so that the disadvantages associated with them be minimized across the spectrum of those affected. In the United States, the Americans with Disabilities Act (ADA) is a powerful legislative attempt to facilitate equality between those who are disabled and those who are currently able.[19] While the legislation does not, because it cannot, eliminate genetic or environmental causes of disability, it acknowledges its social causes and mandates efforts to alleviate them. It does not, however, address the disadvantages experienced by many of those who care for the disabled.

Many people with disabilities view the escalation of genetic tests as a means of reinforcing social stereotypes against them. Prenatal tests, which are hardly new, are generally undertaken to avoid the birth of a child with a genetic or chromosomal anomaly. Since the great majority of genetic disorders are incurable, the only means by which they can be avoided is by terminating the pregnancy, which eliminates the possibility of existence of a particular person with a particular disability. Women who are thirty-five years of age or older are routinely tested for anomalies that involve mental retardation, and positive test results usually lead them to abort the pregnancy. Whether or not such decisions are consistent with genetic equality depends, in part at least, on whether human fetuses, whether able or disabled, have the same value as other human beings.

Genetic testing and interventions are not only possible for genetic diseases, many of which entail disabilities, but for normal conditions and characteristics that may be socially enabling or disabling. The most salient example of a healthy condition for which some people choose to provide or obtain prenatal testing is sex designation. Genetic tests for susceptibility to specific disorders are already available and have been utilized discriminatorily towards people who have not and may never be affected by the disorder in question. Recognizing the injustice of such discrimination, the ADA interprets the perception of disability as a de facto disability.[20] As an increasing number of conditions unrelated to health are identifiable prenatally, however, even normal behavioral traits and characteristics may become socially disabling. To the extent that genetic testing and interventions are utilized to select for traits that are more valued than others for no morally or functionally relevant reason, people with traits not selected for may be disadvantaged. Thus, differences that ought to be neutral in their impact may increase the capability of some individuals at the expense of others.

DIFFERENCES AND EQUALITY

The previous sections have outlined empirical differences based on gender, class, and ability, all as related to genetics. As already suggested, the differences themselves do not render the individuals who embody them unequal to one another. Nonetheless, inequalities occur so prevalently in the context of these three types of differences that it is easy to pick the ones that often entail advantages: maleness, middle classness, and physical or mental ability.[21]

Some differences in genetics entail disadvantages for men, others entail disadvantages for women, and others are equally burdensome or beneficial for both sexes. If genetic equality is to be promoted, the last category can be ignored, but both of the other categories need to be addressed. So, for example, efforts to avoid or effectively control diseases that mainly or only affect men should not be compromised on grounds that only men are affected. For that matter, they should not be compromised on grounds that they only affect a minority of men. To the extent that other conditions mainly affect women or affect pregnant women more severely than others, it needs to be made clear to women themselves that such conditions (e.g., cystic fibrosis and sickle cell anemia) are not gender-neutral but likely to be exacerbated by pregnancy.

Men are unable to share the physical risk and discomfort of prenatal testing and interventions, but they are able to share the expense of these procedures. It may, in fact, be argued that their paying for such procedures is a means of reducing the inequality between men and women in their reproductive roles. As for changeable gender-based differences in child rearing and care of the disabled, genetic equality demands whatever changes are necessary to reduce the overall disadvantages of women vis-à-vis their male partners. This could be done, for example, by increasing the prestige and income level of women who are caregivers or by increasing the number of men who do the caregiving. To promote genetic equality with regard to class, both alternatives should be pursued. To promote genetic equality with regard to ability, the social causes of disability must be eliminated so that everyone's abilities may be maximally developed or exercised.

Genetic equality is unlikely to be realized in a society that champions a competitive framework as most conducive to progress. It is, however, supportable by a social milieu that values all individuals equally and subordinates competition to democratic process. Rawls's theory of justice attempts to reduce but not eliminate the inequality that inevitably occurs when liberty is maximized without addressing the disparate needs and talents of individuals. Reduction rather than elimination of inequality may be all that advantaged people are willing to tolerate, but to the extent that we are satisfied with mere reduction, we condone or are complicit in the inequality.

A Rawlsian attempt to reduce genetic inequality would substantively support the status quo, a system that maximizes individual options regarding genetic tests and interventions while constraining the exercise of options that might increase disadvantages for some. Those who can afford new tests or interventions can and do obtain them, while those who cannot afford them do not. The following cases illustrate this class-based discrepancy and its overlap with gender-based differences:

Case 1: A poor couple

Maria and Reinaldo Sanchez, twenty-seven and thirty years old, respectively, arrived in Brooklyn, New York, from Puerto Rico with their four school-age children. Although they knew little English, both got jobs in a restaurant earning minimum wages. Within a month, Maria discovered she was pregnant. After a routine triple screen, she was advised to see a genetic counselor and undergo chorionic villus sampling or amniocentesis. Most of her visits to the prenatal clinic were delayed by her inability to find appointments that did not conflict with her childcare and job responsibilities and by the unavailability of a Spanish interpreter. By the time Maria was told that her fetus had Down syndrome, she was twenty weeks pregnant. The clinic did not provide second trimester terminations, but she was given the name of a clinic in another city where she might obtain the procedure. Maria called the clinic and was told that a second trimester abortion would cost considerably more than her family could afford.

Case 2: An affluent couple

Sonya and Rob Smith, both thirty-six years old, had two children, ages six and two. Rob was a community obstetrician with a successful practice; Sonya was a full-time homemaker. Their younger child, Alex, had problems learning to walk and appeared delayed in his speech development. At a routine visit to the pediatrician with both children, Sonya expressed her concern about Alex's slow development. The pediatrician suggested consultation with a geneticist. When Sonya called the genetics center, she was asked if she would like both children to be fully evaluated. She was also asked to have her pediatrician send complete copies of both children's medical records. Both parents attended their ensuing appointment at which extensive family histories were taken and physical exams performed on both children. A "routine" set of genetic tests was ordered for Alex, and the result indicated that he had fragile X syndrome, a condition involving mental retardation, occurring mainly in males. His sister was tested next and found not to be a carrier for the condition. Follow-up counseling prompted Sonya to contact various relatives to alert them to the risk of fragile X syndrome in family members. The Smiths' insurance plan covered all appointments and all of the recommended testing.

More than the cases considered separately, the differences between them exemplify the allocation issues raised by rapid advances in genetics: Poor people will have decreased access to the benefits of genetic information, while affluent people will have greater access. If the economic situations of the two couples had been reversed, there is little doubt but that Sonya would have had prenatal diagnosis earlier than Maria had it and would have been able to obtain an abortion even if the diagnosis had been obtained later. Maria and Reinaldo would not have been offered a test for fragile X syndrome or carrier status in their children, even if there were a family history of the condition, unless perhaps the genetics center had a research protocol that they might be solicited to join as test subjects.

Additional details might demonstrate the gap between the cases even more. For example, the Sanchez family has no car, and the clinic to which they are referred is not accessible by public transportation. Or when Maria arrives at the clinic, the physician finds her pregnancy too advanced to perform the abortion. If Maria had been Sonya, she would probably be able to travel to another state or even another country to obtain the procedure. In the United States, abortion is legal in several states during the third trimester. With regard to the fragile X test, consider the possibility that Sonya was adopted; she therefore has no family history of the disease and neither does Rob. If, as is improbable, they nonetheless wanted to have themselves or their children tested for the condition, they could probably find someone willing to perform the test so long as they were willing and able to pay for it. Testing for cystic fibrosis and breast cancer have been offered to low-risk populations on this basis.

The options open to Maria are obviously limited by her economic situation; the lack of language facility on the part of clinicians has probably curtailed her options as well. While the case described illustrates these constraining factors, it ignores another probable constraint, namely, anticipation that the family's already limited resources would be severely taxed by responsibility for a child with Down syndrome.[22] Ideally, the genetic counselor would have provided a positive but realistic account of children with Down syndrome and their parents, along with information on sources of assistance. In keeping with the nondirective model, however, the counselor would also convey support for a decision to terminate the pregnancy. Unfortunately, nondirectiveness does not cancel the real constraints of the situation. Maria is not as free in making this decision as she would be if she were Sonya or if societal supports for raising a child with Down syndrome were sufficient to neutralize the decision for her. Raising a child, whether chromosomally normal or not, is never neutral; it has its rewards as well as burdens. For Maria, however, the financial burden is accentuated by the lack of resources on which to draw and the demands of raising a child with special needs.

In contrast with Maria and Reinaldo, the advantages that Sonya and Rob enjoy because of their higher socioeconomic status are manifest: access to routine health care, easy referral to a specialist, availability of complete medical records of both children, ability of both parents to participate in the genetics appointment, sufficient time and language facility for the specialist to do a complete investigation, insurance coverage, even for expensive testing, and ability to contact at-risk family members so that there is benefit to the extended family. Only rarely are all or even most of these options available to poor women or couples.

From an egalitarian standpoint, at least some of the factors that reduce Maria's autonomy in this situation are changeable and should be changed so that she does not feel compelled to end her pregnancy because she and Reinaldo cannot support another child, especially one with Down syndrome. By that same standpoint, Maria should neither feel nor be compelled to continue her pregnancy, and factors that might constitute pressure in that direction are wrong as well. Most probably, the sequel to the case described would show that Maria was prevented from making either decision. Rather, the fact that she could not obtain an affordable, legal abortion would itself determine the outcome: continuation of the pregnancy and giving birth in due course to an infant with Down syndrome. The sequel to this sequel would probably show an even greater economic inequality between the Sanchez and the Smith families. In other words, whether Maria continued or terminated her pregnancy, the underdistribution of resources compromised her autonomy.[23] Affluence, probably abetted by alliances within the medical profession, allowed the Smiths access to genetic services denied to most, thereby increasing the disparity between the "haves" and "have-nots" of the US health care system.

Would a decision by Maria alone to undergo genetic testing and pregnancy termination in order to avoid the birth of a child with mental retardation constitute discrimination against men? Would it constitute discrimination against those who are disabled? In light of the prevalence of testing and termination for that purpose, both questions are important, but the former is easier to answer, at least from the standpoint of social equality. The right of women and not men to make decisions involving pregnancy is based on the physical and social impact of such decisions on them, as described earlier. To the extent that women are more disadvantaged than men by pregnancy and its consequences, equality within that context argues for giving women's decisions priority over those of their partners.

The question of discrimination against those who are disabled by testing and termination of fetuses with genetic anomalies is particularly unsettling to feminists who, as such, support equal rights for women as well as for the disabled. Feminists have not always recognized that advocacy for people with disabilities is logically and practically required by our commitment to women and gender justice. This is unfortunate not only because so many women are disabled or will eventually become disabled but also because we share the same battle against stereotypes of dependence, passivity, and inferiority.[24] In general, men who are disabled are dominant vis-à-vis women who are disabled. As Adrienne Asch and Michelle Fine put it, "concerns with 'emasculation' may promote efforts directed towards those at the locus of the masculinity-dependence contradiction, not towards those at the redundant intersection of femininity and dependence."[25]

The major issue with which some versions of feminism seem to be at odds with advocacy for those who are disabled is prenatal testing for fetal anomalies.[26] A libertarian version fully supports the decisions of autonomous women, whether currently able or disabled, to initiate, terminate, or continue pregnancies for any reason. In cases involving prenatal diagnosis and termination of pregnancies because of fetal anomaly, this view is incompatible with advocacy for persons with disabilities unless the fetus has no moral status or obligations that follow from its moral status are not as compelling as the woman's choice. To the extent that some women lack autonomy (e.g., because of retardation or mental illness), libertarian feminism ignores their interests if those interests are not pursued by autonomous individuals, such as family members.

An egalitarian version of feminism, that is, one that places greater emphasis on equality, broadly construed, implies that other values besides women's autonomy are morally relevant to decisions about initiation, continuation, or termination of a pregnancy. With regard to prenatal diagnosis and termination of affected fetuses, this view is consistent with the pregnant woman's right to choose and with the rights of the disabled, if the fetus has no moral status. But if the fetus has moral status or standing, egalitarian feminism can only be consistent with advocacy for women's choice and for the interests of those who are disabled if either the moral status of a fetus is deemed less compelling than the pregnant woman's autonomy or the decision is not based on the ability or disability of the fetus. Concerning the latter factor, the decision may be based on the inability of the caregiver or of society to provide adequate care for the potential child. To an egalitarian feminist, choice is not an absolute value. From that perspective, therefore, pregnant women, whether they are currently able or disabled, are morally obliged to consider the welfare of the potential child in their decisions about initiating, continuing, or terminating pregnancy. This does not imply that they should be legally obliged or coerced to do so.

With regard to decisions to terminate pregnancies, an egalitarian framework is as applicable to fetuses without disabilities as it is to those with disabilities. The applicability to both suggests a criterion to be followed if advocacy for women's choice and advocacy for persons with genetic disabilities are to be reconciled: The mere fact of the disability is irrelevant to the choice. Admittedly, there are cases during and beyond gestation in which unrelievable suffering, whatever its cause, may be so overwhelming that letting the suffering individual die seems like a merciful or humane act on his or her behalf. Consider, for example, an infant with a profoundly devastating, incurable, progressive, genetic condition such as Tay-Sachs disease or Lesch-Nyhan syndrome or someone who is dying of an incurable, painful cancer. The criterion in those cases, however, is not the disability itself but the pain and suffering of the person with the disability. Moreover, the crucial caveat in situations of overwhelming pain or suffering is that it be unrelievable by others. As many authors attest, much of the pain and suffering associated with disabilities is socially induced and relievable.[27] For autonomous persons with disabilities, another crucial variable is respect for autonomy; this consideration is relevant to pregnant women but not to fetuses.

My suggested criterion for reconciling advocacy for women with advocacy for people with genetic disabilities is also applicable to the issue of assisted suicide, which presents another possibility for discrimination against them. One disabilities activist articulated this concern by claiming that supporters of the legalization of assisted suicide "just want to get rid of us."[28] From an egalitarian standpoint, however, if assisted suicide is a legal right of those who are currently able, it should also be a right of those who are disabled. For both groups, measures must be taken to insure that the decision is made autonomously. Circumstances that compromise autonomy, such as treatable depression, and social causes of disability must be adequately addressed before an individual's decision is regarded as genuinely autonomous.

An egalitarian version of feminism is more coherent in its own right and more compatible with advocacy for those who are genetically disabled than a libertarian version. It is more coherent because individual choice is not an absolute moral right; other rights and others' rights may be more compelling. Egalitarian feminism is compatible with advocacy for the disabled because it embraces all of the disabled, including those who are not autonomous. People with disabilities, like persons who are currently able, are not always autonomous or equally autonomous any more than they are equally intelligent, talented, or attractive. The goal of an egalitarian feminism is to treat different individuals fairly in the face of these differences, both changeable and unchangeable. This returns us to the notion of genetic equality as essentially tied to issues of gender, class, and ability. Subscribing to that notion means that anyone who fully supports social equality is necessarily a feminist, whether or not that is acknowledged. An obligation to treat everyone equally assumes that no one's autonomy is absolute, whether women or men, able or disabled, young or old, whatever their class, color, ethnicity, or sexual orientation. In addition, treating everyone equally requires the persistent attempt by all reasonable means to reduce whatever disadvantages individuals or groups experience vis-à-vis one another.

Asch and Fine illustrate the compatibility between advocacy for women and advocacy for people with disabilities while identifying a concrete measure by which an egalitarian feminist standpoint may be promoted: the provision of adequate and balanced information to potential parents of children with disabilities about the experience of raising such children and their potential for satisfying and productive lives. Assessing the counseling typically provided as inadequate and biased against the birth of a disabled child, they contend that "given the proper information about how disabled children and adults live, many women might not choose to abort."[29] As already suggested, however, their support for a woman's right to terminate her pregnancy depends on a denial that fetal interests ever outweigh a pregnant woman's interests. According to Asch and Fine, "we must recognize the crucial 'line' separating the fetus—residing in the body of her mother—and the infant, viable outside the womb."[30] Once the infant is born, Asch and Fine's position shifts drastically. While staunchly defending the right of disabled infants to be treated over the objection of their parents, they argue just as forcefully for the right of every woman to abort a disabled fetus so long as she has adequate information about its actual potential.

Unfortunately, even if pregnant women are provided with adequate information about the prospects of life with a disability, they are rarely adequately supported in the caregiving responsibilities they face if they decide to give birth to children whose serious genetic disorders have been identified prenatally. Recognition and remediation of this social disparity calls for an egalitarian standpoint. As we shall see in the next section, that standpoint is epistemologically and ethically crucial to theoretical justification and practical implementation of genetic equality.

An Egalitarian Standpoint

The term *standpoint* has been used to define any perspectival view of the world. *Standpoint theory* refers to the theoretical justification for utilizing particular standpoints and strategies to implement them. Classical pragmatists such as William James and Charles Sanders Peirce insisted that human knowledge is unavoidably perspectival.[31] In light of a doctrine he called "fallibilism," Peirce argued for collaborative inquiry, based on scientific method, in order to maximize our potential for understanding reality.[32] However, he did not use the terms *truth* or *knowledge* to signify the result of his pragmatic, maximizing method; rather, he called the result "belief," defining this as a plan or habit of action.[33] Peirce thus distinguished between truth as the ultimate goal of inquiry and the conclusions that human beings reach in their ongoing search for knowledge. What is known and knowable through experience in this unfinished world is inevitably partial but not relative. Although we cannot achieve omniscience, we can minimize our errors or mistakes through collaboration.

Because of the intellectual advantage provided by collaboration, Peirce considered it illogical to be antisocial in the quest for knowledge. "Logic," he wrote, "is rooted in the social principle," which requires that the interests of investigators not be limited to their interests as individuals or even to their own area of research.[34] Consistent with the pragmatic tenet that theory and practice are inseparable, he affirmed the congruence of the two in his conception of inquiry. The goal of inquiry, he wrote, is to enhance "the whole community," that is, "all races of beings with whom we can come into immediate or mediate intellectual relation."[35] Pursuit of this goal through a collaborative methodology requires a certain selflessness, a willingness to sacrifice one's own ego satisfaction in order to increase the total fund of human knowledge. Peirce viewed science as a kind of religion in the demands it makes of the individual: "He who would not sacrifice his own soul to save the whole world, is as it seems to me, illogical in all his inferences, collectively."[36]

While stressing the practical importance of generalizations, or "generals," as he called them, Peirce did not insist on universalizability. "Generals" are generalizations that are epistemologically necessary and indispensable to resolution of ambiguities or conflicts, but they do not demand applicability always and in all circumstances, as they would if they were universalizable. In contrast, most nonpragmatist philosophers have maintained that universalizability and impartiality are not only achievable but essential to the justification of ethical decisions. Immanuel Kant is one of the strongest exemplars of this view, but the majority of contemporary bioethicists, whether trained in philosophy or not, follow suit. For example, in all five editions of *The Principles of Biomedical Ethics,* Tom Beauchamp and James Childress identify universalizability as a necessary condition of moral decision making.[37] Impartiality, as reflected in the image of justice as blind, is construed as a condition of universalizability. If and when the interests of one party are the same as those of another, weighing the interests of either as greater than those of the other compromises the impartiality and universalizability that ethical judgments demand.[38] Justice, which some consider the most important of Beauchamp and Childress's proposed principles of biomedical ethics, is thus dependent on universalizability and impartiality. As they recognize, however, justice is open to a number of conflicting interpretations.[39]

Impartiality is also interpreted as requiring that we prescind from personal considerations in moral decision making. Thomas Nagel, for example, distinguishes between a personal and an impersonal standpoint, arguing that the latter is indispensable to ethics.[40] A personal standpoint inevitably involves particular relationships and a unique position in the world. Ethics and political theory, according to Nagel, begin with the ability "to think about the world in abstraction from our particular position in it."[41] Only from this "impersonal standpoint" can we recognize and pursue values that are common to all persons, whatever their relationships and position. In other words, morality requires persons to act impersonally, with deliberate disregard for whatever needs or interests may be unique to them. Yet if ethics focuses on the moral responsibility of persons, it seems ironic as well as illogical to insist that personal considerations be excluded from ethical judgments.[42] Moreover, personal considerations are not equivalent to individualistic considerations; the former often address the interests of others, while the latter only address those of the lone individual.

In the 1980s, Nancy Hartsock developed a notion of standpoint that identifies the disparities that arise between those who occupy different positions vis-à-vis one another.[43] Applying Marx's view of the relationship between the bourgeoisie and the proletariat to the relationship between men and women, Hartsock imputed the following related claims to the standpoint she proposed:

1. Material life or social position structures and limits everyone's understanding of social relations.

2. When material life is structured in fundamentally opposing ways for two different groups, the vision of each represents an inversion of the other, and in systems of domination the vision available to the rulers is inevitably partial.

3. The vision of the ruling or dominant group structures the material relations in which all parties participate.

4. Members of the nondominant or marginalized group are capable of seeing beneath the surface of the oppressive social relations they experience; this vision is facilitated by the educative impact of their struggle to change those relations.

5. The standpoint achieved by the dominated group allows them to see beyond the present, exposing to others as well as themselves the dehumanizing aspects of existing social relations; this enables them to fulfill "a historically liberatory role."[44]

The fourth and fifth of Hartsock's claims provide the rationale for seeking and utilizing marginalized standpoints to reduce the inevitable nearsightedness of those who occupy the privileged or dominant side of a relationship, that is, the side that defines its terms. Hartsock would reverse the privileged status of the parties involved, granting superior status to the nondominant or dominated point of view because it constitutes a means of overcoming the inevitable limitations of the dominant view. Both groups are advantaged through the reversal of privilege: Members of the dominant group are empowered to correct and expand their vision, and members of the dominated group are empowered to liberate themselves. Although Hartsock's original account targeted the man-woman relationship, her later work acknowledges the need to extend this analysis to other dominant-nondominant relationships. "My focus on a simplified model of masculinist and feminist perspectives," she writes, "left out of the account other important social relations."[45] Other groups to whom a privileged status should be assigned so as to overcome the nearsightedness of the dominant perspective are ethnic minorities, those who are disabled or poor, people of color, gays, and lesbians. Hartsock has thus amended her view to account for the plurality of dominant and nondominant standpoints that an egalitarian version of feminism needs to address.

While supporting Hartsock's rendition, Donna Haraway observes that "the standpoints of the subjugated are not 'innocent' positions." Nonetheless, she considers them "preferred positions because in principle they are least likely to allow denial of the critical and interpretive core of all knowledge."[46] This "core" derives from their widespread and diverse experience of nondominance in a culture of dominance. Nondominant standpoints are justified, or rather, demanded, on ethical as well as epistemological grounds because of the relationship between knowledge and decision making. Ethical decisions, after all, require an adequate grasp of pertinent information, which can only be obtained through the corrective lens of those who are nondominant.

Admittedly, nondominant groups and individuals are sometimes so suppressed that they are incapable of recognizing, let alone utilizing, the perspective that is available to them. Whether they are able to access the "core of knowledge" to which Haraway refers depends crucially on the degree to which they are intellectually and psychologically capable of comparing and contrasting their own situation with that of the dominant group. Women, for example, need to be free enough to recognize their marginalization vis-à-vis men. Increased education and consciousness-raising techniques serve the purpose of enabling women to identify their own standpoint as different from, and dominated by, the supposedly impersonal standpoint of men.

For Nagel and his ilk, an impersonal standpoint is achieved through a process of abstraction that is indispensable to moral judgment. Referring to the majority of those who embrace this view, Hartsock calls the process one of "abstract masculinity."[47] Other standpoint theorists concur in her denial that an impersonal standard is feasible or desirable. Haraway, for example, affirms the "embodied nature of all vision" against the pretense of objectivity that denies the overall situatedness of human experience.[48] The concept of an impersonal standpoint, she says, suggests the "god trick of seeing everything from nowhere."[49] To a believer, performers of this "god trick" act blasphemously. Moreover, their attempt to impose their vision on everyone, on grounds that judgments drawn solely from their experience are universally applicable, is ethically objectionable because it fails to respect the autonomy of those whose standpoints are different from their own.

Haraway's proposed alternative is a doctrine of "embodied objectivity" that involves "partial, locatable, critical knowledges." These "knowledges" sustain "the possibilities of webs of connections called solidarity in politics and shared conversations in epistemology."[50] Only through such partial perspectives, she claims, can we approach genuine objectivity. Haraway defends her proposal against the anticipated charge of relativism by pointing out that, like the concept of an impersonal standpoint, relativism is "a way of being nowhere while claiming to be everywhere equally."[51] Her concept of "situated knowledges" does not conform to this definition of relativism because it denies the adequacy of anyone's inevitably partial perspective. The difference between partial knowledge and relativism thus supports the epistemological validity of standpoint theory.

Critics of an impersonal standpoint include authors who are not explicitly feminist. John Ladd, for example, develops a distinction between objective and subjective points of view that is comparable to feminist accounts of dominant and nondominant standpoints. Like Haraway, Ladd equates the "God's eye point of view" of those who claim to be objective with the dominant perspective of "social engineers," who see themselves, and whose supporters describe them, as "sincere and dedicated public servants selected on the basis of their professional expertise."[52] Although their approach is inevitably speculative, the social engineers or programmers regard their perspectives as overwhelmingly superior to those of ordinary, nondominant individuals. As objectivists, they think that their own "formal organizations of expert administrators" are indispensable to achievement of their goal, namely, a true and adequate account of "the way things are."[53] Participation by those who see the world subjectively, that is, differently or from nondominant perspectives, can only impede that achievement.

For Ladd, the preceding rationale ignores the fact that, typically, the individuals who formulate decisions and policies are fallible human beings like the rest of us and "frequently misinformed and stupid to boot."[54] However, the most significant flaw of this approach is that dominant individuals often "lack the kind of involvement in the outcome that is forced on the recipients of the decision," who are nondominant.[55] While the latter are fallible also, they have a personal moral stake in what is decided, and that in itself constitutes a moral argument for their participation. On democratic as well as utilitarian grounds, their input should be weighed more heavily than that of those who are less affected precisely because of the differential impact.[56]

The critical question that Ladd's objectivist fails to address is "Who is to decide?" This question, he says, is even more important today than in the past because those who make decisions are farther removed than ever from those to whom their decisions apply. As proof of a long-standing tendency to ignore the question, Ladd offers examples of old men who decide that young people should kill innocent people in war, rich men who decide what kind of welfare the poor should receive, and white men who decide who should police the streets in a black neighborhood.[57] Although all of his examples are pertinent to standpoint theory, so is one not mentioned: Men in general decide what women in general may do or not do.

Aware that the "objective approach" threatens the autonomy of nondominant groups, Ladd maintains that participation in decision making is a means of reducing the alienation they experience through domination. He credits minorities, students, and workers with contributing to "disalienation" through their demands for participation in the communities to which they belong, at home, school, or their places of employment,[58] imputing to them a position of ethical as well as epistemological privilege. The same point may of course be made for women whose efforts to participate in various levels of community governance serve as an antidote to the alienation that might otherwise prevail.

In short, the epistemological reasons for subscribing to standpoint theory reflect recognition that the experiences on which knowledge is based are incomplete and partial; they also reflect the pragmatists' insistence on collaborative inquiry as a means of overcoming the limitations of individual quests for knowledge. The ethical warrant for standpoint theory derives from prima facie obligations to respect the autonomy of, and practice beneficence and nonmaleficence towards, those who are nondominant as well as those who are dominant. While acknowledging the liberatory potential of standpoint theory for dominant groups, the theory assumes that justice has priority in ethical and social decision making. As we shall see in the next section, however, justice towards all of the individuals for whom the theory is intended requires its extension beyond dominant and subjugated groups.

Feminist Standpoint Theory and Its Extension

Women in general are a nondominant group because they are hugely underrepresented among those in positions of power in the world. Feminist standpoint theory involves the arguments cited above for imputing privileged status to women in decisions and policies that affect them along with men. However, these arguments are even more compelling when women are affected more significantly than men, as in many areas of reproduction and genetics. The ethical argument is rendered stronger still by the rejection of relativism that feminism, in all of its diverse manifestations, adds to Haraway's refutation through its affirmation of gender equality as an objective, universalizable ethical norm.[59] As Susan Sherwin puts it, even if feminists remain relativist on other moral matters, they remain "absolutist on the question of the moral wrong of oppression."[60] So long as feminism is absolutist on that matter, it is in fact incompatible with relativism.

Sara Ruddick posits the roots of a feminist standpoint in the experience and activity of mothering. She develops a concept of "maternal thinking" that is applicable to men as well as women. Maternal thinkers do "maternal work" through preservative love, nurturance, and socialization of those for whom they care.[61] This work necessarily involves resistance to the spirit and practice of militarism, which impedes the growth and development of oppressed or vulnerable people. For Ruddick, a feminist standpoint thus involves pacifism. Not all women, of course, are pacifists, and not all women are feminists. Women's standpoint differs from a feminist standpoint in that the latter entails a prescriptive element, namely, resistance to oppression.

Acknowledging the difference between a feminist standpoint and women's standpoint, Hartsock embraces the former rather than the latter because she interprets women's experience and activity as including both negative and positive aspects. In contrast, a feminist standpoint "picks out and amplifies the liberatory possibilities" contained within women's standpoint, that is, the negative aspects that may be effectively changed into positive possibilities for women.[62] On such a reading, a feminist standpoint is narrower than women's standpoint unless the former includes the standpoint not only of women as a group but also of women as individuals who belong to other nondominant groups and, in many cases, to dominant groups as well. Thus understood, a feminist standpoint embraces the standpoint of all of those who are nondominant or marginalized, whether by gender, race, class, ability, or sexual orientation.

Hartsock admits that her delineation of a feminist standpoint assumes commonalities among women despite their differences. In general, those commonalities are associated with nondominance. However, a narrow interpretation of a feminist standpoint cannot adequately reflect all of the standpoints of individual women who, in addition to the above, are distinguishable by size, age, politics, religion, and multiple other factors. Like men, women are unique in the compilation of standpoints that each embodies. A broad interpretation of a feminist standpoint collects all of the nondominant standpoints together and imputes to them a privileged status vis-à-vis whatever dominant standpoint prevails, regardless of whether gender or another characteristic, or set of characteristics, determines the dominance.

Hartsock's feminist standpoint applies to groups rather than to individuals. However, an extension of standpoint theory to individuals is consistent with most versions of feminism because of their common emphasis on attention to context and relationship, as well as their critique of gender roles, stereotypically conceived. It also serves as a response to a criticism of Hartsock's account, namely, that it leads to a form of essentialism, representing women from different cultures and classes as if they were fundamentally the same.[63] Hartsock defends herself against this criticism when she asserts that "a standpoint is constituted by more than oppression and cannot be reduced to identity politics as usually understood."[64] In other words, other characteristics are relevant to the standpoints of diverse oppressed groups. While this acknowledgment makes Hartsock's position more acceptable to those other groups, extending the theory to individuals constitutes, in my view, an even stronger defense.

Individual women are not adequately definable as a group or even as members of multiple groups because of the uniqueness of each one's context and relationships. An adequate feminist standpoint calls for attention to the variety of contexts and of relationships in which women find themselves. While insisting on the importance of relationships that women alone have to others (e.g., pregnancy, motherhood), a broad interpretation of feminist standpoint theory maintains a critical attitude toward relationships and roles that support the subordination of women to men, whether as individuals or as a group. Simultaneously, it maintains a critical attitude towards generalities that mask the disparate needs and advantages of individual women.

Contemporary feminist scholarship has been self-conscious about its own limitations, attempting to reduce these through careful, criti-

cal consideration of the diversity of women's experience. Among
others, Maria Lugones and Elizabeth Spelman offer compelling arguments for paying attention to cultural, racial, and class differences
among women.[65] But generalizations regarding cultural, racial, and
class differences may ignore significant differences among women
who belong to the same culture, race, and class. Lesbian women and
women with disabilities, for example, are often overlooked when
cultural, racial, and class differences are addressed.

Taking account of differences among women also means taking
account of different versions of feminism. Alison Jaggar suggests that
consideration of women's standpoint may provide a criterion for
evaluating different feminist theories.[66] For Jaggar, the "socialist
feminist concept of the standpoint of women" is crucial to such
evaluation.[67] In general, I agree with this view. Among other versions
of feminism, however, postmodern feminism is most strongly supportive of an extension of feminist standpoint to individuals. For
postmodern feminists, the privileged standpoint of women is bor-
rowed from Simone de Beauvoir's category of *otherness*, which they
extol rather than reject.[68] For de Beauvoir, the category of otherness
applies to women as a group; for postmodern feminists, the category
applies to individuals as well. Rosemarie Tong describes the more
positive interpretation of women's otherness as enabling "individual
women to stand back and criticize the norms, values, and practices
that the dominant culture (patriarchy) seeks to impose on everyone,
including those who live on its periphery."[69] In other words, the very
otherness of women, both as individuals and as a group, introduces
a potential for change and difference that justifies the privileged
status of their standpoints.

Through its link with deconstruction, postmodern feminism is
antiessentialist. The antiessentialism entails a rejection not only of
universal definitions but also of traditional male-defined dichotomies between reason and emotion, beautiful and ugly, self and other
and of rigid boundaries between disciplines such as art, biology, and
psychology.[70] A dichotomy between maleness and femaleness is chal-
lengeable not only on postmodernist grounds but even on biological grounds because of the different chromosomal arrangements that
may characterize members of either sex.[71] While categorizations may

be inevitable and useful, rigid distinctions and dichotomies tend to be stereotypic and artificial, betraying the complexity of real individuals and adequate accounts of them.

Through its insistence on uncategorizable differences among individuals, postmodern feminism may be particularly supportive of nondirectiveness in genetic counseling. However, so radical a critique raises enormous epistemological and communicative problems. Some postmodernists even reject the term "feminism"; nonetheless, their views are profoundly feminist in that they propose for women the most fundamental liberation of all: "freedom from oppressive thought."[72] Individual women, after all, cannot be adequately defined by the thoughts of others, even when the others are feminists.

Taking account of differences between individuals as well as groups means proceeding on two tracks at once. On one track, we pay attention to the actual standpoints of individuals; on the other, we also look for patterns of oppression or domination in different groups in order to identify and rectify systemic injustice or exploitation. Sandra Harding recognizes the tension that occurs when the standpoint of an individual is at odds with that of a group with which she is identified. She maintains, however, that this "apparent tension in feminist thought is simply one we should learn to live with."[73] On both tracks, women's experience is the starting point of the critique.

To the extent that a feminist standpoint applies to women as a group and to women as individuals through an egalitarian perspective, it takes account of all of the differences that arise in people's lives. In the conception of equality that I have elaborated, however, an egalitarian standpoint already includes feminist concerns, making it unnecessary to add the term *feminist* to its description. If other conceptions of equality are assumed, a feminist standpoint may not be equivalent to an egalitarian standpoint.

Implementing an egalitarian standpoint in the context of genetics is difficult (as it is in other contexts) because of the pervasive tendency of dominant individuals and groups to assume that they already endorse and practice social equality. If the epistemological and ethical arguments in its behalf are persuasive, however, concrete measures to overcome or reduce nearsightedness are demanded. In conclusion, therefore I propose a modest strategy for implementing an egalitarian standpoint to promote genetic equality toward women, the poor, and the disabled.

Soliciting and Listening to Nondominant Voices

In American society, we are familiar with the concept and strategy of proportionate representation. Despite failures in implementation of this strategy, it is potentially a means by which each individual exerts some influence in policy decisions that apply to everyone. At an earlier point in history, direct participation of citizens in town meetings offered a purer form of democracy than we have now; that model ceased to be operable when society became too large and complex for every competent adult to be directly involved in its governance. Proportionate representation remains a mechanism intended to ensure as much democracy as possible under the circumstances.

Democratic process is considered a good not only because it maximizes the participation of individuals but also because it manifests equal regard for each one's participation. Even within a system of equal voting rights, however, it is hardly true that each one's participation is, or is even considered, equal to everyone else's. A similar discrepancy is observable in health care, where the traditional paternalistic relationship of inequality between practitioner and patient prevails and the income, prestige, and power of physicians is greater than those of other health practitioners.[74] Since most physicians are white, affluent, able men, their dominance involves the dominance of race, class, ability, and gender.

An egalitarian standpoint suggests a means of countering the inevitable nearsightedness of the dominant class: ensuring that those who are not part of that class are included among the decision or policy makers. If such a strategy were implemented, the voices of women, poor people, those who are disabled, and others whose perspectives are different from those who are dominant would be heard in the development of policies and clinical decisions about genetic services. These voices would also be heard as teachers of those who dominate the field of genetics: geneticists, genetic counselors, and other caregivers who provide genetic services.

Proportionate representation means inviting the input of people with whom members of the dominant class do not themselves identify, whose presence may reduce their level of comfort, and whose views may challenge theirs. It also means that tokenism, such as having one woman or one person with disabilities on a policy-making committee, is not enough, particularly when the group's decisions disproportionately affect those who are not dominant. Truly proportionate representation extends beyond gender and race, which are often "covered" by tokenism, to differences in sexual orientation, political orientation, and mental as well as physical disability. It extends beyond the decision making of formally established groups such as academic committees and centers to the informal contexts of clinic management. Ideally, proportional representation also takes account of the fact that the same individual may belong to both dominant and nondominant groups. For example, while I belong to the nondominant gender, I am dominant by class, race, ability, and sexual orientation. To be fully reflective of the engaged vision of the world that an egalitarian standpoint offers requires participation of all the nondominant counterparts to dominance. Accordingly, the limitation of vision occasioned by my participation in dominant groups needs to be overcome, or at least reduced, by soliciting and listening to the input of other nondominant individuals.

Unfortunately, situations arise in which too few nondominant persons are available to provide proportionate representation. Sometimes the claim that there are too few is refutable, but sometimes it is not. Self-consciousness is then especially demanded of the dominant individuals who render the representation disproportionate. Minimally, such self-consciousness means acknowledgment of differences between dominant and dominated perspectives and efforts to learn about the latter. With regard to gender differences, it means acknowledgment of a possible sexist bias even by those who consider themselves free of such bias. As Virginia Warren observes, "Sexist ethics would never appear sexist [even to the person practicing it]. It would be clothed in a cloak of neutrality because favoring some group or position would be unthinkable."[75] A similar observation applies to groups distinguishable by race and class and often to those distinguishable by their mental or physical ability or sexual orientation.

The postmodern insight regarding the inadequacy of categorizations is an important reminder that proportionate representation cannot entirely eliminate nearsightedness, because nondominant persons are nearsighted also. Those of us who belong to the nondominant gender need to be self-conscious about this limitation, thereby avoiding, or at least reducing, arrogance. When we make decisions and formulate policies, our judgments remain fallible. Accordingly, from time to time, we need to reconsider and revise our judgments in response to changing circumstances and new insights or critique.

In applications of genetics as in other areas of life, decisions and policies need to be developed by democratic means, inviting the standpoints of diverse individuals in order to maximize their ethical and epistemological validity. Thus, soliciting and listening to women, poor people, and the disabled is a means of overcoming the inevitably inadequate perspectives of men, those who are affluent, and those who are currently able.

Because of inequalities that arise even within nondominant groups, soliciting and listening to the input of other nondominant individuals is as important for them as it is for those who are dominant. Such listening is often demanding because it requires the listener to suspend his or her own speech temporarily. It also requires psychological openness to new and critical ideas, that is, a kind of intellectual humility. At times, the learning that comes from listening changes our views of ourselves as well as others. Even as individuals grow through listening, so do the others—women and men, able and disabled, rich and poor—from diverse backgrounds and circumstances. Ongoing listening to marginalized or nondominant groups and learning from and acting on what we hear from them is indispensable to genetic equality.

NOTES

Substantial portions of this article are drawn from Mary B. Mahowald, *Genes, Women, Equality* (New York: Oxford University Press, 2000). I am grateful to Oxford University Press for permission to use this material.

1. John Rawls, *A Theory of Justice* (Cambridge: Harvard University Press, 1971), 3–53. Although Rawls also subscribes to this view in his

Political Liberalism (New York: Columbia University Press, 1993), he gives less emphasis to equality in that text.

2. See Aristotle's *Nichomachean Ethics* 5.3–5, trans. W. D. Ross, in *The Basic Works of Aristotle,* ed. Richard McKeon (New York: Random House, 1941).

3. Aristotle defines *equity* as "a correction of law where it is defective owing to its universality" (*Nichomachean Ethics* 5.10.1137b27).

4. By using the term *individuals* rather than *persons* or *human beings,* I am open to the inclusion of nonpersons and nonhumans in considerations of equality.

5. Amartya Sen, *Inequality Reexamined* (Cambridge: Harvard University Press, 1995), 3 (italics in original).

6. Sen, *Inequality Reexamined,* 22–23 (italics in text).

7. Sen, *Inequality Reexamined,* 83.

8. Rawls, *Theory of Justice,* 62.

9. Sen, *Inequality Reexamined,* 85–86.

10. Mary B. Mahowald et al., "The New Genetics and Women," *Milbank Quarterly* 74, no. 2 (1996): 239–83.

11. For an excellent account of the risks of fetal surgery to both women and fetuses, see Monica J. Casper, *The Making of the Unborn Patient: A Social Anatomy of Fetal Surgery* (New Brunswick: Rutgers University Press, 1998).

12. Amy Ravin, Mary B. Mahowald, and Carol Stocking, "Genes or Gestation: Attitudes of Women and Men about Biological Ties to Children," *Journal of Women's Health* 6 (1997): 1–9.

13. Diana Pearce, "The Feminization of Poverty: Women, Work, and Welfare," *Urban and Social Change Review* 11 (February 1978): 28–36.

14. See Mahowald et al., "New Genetics and Women," 249.

15. National Society for Genetic Counselors, Professional Status Survey, *Perspectives in Genetic Counseling* 18 (1996, suppl.): 1–8. This article also delineates the racial composition of genetic counselors, as mentioned in the next paragraph.

16. Genetic counselors tend to refer to those they counsel as *clients;* physicians refer to the same individuals as *patients.* The distinction supports nondirective and directive conceptions of their respective roles.

17. Anita Silvers, "Formal Justice," in Anita Silvers, David Wasserman, and Mary B. Mahowald, *Disability, Difference, Discrimination: Perspectives on Justice in Bioethics and Public Policy* (New York: Rowman and Littlefield, 1998), 54.   .

18. Silvers, "Formal Justice," 54.

19. *Americans with Disabilities Act,* enacted July 1990 by 101st Congress, 1st sess., cited in PL 101-336, sect. 2, 104 Stat. 327. See also Silvers, *Disability, Difference,* 75–76, 82.

20. See Silvers, *Disability, Difference,* 122; and Committee on Assessing Genetic Risks of the Institute of Medicine, *Assessing Genetic Risks: Implications for Health and Social Policy* (Washington: National Academy Press, 1994), 272–73.

21. Other differences that typically confer advantages are whiteness, heterosexuality, tallness, and good looks (as defined by some stereotypical standard).

22. Additional constraining factors may include Maria's husband and her religious or cultural tradition. These factors might influence not only whether she is open to prenatal testing or abortion but also whether physical or cognitive disability is perceived as the greater burden.

23. A conception of autonomy that fits this interpretation is developed in Susan Sherwin, *The Politics of Women's Health: Exploring Agency and Autonomy* (Philadelphia: Temple University Press, 1998), 19–44.

24. People with disabilities in the United States number from 35 to 43 million, depending on how disability is defined. Of these, one-third are over sixty-five years of age, and women comprise the bulk of that population. See Joseph P. Shapiro, *No Pity* (New York: Random House, 1993), 6.

25. Adrienne Asch and Michelle Fine, "Introduction: Beyond Pedestals," in Michelle Fine and Adrienne Asch, eds., *Women with Disabilities* (Philadelphia: Temple University Press, 1988), 3.

26. In addition to Asch and Fine, "Introduction," see also Marsha Saxton, "Disability Rights and Selective Abortion," in *Abortion Wars: A Half Century of Struggle, 1950–2000,* ed. Rickie Solinger (Berkeley: University of California Press, 1998), 374–93; and Adrienne Asch and Gail Geller, "Feminism, Bioethics, and Genetics," in *Feminism and Bioethics,* ed. Susan Wolf (New York: Oxford University Press, 1996), 318–50.

27. For example, see Asch and Fine, "Introduction," 5–6; and Susan Wendell, *The Rejected Body: Feminist Philosophical Reflections on Disability* (New York: Routledge, 1996), 35–56. The extent to which the pain and suffering associated with disability is relievable depends also on the nature of the disability and the variability of its impact on different people. Those who are able to write about their own experience of disability probably constitute both a numerical minority and a dominant group within the community of those who are disabled.

28. This statement was made by a woman with disabilities who attended a workshop funded by the Ethical, Legal, and Social Issues Program of the National Center for Human Genome Research in Zanesville, Ohio, May 16–19, 1996. The principal investigator for the workshop on Women and Genetics in Contemporary Society (WAGICS) was Helen Bequaert Holmes.

29. Adrienne Asch and Michelle Fine, in Fine and Asch, *Women with Disabilities,* 302. Shapiro (*No Pity,* 278) says that less than 50 percent of women told that their fetus has a serious genetic defect choose abortion.

30. Asch and Fine, in Fine and Asch, *Women with Disabilities,* 302.

31. See John J. McDermott, ed., *The Writings of William James* (New York: Modern Library, 1968), 629–45, 227–32, 136–52.

32. See Justus Buchler, ed., *Philosophical Writings of Peirce* (New York: Dover Publications, 1955), 4, 38, 42–59, 160, 288, 356.

33. Buchler, *Philosophical Writings,* 9–10, 28.

34. Charles Hartshorne and Paul Weis, eds., *The Collected Papers of Charles Sanders Peirce,* vol. 2 (Cambridge: Belknap Press of Harvard University Press, 1960), #654.

35. Hartshorne and Weis, *Collected Papers.*

36. Hartshorne and Weis, *Collected Papers.*

37. Tom L. Beauchamp and James Childress, *The Principles of Biomedical Ethics* (New York: Oxford University Press, 1979, 1983, 1989, 1994).

38. The *if* in this statement is intended to allow for the possibility that the interests of one party are never precisely the same as those of another.

39. Beauchamp and Childress, *Principles of Biomedical Ethics* (5th ed., 2001), 226–35.

40. Thomas Nagel, *Equality and Partiality* (New York: Oxford University Press, 1991), 10–20.

41. Nagel, *Equality and Partiality,* 10.

42. Nagel could respond to this criticism by claiming that the things that matter most to individual persons matter to all of them (see *Equality and Partiality,* 11). My rejoinder to this response is that morality asks more, and sometimes less or other, than merely dealing with what matters most to everyone.

43. Nancy C. M. Hartsock, *Money, Sex, and Power* (Boston: Northeastern University Press, 1985), and *The Feminist Standpoint Revisited and Other Essays* (Boulder: Westview Press, 1998), 105–32.

44. Hartsock, *Feminist Standpoint Revisited,* 108.

45. Hartsock, *Feminist Standpoint Revisited,* 235.

46. Donna Haraway, "Situated Knowledges: The Science Question in Feminism and the Privilege of Partial Perspective," *Feminist Studies* 14 (1988): 584.

47. Hartsock, *Feminist Standpoint Revisited,* 117–25. Hartsock draws on psychoanalytic theory in developing this critique.

48. Haraway, "Situated Knowledges," 581.

49. Haraway, "Situated Knowledges," 581.

50. Haraway, "Situated Knowledges," 584.

51. Haraway, "Situated Knowledges," 584.

52. John Ladd, "The Ethics of Participation," in J. Roland Pennock and John W. Chapman, eds., *Participation in Politics,* Nomos, vol. 16 (New York: Lieber-Atherton, 1975), 101. Ladd imputes this view to Kurt Baier in *The Moral Point of View* (New York: Random House, 1965), 107.

53. Ladd, "Ethics of Participation," 102.

54. Ladd, "Ethics of Participation," 103.

55. Ladd, "Ethics of Participation," 103.

56. The democratic justification for participation may be construed as a deontological argument, e.g., one based on the inalienable right of persons to participate in the development of social policies that affect them. Admittedly, utilitarian arguments may be invoked to curtail as well as to demand participation by nondominant groups. The utilitarian rationale for their participation gives priority to the greatest number of subjects to whom utility is to be applied; this is a democratic interpretation of utilitarianism. The utilitarian rationale opposing their participation gives priority to the best consequences (greatest happiness), which may be achieved undemocratically by allowing the exclusion of specific groups or individuals.

57. Ladd, "Ethics of Participation," 103.

58. Ladd, "Ethics of Participation," 102.

59. Note that I have identified equality as an *ethical* rather than a *psychological* or an *empirical* norm. Paradoxically, equality deserves to be supported, and is in fact supported, as an ethical norm by people who are *psychologically* attracted to inequality and pursue it in their empirical affairs. Most of us tend to promote the advantaged side of inequality in our own behalf.

60. Susan Sherwin, *No Longer Patient: Feminist Ethics and Health Care* (Philadelphia: Temple University Press, 1992), 75.

61. Sara Ruddick, *Maternal Thinking: Toward a Politics of Peace* (New York: Ballantine, 1989).

62. Hartsock, *Money, Sex, and Power,* 232.

63. Hartsock, *Feminist Standpoint Revisited,* 231.

64. Hartsock, *Feminist Standpoint Revisited,* 238.

65. Maria C. Lugones and Elizabeth V. Spelman, "Have We Got a Theory for You! Feminist Theory, Cultural Imperialism, and the Demand for 'The Woman's Voice,'" *Women's Studies International Forum* 6 (1983): 573–81; and Elizabeth V. Spelman, *Inessential Woman: Problems of Exclusion in Feminist Thought* (Boston: Beacon Press, 1988).

66. Alison Jaggar, *Feminist Politics and Human Nature* (Totowa, N.J.: Rowman and Allanheld, 1983), 371.

67. Jaggar, *Feminist Politics,* 377.

68. See Simone de Beauvoir, "The Second Sex," in *Philosophy of Woman,* ed. Mary Briody Mahowald (Indianapolis: Hackett, 1992), 82.

69. Rosemarie Tong, *Feminist Thought* (Boulder: Westview Press, 1998), 7 (parentheses in original).

70. See Linda J. Nicholson, ed., *Feminism/Postmodernism* (New York: Routledge, 1990) for an excellent collection of articles on postmodern feminism.

71. Moreover, gender identity and sex identity (as defined by chromosomes) may be different in the same individual.

72. Tong, *Feminist Thought,* 223.

73. Sandra Harding, *The Science Question in Feminism* (Ithaca: Cornell University Press, 1986), 195.

74. Mary B. Mahowald, "Sex-Role Stereotypes in Medicine," *Hypatia* 2 (summer 1987): 22.

75. Virginia L. Warren, "Feminist Directions in Medical Ethics," *Hypatia* 4 (summer 1989): 74.

4

What Is Environmental Ethics?

Max Oelschlaeger

Let me begin with a remembrance of Wayne Leys, which may seem to be an indulgence—how could anything personal be philosophical?—yet, I think, on second look is germane. Philosophers tend to think that only ideas are significant, thus overlooking the importance of example—the actual behavior of a particular person. Whatever the philosophical pretense, the culturing of human beings involves the inspiration that comes from the particularities of relationships. Of course, the role of examples in relation to human conduct has been suspect since the *Euthyphro*. It is not relationships philosophers have wanted but universal definitions and principles, that is, knowledge free of historical context and social entanglement.[1] Yet the influence of Leys on my life has more to do with example, with his actual behavior, than with any formal principle he codified in a philosophical journal.

No doubt, I impose an interpretive frame upon my remembrances. One might think of it as Aristotelian, since Leys always sought a reasoned middle ground. He was a man who encountered life and reflected upon it in a steady, measured way. He was never in a hurry, always gracious, and for a person of achievement, enormously humble. Why, he would even have lowly graduate students to his house

for supper and an evening of conversation. On these occasions, the
graduate students would sometimes, as is the bent of young people
inspired by the company of a distinguished philosopher, attempt to
rise above doxa and speak of foundational truths. But in his patient
way, Leys would usually suggest that a second look might be in order
and would gently but incisively poke holes in any and all "first principles." And when the opportunity came for one-to-one conversation, he would redirect the conversation to practical concerns, such
as asking you who you were, where you were headed, and why you
thought that such was important.

Of course, on no occasion during my tenure at Southern Illinois
University could I have told him that I intended to become an environmental ethicist. Environmental ethics simply did not exist; in
those days, we were concerned with issues like world peace, civil
disobedience, the war in Vietnam, and the incidents at Kent State.
Still, even at that time, having read Wordsworth and Thoreau and
some of the nature philosophy of Spinoza, Hegel, and Collingwood,
I was already inclined to take the path that I ultimately took. But
there was no possibility that any graduate student in the late 1960s
and early 1970s could have said, "I want to write my dissertation
on a problem in environmental ethics." No dissertation committee
would have known what such a proposal meant. Please note that
the first volume of the journal *Environmental Ethics* was published
in 1978, some five years after I left SIU.

It makes more sense, then, to imagine my remarks occurring in
an encounter with Leys where—some twenty years after leaving
SIU—I have returned, professing that I have become an environmental ethicist. My guess is that Leys, upon hearing my remark, would
deliberately pause and puff on his pipe and then ask, "What is this,
what did you call it, 'environmental ethics,' all about?"

Such a question is not one that I customarily address. I normally
speak before audiences of the "already converted," the "if not ecologically saved at least repentant sinners." Posing such a question
confirms the steady, reflective judgment that was characteristic of
Leys. Has the unexamined life ever been complete?

As I begin to engage the question "What is environmental ethics?" I confess that environmental philosophers, like most of their

philosophical brethren, are enormously confident that they have the rational answers to issues of ultimate consequence. They believe that by providing philosophical arguments that obligate humankind to care for the planet, a greener future, indeed, a sustainable culture can be created. Regrettably, to date, environmental ethicists seem to have accomplished little of ecological consequence. To the credit of the journal *Environmental Ethics,* recently published papers and editorials acknowledge that ecophilosophy has not been socially efficacious.[2] In truth, environmental ethics is still struggling for acceptance not only within the larger society but within the philosophical community itself. Consider that the same familiar faces appear again and again at the American Philosophical Association meetings organized by the International Society for Environmental Ethics as well as at international ecological meetings, such as the Society for Conservation Biology. Environmental ethicists seem like mainline Protestant ministers, preaching to an aging and already committed audience.

More seriously, despite the hundreds (if not thousands) of books on environmental ethics, Western society still careens toward a potentially catastrophic ecological future. Salient indices of ecocrisis, such as the loss of species, the thinning of stratospheric ozone, the growth of human population, the destruction of rain forests, and the increase in levels of atmospheric CO_2, continue to escalate. E. O. Wilson warns that humankind has itself initiated the sixth mass extinction of life on earth,[3] an extinction event that will likely take the human species with it. Interestingly, Wilson, now turned conservation biologist but an entomologist by academic training, is one of the strongest proponents for environmental ethics. At least two of his books close with chapters on environmental ethics, and he argues more generally that our field is crucial to creating a sustainable future.[4]

Clearly, there is a call for environmental ethics. One thinks that a pragmatic justification, if no other, is in order, since the very circumstances of life, the environmental contingencies of human existence, are threatened.[5] Just as clearly, there has been an underwhelming response from the professional philosophical community to these circumstances. At this juncture, there are only two programs (at Colorado State University and the University of North Texas) where a student can pursue a master's degree with a concentration in environmental ethics. There are no doctoral programs offering such a specialization; although a few students write dissertations on the subject, such efforts are made despite rather than because of programmatic structures.

More problematically, Bryan Norton, a leading environmental ethicist, argues that our likes do not really belong in departments of philosophy. He claims that if environmental ethicists are to contribute anything more than an endless series of theoretical conjectures (and refutations) that are almost always ignored by the institutionalized actors who actually make environmental decisions, such as corporate executives and governmental resource managers, then it is time for us to involve ourselves with practical ethics. Norton distinguishes applied ethics, which attempt to establish and then apply foundational principles to the resolution of particular problems, from practical ethics, which do not assume that philosophers can establish any kind of theory that is actually relevant to environmental decision making apart from involvement within the process. The practical philosopher, on Norton's account, attempts to facilitate the identification of "a general policy direction that can achieve consensus and define a range of actions that are morally acceptable to a wide range of worldviews."[6] Accordingly, Norton maintains, environmental ethicists must jump into environmental policy debates where they can test philosophical principles. But the consequence of this pragmatic move, he continues, "may be the abandonment of philosophy departments by environmental philosophers, who may instead take up residence in schools of natural resources, schools of planning, and schools of public policy."[7]

In some ways, I think Norton may be right.[8] In part, this stems from my own Deweyan notion that, whatever else it might be, philosophy is about the world, the things in the world, and the relations among the things in the world. Environmental crisis, if anything, is an open invitation to begin the reconstruction of culture. In the recently published *Philosophy and the Reconstruction of Culture*, John Stuhr argues that philosophy "must serve today as an impetus to action, and it can and must enrich and inform this action in service of desperately needed reconstructions of culture."[9] Yet my sense of my mainstream philosophical brethren is that they have grown too insular, too isolated, too remote from the affairs of the larger society, indeed, from the earth processes that sustain and nurture culture. Charles Taylor argues that contemporary philosophy seems scholastic, not so much concerned with the numbers of angels that can dance on the heads of a pin but consumed with "meta" questions, that is, questions that define theories of justification and explanation rather than constructive proposals dealing with the good society and the means to its realization.[10] Alasdair McIntyre, in a similar vein, argues that post-Enlightenment ethical discourse is a failed project. "The most striking feature of contemporary moral utterances is that so much of it is used to express disagreements; and the most striking feature of the debates in which these disagreements are expressed is their interminable character."[11]

The Lay of the Land

If the scandal of philosophy is that no two philosophers ever agree about anything, then environmental ethics is scandalous. There are so many different approaches to environmental ethics, most of which claim the status of foundational narratives or master discourses and delight in showing what foolish blunders of fact and egregious errors of logic that others have made, that outsiders—including philosophers who are not environmental ethicists—must wonder just what, if anything, it all means. Nonetheless, it is this diversity with which I reckon.

The limits of space preclude an extended discussion of the many types of ecophilosophy; an inventory must suffice. Let me identify ten species of the genus environmental ethics. Two caveats: First, within certain species, no defining criterion is uniformly agreed on among proponents. Second, there are considerable overlaps among species, for example, between postmodern approaches and philosophical anthropology, or between ecofeminists and deep ecologists.

Perhaps the best known variety of environmental ethics is deep ecology, as articulated by its primary proponent, Arne Naess, a Norwegian, and the leading American philosophical advocate, George Sessions.[12] One indication of the familiarity and popularity of deep ecology is that lay publics recognize the term; a second is that professional communities, such as conservation biologists, use deep ecological arguments as the justification for the conservation of biodiversity.[13] But deep ecology is not a single enterprise; a recent publication shows no less than eight variants of deep ecology in Norway alone.[14] However, virtually all proponents of deep ecology argue that nature has an intrinsic value or inherent worth that trumps human claims to unlimited access to natural resources beyond those that satisfy basic needs.

A second species can be labeled land ethics, conceptualized as beginning with Aldo Leopold's *Sand County Almanac* and extending to include the many philosophical commentators on Leopoldian land ethics, some of whom offer inconsistent or even contradictory interpretations of it. For example, J. Baird Callicott reads Leopold as an ecocentrist, while E. C. Hargrove interprets him as a therapeutic nihilist.[15] No commentator, however, has achieved the simple elegance of Leopold's original formulation that a human action is right when it preserves the integrity, stability, and beauty of the land community. Leopoldian land ethics is perhaps the most accessible environmental ethics for lay publics. Land ethics also has a considerable following among the diverse kinds of professionals engaged in natural resource management.[16]

A third kind of environmental ethics is ecofeminism. Ecofeminism has no single, widely acclaimed, original proponent, as do deep ecology and land ethics. But the species can be identified by the convergence of virtually all theorists on the premises that environmental problems and social problems are rooted in patriarchy, and that there are no solutions for environmental pathologies apart from solutions of the social problems created by patriarchy. Among the philosophical ecofeminists are Susan Griffin, Ariel Salleh, Karen Warren, Carol Bigwood, and Rosemary Ruether.[17]

A fourth type of environmental ethics is traditionally philosophical—traditional in two senses. First, traditionalists attempt to develop a master theory in terms of which all environmental problems might be solved. And second, they attempt to extend established ethical theory to environmental ethics. For example, Paul Taylor's *Respect for Nature* extends Kantian theory along the lines of ecological science to reach a position he terms *biocentrism*. In the same vein, Arne Naess's deep ecology can be read as an extension of

Spinozist ethics to issues of environmental concern. And some ethicists, such as Kristin Shrader-Frechette, extend the work of contemporary ethical theorists, such as John Rawls's theory of justice, into areas of environmental theory, such as risk-cost-benefit analysis.[18]

A fifth kind encompasses aesthetic theories, such as those of Yrjö Sepänmaa, Aldo Leopold, Eugene Hargrove, and Erazim Kohák.[19] These ethicists find a source for environmental ethics in natural beauty. Their theories tend to cloud clear distinctions between aesthetics and ethics in favor of qualitative dimensions of experience, that is, the experience of natural entities (as distinct from the built environment and humanly made art objects), although some emphasize the objective dimensions of the beauty of natural entities.

A sixth sort of environmental ethics is rooted in philosophical anthropology, deriving primarily from Native American and other aboriginal cultures. Theorists like Vine Deloria, Calvin Martin, and Jim Cheney argue that the West is culture-bound, stuck inside the belief that nature has only instrumental value.[20] Aboriginal lifeways and belief systems are held up as countervailing philosophies, as alternatives to the Eurocentric beliefs that reduce nature to commodity and create the conditions of human estrangement from nature. Native American theorists believe that the old ways can be recovered by contemporary indigenous peoples. In contrast, the Anglo theorists characterize the ecophilosophies of indigenous peoples more as springboards to change in the dominant worldview than as a call for Americans to go native.

A seventh type derives from religion, including Jewish, Christian, wiccan, Native American, and goddess traditions. In part, these theories are a response to the criticism leveled by Lynn White Jr. that Judeo-Christianity, with its belief that man was the son of God and with its other worldly attitudes, encouraged environmental ruination.[21] Today, virtually all Protestants, Jews, and Roman Catholics acknowledge an ethical obligation to care for the creation in their creedal statements. However, the specifics of these statements are enormously varied, ranging from conservative biblicists like Francis Schaeffer, who cite God's word as mandating environmental ethics, to radicals like Thomas Berry, who, like the biblical prophets, castigate the conventionally pious.[22]

An eighth species of environmental ethics comes from Third World philosophers, partly in response to arguments from First World ethicists, who claim Third World peoples have failed to control their explosive population growth and are thus overwhelming biogeophysical systems, such as rain forests. Third World theorists, however, challenge Western environmental ethicists, contending that they are in no position to criticize the Third World. Ramachandra Guha, for example, argues that deep ecologists, in their concern for the protection of biodiversity and wilderness habitats, marginalize the socially legitimate and economically vital concerns of Third World citizens. He also charges Western ethicists with hypocrisy, since a single citizen in the industrialized West consumes fifteen to thirty times as much energy and other resources as the typical Third World citizen.[23] Vandana Shiva, to take another example, argues that the Third World does not need Western environmental ethics but can find its own sources of inspiration within indigenous traditions, such as the Upanishads.[24]

A ninth variety of environmental ethics utilizes the idea of wilderness as the grounds for responsibility to nature. E. O. Wilson, for example, identifies the idea of wilderness as one of only two sources of environmental ethics (the other being "biophilia"). He contends that the idea of wilderness is essential to the development of a deep conservation ethics that naturalizes history and reconnects human beings with ecological processes, if for no other reason than wilderness is fundamentally beyond human contrivance.[25] Susan Bratton, to take another example, argues that appeals to wild nature, as the grounds for the caring stewardship of the earth, have a long association with Judeo-Christianity, beginning in the Old Testament itself.[26]

Last but not least are reconstructive postmodern approaches to environmental ethics. Postmodern environmental theorists believe that "ecomalaise" is grounded in language, and that it is also through language that the fissure between nature and culture might be healed.[27] Since my answer to the question "What is environmental ethics?" expands on postmodern approaches, no further commentary is required now.

Two last points. First, some environmental ethicists offer arguments, such as Mark Sagoff's *The Economy of the Earth* and Murray Bookchin's *Remaking Society,* that cannot be readily categorized in terms of the ten types above.[28] Second and crucially, since mainstream philosophy has yet to recognize environmental ethics, there are philosophers who have virtually no reputation as environmental ethicists yet whose work bears both methodologically and substantively upon the field. I am thinking particularly of Charles Taylor. I emphasize Taylor in hopes that some avenue of communication might be established between environmental ethics and the wider domain of philosophical inquiry. I still hold out some hope that Norton is not entirely right in contending that environmental ethicists have no place in "academic philosophy."

In any case, the enormous array of ethical theory outlined above has proven an embarrassment to some ecophilosophers, who argue that if environmental ethics is to become cognitively respectable and socially efficacious, then it must develop a single knockdown theory that will vanquish all pretenders to the ethical throne in favor of the one, true theory.[29] The advantage, according to the advocates of moral monism, is that by developing one master theory, ecophilosophers might present a united front to the sociopolitical world, the consequence being that politicians and bureaucrats in the many natural resource agencies, as well as environmental economists, lawyers, and engineers and corporate decision makers, might conclude that ethicists actually know what they are talking about. Further, as the argument goes, a single theory would allow philosophers to proceed deductively from basic principles to specific issues, such as human population levels, atmospheric pollution, mining of groundwater, obligations to future generations, North-South equity issues, and so on. If applied ethics is conceived as the derivation of second-order principles that fit universal ethical principles to particular situations, then the moral monism model would be particularly appealing.

Predictably, although proponents of one kind or another of environmental ethics, whether deep ecology or ecofeminism, land ethics or ecotheology, have been attracted by the moral monist argument—who wouldn't like to be cognitive king?—there have been dissenters, known in the trade as the moral pluralists. The pluralists, who have been influenced by twentieth-century intellectual culture and thus function in a post-Gödel, post-Heisenberg, post-Wittgenstein, post–chaos theory milieu, argue that no philosophical approach specifically, and no intellectual paradigm more generally, can ever achieve a position of intellectual preeminence or knockdown superiority. More pragmatically, moral pluralists have also examined the actual ways in which environmental decisions have been legitimated; the results indicate more of an ad hoc approach (much like casuistry), where environmental decision makers have used justifications ready to hand, rather than any constant, methodologically rigorous, and theoretically grounded paradigm.[30] The moral pluralists are largely pragmatists as well, in the sense that they think that, above all else, moral philosophy generally and environmental ethics specifically should be useful, in the sense of helping human beings, considered either individually or collectively, come to grips with the challenging circumstances of cultural existence.

After the Linguistic Turn

In the introductory essay to *Postmodern Environmental Ethics,* I contend that the moral pluralists (as I categorized them) have fallen into a reconstructive and pragmatic, that is, postmodern way of doing environmental ethics. I can here recount only a few aspects of the analysis that underlies that categorization.[31] Postmodern environmental ethicists take language seriously. When I say that postmodern environmental ethics has taken the linguistic turn, I mean that it's difficult to envision any solution for ecomalaise that is not explicitly linguistic. Will Wright captures this idea succinctly, if abstractly, in his book *Wild Knowledge:*

> language always constitutes our world, the world we know, the world we live in—not in the sense that the world is language, or that language controls the world, but in the sense that the structure of language must be an inherent part of any world we can know. If knowledge is to be possible, the structure of language must be compatible with the structure of the world, and in this sense the world must be linguistic. . . . the idea of nature must be understood as first of all an aspect of language, so that the idea of nature is understood as a necessary aspect of the way language successfully mediates between

actions and the world. It is in this sense that both social theory and natural theory must be explicitly referred to the formal structure of language, as constituting the possibility of both. And it is in this sense that the idea of knowledge can generate a social-natural theory, where the validity of knowledge must involve a formal judgment of successful social-natural mediation, successful in the sense of sustaining the possibility of language, the possibility of social life.[32]

Yet as noted above, there are many kinds of environmental ethics, such as aesthetic theories and land ethics, that do not explicitly consider the question of language. Language in this sense is transparent to the ethicists who propose these theories, much like water is transparent to fish.[33] Of course, it is not only environmental ethicists who refuse to recognize their immersion in language; the vast majority of our fellow human beings do so as well. Nonetheless, placing an explicit emphasis on language allows the possibility of conceptualizing the many different varieties of environmental ethics as engaged in the reconstruction of culture through language to emerge. And it is also possible to at least outline how it is that the citizens who constitute the masses might move from where they are now, mired in an ecologically dysfunctional culture, toward a sustainable society. I develop these ideas in ensuing sections.

The immediate question is the relation of language to environmental ethics. My claim that all human beings, including environmental ethicists, are linguistically situated does not dictate either the form or the content of any philosophical theory. While the notion that all philosophical theories are linguistically formulated is minimal, it is not trivial, since language is necessarily the means of adaptation to the circumstances of existence.[34] Therefore, the self-conscious realization that nature and culture are linguistically mediated offers practical advantages over theories that privilege either linguistically naive or representational views of nature for a number of reasons.[35] For one, it works against philosophical arrogance: No language game, recognized as such, can maintain an argument that it is privileged, that is, metaphysically (in the sense of extralinguistically) correct. For another, it means that philosophical inquiry can be reconceptualized reflexively in a way that recognizes the social construction of knowledge and the possibility that environmental ethicists might actively participate in the knowledge-creating process.[36] And finally, ecocrisis itself can be reconceptualized as a problem of language rather than as a problem of environmental engineering, economic externalities, or public policy per se. Or more pointedly, after the linguistic turn, we realize that problems of environmental engineering, economic externalities, and public policy are themselves linguistically mediated.

However, in the remainder of this paper, I go beyond any minimalist interpretation of language in its relation to environmental ethics. Not only do I take language seriously but my argument pivots on the idea that whatever else human beings are, they are self-interpreting language animals. This phrasing comes, of course, from the work of Charles Taylor.[37] In some ways, Taylor's ideas are not entirely novel. Similar (although not identical) ideas have been stated in a variety of ways by other philosophers; for example, Heidegger's notion that language is the house of being, and Wittgenstein's aphorism that to imagine a language game is to imagine a way of life. I come close to making the same point as Taylor with the premise that, insofar as we are specifically human beings, we are biologically underdetermined (note I don't say undetermined) and culturally overdetermined. But Taylor's exposition of the notion that human beings are self-interpreting language animals has reached a level of analytical detail and intellectual comprehensiveness that few philosophical theorists reach. And while it might be argued that Gadamer or Habermas are as analytically astute and conceptually comprehensive as Taylor, they are less relevant to the purposes of doing environmental ethics in North America.

Gadamer does make one point that Taylor does not explicitly make, suggesting that we teeter on the precipice of ecocatastrophe "because of the baleful influence of language." The suspicion is all too real, he continues, that "if we continue to pursue industrialization, to think of work only in terms of profit, and to turn our earth into one vast factory as we are doing at the moment, then we threaten the conditions of human life in both the biological sense and in the sense of specific human ideals [love, justice, charity, peace] even to the extreme of self-destruction." But language also carries the possibility of changing the status quo. As Gadamer puts the point, "Language is not [only] its elaborate conventionalism, nor the burden of pre-schematization with which it loads us, but the generative and creative power unceasingly to make this whole fluid."[38] On this point, Taylor and Gadamer (as well as all others who have taken the linguistic turn) agree.

Two caveats: I am not claiming that Taylor's theory of language is *the* theory per se, rather I use it to flesh out the idea that the linguistic turn offers a way in which environmental ethics might be reconceptualized—to the end, I should emphasize, of making it more evident how ecophilosophy bears on the reconstruction of culture. Neither do I claim that all environmental theorists must take the linguistic turn. I am claiming that the idea that humans are self-interpreting language animals might change the way that some ethicists conceive of their mission. Ecophilosophers who accept this idea might also accept the responsibility to participate in the conversation that comes with membership in a discourse community, such as liberal-democratic industrial culture. And they might also acknowledge that insofar as ethical inquiry is to make a difference, then it must be effective within that discourse community. It must, that is to say, promote constructive change. On this account, then, environmental ethics must confront the question of effective discourse. After expanding in the next section on the idea that human beings are usefully conceptualized as self-interpreting language animals, I will take up the idea of effective discourse in the section that follows.

ECOPHILOSOPHY AS STRONG EVALUATION

No simple summary of Taylor's work is possible. In truth, I am attempting an overview of a thicket of issues that leads Taylor himself to occasionally despair of clarity. With Taylor and many other commentators on language, I find incomprehensible the idea of an absolute vantage point on language.[39] So some lack of clarity, some lack of formal consistency, is inevitable, as Gödel's proof perhaps reminds us. What I offer is a reading of Taylor's texts in the context of the question "What is environmental ethics?" Although many, many issues germane to the philosophy of language are not included in my discussion, my contextualized reading of Taylor's work is, I think, legitimate, since he brings his theory of language to bear—if obliquely—on issues of ecocrisis. In the course of my discussion, I single out some of these places. But what is most important for my purposes is that Taylor offers deep insights into human agency, insights that empower an alternative to the dominant cultural ethos, which categorizes ecomalaise as either a set of technological dysfunctions or a set of problems requiring market adjustments. By extending Taylor's notion that human beings are self-interpreting language animals, ecological crisis can be contextualized more as a crisis of language—or what might be called a crisis of legitimacy—than as a question of either engineering or economics.[40]

What, then, does Taylor's notion mean in the context of environmental ethics? Several things, obviously, so many things that it is relatively easy to get lost in the forest because of all the trees. First, since language is the modality of specifically human being, the very means by which we invent ourselves in our cultural projects, it is the means also by which humans can adapt (politically, economically, technologically, ethically) to the circumstances of ecocrisis. Moreover, those circumstances themselves have been created through language, such as the language of physics, as in Descartes's proposal that through the new science humankind could become the master and the possessor of nature, or the language of religion, as in Genesis, where Adam is given dominion over the flora and the fauna.[41]

This notion leads, then, to the second point. Closely examined, as Taylor does in *Sources of the Self,* the languages of physics and religion are themselves revealed as self-interpretations, that is, projections of human being in one configuration rather than another. That is, neither the discourse of physics nor the language of religion exist by nature but only through history and society. But the possibilities for imaginative responses to the circumstances of life—or alternatively, the possibilities for self-definition—are not fixed by one place and time but remain, to a greater or lesser extent, open. Previous interpretations can be reinterpreted. In Taylor's terms, strong evaluations can be made of the present modalities of human being to the end of future possibilities, such as the creation of a sustainable culture that is ecologically healthy, socially just, and economically sufficient.

That is the "big picture" of my reading of Taylor, a sketchy overview to be sure. Now for some details. One is his argument that the socially and politically dominant conception of human being is instrumental and utilitarian. It defines the dignity of human being in terms of our ability to "control . . . an objectified universe through instrumental reason."[42] The outcome is our materialistic way of life, since humans are conceived essentially as greedy little pigs, whose happiness and well-being depend upon the relentless conversion of the earth into economic goods. North American culture is fixated, Taylor argues, "on brute quantitative growth, unalloyed by judgments of priority. The justification of this has to be an image of the good life, where the acquisition of more and more consumer goods—what the system is good at producing—is seen as a central purpose of life."[43] It is precisely this scheme to which environmental ethicists object.

That the consumerist conception of human being relates directly to ecocrisis can be intuited in terms of the (too simple) formula, $E_{(total)} = D \times P \times T$, where $E_{(total)}$ represents the biogeophysical consequences (such as the destruction of rain forests, extinction of species, rending of holes in stratospheric ozone, and so on) of the interactions among three variables—namely D, the level of demand placed on the ecosphere, P, the number of people making the demand, and T, the technologies employed to exploit the earth. Beyond basic metabolic needs, as Taylor makes clear, demand (D) is a function of our self-conception.[44]

The problem is that the established consumerist lifestyle is not subject to strong evaluation. Taylor writes, I think with a high degree of humor, that "the definition of the good life as continuing escalation in living standards has an inescapable appeal to unregenerate men, which we all are. This Plato knew well. Appetite tends to run on to infinity, unless controlled by reason."[45] Little wonder that the typical American produces fifteen hundred pounds of waste and requires forty thousand pounds of various resources per year, and that collectively Americans, although only 5 percent of the world's population, consume more than 30 percent of the earth's resources. But the plot is even thicker than this, since the psychological hook of the consumerist society goes beyond consumption for the sake of consumption to the notion of human freedom, that is, the individual's ability to control his or her own life. As Taylor puts the point, "The promise of greater control over nature which our civilization holds out is naturally translated . . . into a promise of increased individual control, which means disposing of an increasing number of individual consumer goods."[46] The social outcome of such unalloyed individualism is pernicious, since the consumer-citizen tends "to look at society as a set of necessary instruments, rather than as the locus in which we can develop our most important potential."[47] Thus, the consumer-citizen withdraws, as many social commentators observe, into his or her own private space. As Taylor puts the point, "a society whose institutions are mainly seen in instrumental terms is one which offers very few intrinsic satisfactions, and which men naturally tend to withdraw from whenever feasible to their own private space."[48] A different conception of human being, one which Taylor favors, rejects the socially dominant one as "a [dogmatic and uninformed] denial of our place in things."[49] As an alternative, Taylor ties human dignity to the recognition "that we are part of a larger order of living beings, in the sense that our life springs from there and is sustained from there."[50] Nature, in other words, makes a moral claim upon us. Whatever the reasons we have had for assigning moral consideration to human beings, human beings themselves are cut from the fabric of life. Thus, to deny moral consideration to that fabric of life is an act of enormous arrogance, if not simply bad manners: that is, radical ingratitude. Here is talk to warm the environmental ethicist's heart. But crucially, it is strong evaluation that supports Taylor's claim.

Here I must further adumbrate my account of Taylor's philosophy, since it involves a long and complex consideration of designative and expressive theories of language.[51] The theory of designative language, on Taylor's account, is the view that words unproblematically hook up with things so that language reveals the world as it is in itself, apart from human beings and their projects. More crucially, the designative theory of language accompanies, indeed, enables the dominant theory of human being. From this point of view, language is essentially a tool in terms of which humankind exercises its rational control of the world, bringing the world of things into the rubric of human meaning. But this, according to Taylor, is a problem that ultimately defeats a designative theory, since the possibility of specifically human meaning, or any adequate account of human meaning, is not possible within the frame of a designative theory. From a designative standpoint, human beings are just objects among objects, and only objective descriptions—or putatively objective descriptions, like neoclassical economics—of human affairs are possible.

The designative theory is also beset with further conceptual difficulties (beyond its inability to account for human meaning). One has do with the implications of reflexivity itself. For once we realize that we are inside language, that there are no specifically human positions outside language, then there is no escape from contingency.[52] And if there is no exit, there is no Parmenidean point from which the whole of language can be disclosed. But more to the point, although language clearly relates us to a world outside the skin— the objective world of things—Taylor believes that this kind of relation is secondary to a more basic function, namely, that language enables the expressive activity that makes us specifically human beings living in a meaningful world of intentions rather than simply existing as objects among other objects. As Taylor puts it, we are "surrounded by meaning; in the words we exchange, in all the signs we deploy, in the art, music, literature we create and enjoy, in the very shape of the man-made environment most of us live in; and not least, in the internal speech we rarely cease addressing to ourselves silently, or to absent others."[53]

For Taylor, then, language is the medium of human agency. Again, his conception of agency is complicated, but it can be glossed here by contrasting strong and weak evaluation. "In weak evaluation," Taylor claims, "for something to be judged good it is sufficient that it be desired, whereas in strong evaluation there is also a use of 'good' or some other evaluative term for which being desired is not sufficient; indeed some desires or desired consummations can be judged as bad, base, ignoble, trivial, superficial, unworthy, and so on."[54] Weak evaluation is, of course, the socially dominant form of judgment, overdetermining public policy and private decisions, dovetailing precisely with the consumerist conception of self and the designative theory of language. As Taylor notes, "The bent of utilitarianism has been to do away with qualitative distinctions of worth on the grounds that they represent confused perceptions of the real bases of our preferences which are quantitative."[55]

In contrast, strong evaluations are qualitative, neither capable of mensuration nor reduction to consumerist preferences. Strong evaluations, Taylor claims, "are articulations of our sense of what is worthy, or higher, or more integrated, or more fulfilling, and so on."[56] And these aspirations are not given to us by our human nature but are formulated in language, in words that form legitimating narratives, stories that give direction and meaning to human existence. Neither are these aspirations simply descriptions that can be subsumed within a designative theory of language, for the very activity of articulating our aspirations gives shape to that which is, at the beginning, vague, confused, unformed, even chaotic. Our strong evaluations, that is, our self-interpretations, "are partly constitutive of our experience."[57]

Clearly, the foregoing discussion is no substitute for an actual encounter with Taylor's texts. I may have so adumbrated his arguments that they perhaps lose plausibility. As Taylor himself notes, the idea that humans are self-interpreting runs against the rationalist grain of modern culture. "It violates a paradigm of clarity and objectivity."[58] Nonetheless, whatever the inadequacies of my account, it enables me to attempt in the following section to recontextualize environmental ethics as effective discourse, that is, as promoting a cultural conversation that portends the reconstruction of culture.

Ecophilosophy as Effective Discourse

If it is the case that human beings are usefully conceptualized as self-interpreting language animals, that we are biologically underdetermined and culturally overdetermined, then ecophilosophy, whatever else it might be, can be conceptualized as effective discourse. But what is effective discourse? Minimally, effective discourse would promote a cultural conversation that would lead from where we are now, mired in an ever worsening ecocrisis, toward a cultural configuration where the activities of human living did not undercut ecosystem integrity. Effective discourse self-consciously attempts, perhaps in a Socratic fashion (although devoid of Socratic epistemological and metaphysical commitments), to disturb society, to loosen the web of belief, the socially legitimated, dominant story, so that new stories might be woven. Alternatively stated, environmental ethics has a major role to play in the cultural response to ecocrisis. It follows that, insofar as ecophilosophers are self-consciously aware of their role, they can better carry it out—better assist culture in the reweaving of basic stories.

The move into language, I think, reveals with startling clarity the details of the social construction of the idea of nature and the ideas of our relations with nature. For example, there are clear differences between nineteenth-century interpretations of Darwin's theory of evolution and our own, early-twenty-first-century interpretations. Herbert Spencer read Darwin's theory as confirmation of the idea of progress. Thus the struggle for survival winnowed out the weak and the unfit in favor of the strong and the adaptable. Today, the idea of progress has largely been abandoned in favor of readings that find a different story in evolutionary theory. Peter Bowler contends that the modern reading of Darwin "extracts a message that has become popular only in the age of environmental awareness. In his own time, the ecological dimension . . . was largely subordinated to the confident progressionism that characterized the Victorian era."[59] That is, theories of nature do not spring up in a vacuum but amid historical circumstances.

To accept our historicity and linguisticality implies that ecophilosophers might abandon the conception of themselves as providing master discourse. So construed, environmental ethics is a lesser enterprise than what ethicists have aspired to over the ages. For, trailing in the wake of Parmenides, they sought the One: the immutably true that all people in all places at all times would have to accept.[60] Yet less, in another sense, is more: By embracing time and language, philosophers might once again place their (figurative) hands upon the fabric from which life is cut, that is, the threads that constitute the woof and warp of an evolving text, or weaving, that is the West. So framed, the question is "Who needs master discourse?"

The notion of effective discourse implies that ecophilosophers, whatever else they might be, might be useful to society. For one thing, philosophers seem better prepared to deal with complexity than almost any other discipline. Perhaps we have an obligation to listen to the cacophony of voices in the contemporary world, voices that have grown specialized and narrow, the voices of law, economics, science, and religion. In any case, rather than being a source of embarrassment, the notion of ecophilosophy as effective discourse is a great triumph. What greater function has philosophy than to be midwife to the birth of an age—the age of ecology, as this has been termed?[61] Such an assertion seems immodest, to say the least, perhaps analogous to Plato's idea that philosopher kings are best suited to rule society. But the notion of effective discourse trumps any claim to the throne, to the status of philosopher king.

Taylor suggests that philosophers are not so much creative geniuses who single-handedly invent new ages as they are members of conversational communities who help articulate an emerging world-view. He notes that René Descartes and Francis Bacon ushered in the modern age not so much through the originality of their thought as by describing the background of the dominant discourse of that age. What is crucial is describing the background of the dominant discourse. For if human beings are language animals, thrown into the circumstances of history and bound by the threads of language, then the past cannot be repudiated. As Ortega y Gasset observes, we are substantial immigrants on a pilgrimage of human beingness.[62] The past, whatever its insufficiencies, dogs our every step. Grasping the background, Taylor contends, is essential to rational change, since it "is the background we assume and draw on in any claim to rightness, part of which we are forced to spell out when we have to defend our responses as the right ones."[63]

Taylor's *Sources of the Self* exemplifies the attempt to develop "the background picture," the many strands of thought and action that undergird the present. On the one hand, Taylor argues that our changed sensibilities, the sensibilities that find moral obligation and inherent worth in nature, grow out of the change of consciousness associated with the Enlightenment and instrumental reason. On his account, we could not have rationally articulated the claims that nature makes upon us as human animals apart from the objectifying moves of the Enlightenment. On the other hand, instrumental reason has, through time, disclosed its own insufficiencies. Contemporary society, the new industrial state, is fixated on economic growth for the sake of growth, that is, it is a slave to commodity fetishism and to the idea that humans are nothing more than Homo economicus: greedy little pigs.

The second moment of ecophilosophical thought conceptualized as effective discourse is the deconstruction of the dominant discourse, criticism that aims not at annihilation of the past but at its transformation in light of present challenges. Deconstruction, in the continental European sense, has been roundly criticized by American pragmatists as a nihilistic, self-defeating kind of philosophy.[64] If history is full of sound and fury, signifying nothing, or nothing more than the discourse of a politically dominant class, then what conceivable purpose does it serve? The very idea of cultural reconstruction implies that history has meaning, if for no other reason than it conditions the ambit of possibility. The dominant discourse cannot be eliminated per se, since history constitutes the fabric of human life. The pragmatic challenge is to loosen the woof and warp of the cultural fabric, the sedimented behaviors and the sanctified conventions, so that adaptive change becomes possible.

All of the ten varieties of environmental ethics discussed above function in a deconstructive vein: Their primary strength is criticism of the status quo. For example, virtually all environmental ethicists criticize the anthropocentric tendencies of modern thought, which privileges human interests over all others. Of course, the deconstruction of anthropocentrism can take different forms. One strategy might be to simply show that strong anthropocentrism is self-defeating, since satisfaction of human interests does not occur in an ecological vacuum; another strategy, based on a close reading of biblical texts, might argue that the Creator did not privilege human interests to the exclusion of other interests. However, the deconstruction of anthropocentrism, in and of itself, is not sufficient. If ecophilosophers do not develop a background picture, then ecophilosophical criticism fails to establish connections with the meaningful experiences of the larger human community. It falls, in other words, on deaf ears, since citizens cannot identify themselves as actors on the stage of history—agents who must take on new roles.

But effective discourse must also move from the first two moments of thought to the third, reconstructive (imaginative) moment, where reflective awareness leads from a past, now recognized as partially failed, toward a future that offers fresh possibilities. Following Taylor's thesis that human beings are usefully conceptualized as self-interpreting language animals, strong evaluations are essential to the reconstruction of culture. For it is strong evaluation that reveals the insufficiencies of the status quo and imaginatively points toward tomorrow. And it is strong evaluation of the status quo that, to a greater or lesser extent (depending on reflexive awareness), environmental ethics attempts to offer. The actual success of environmental ethics is beside the point; pragmatically considered, environmental ethics is a catalyst for cultural conversation that is alert to the manifest ecosocial insufficiencies of today and the possibility of overcoming those deficiencies tomorrow.

Obviously, the reconstruction of culture through effective discourse presupposes the enabling moves of the linguistic turn. From inside language, language can be conceptualized as a middle way between humankind and the more than human: an open, fluctuating system of signs upon which survival depends. And from such a position, human beings might reestablish themselves as natural animals while remaining distinctively human. Thus, effective ecophilosophical discourse is not entirely inconsistent with traditional definitions of human being, such as the notion that human beings are rational animals or the children of God. Where the linguistic turn pinches traditional definitions is in recontextualizing them as contingencies, as artifacts of cultural conversations, rather than as apodictic truths, as necessary features of the universe, as universals good for all people in all places at all times. But as I have argued elsewhere, these issues are more rhetorical than philosophical for the ecophilosopher who takes the linguistic turn. Persuasion does not depend on abandoning a human point of view but rather on making strong evaluations that change the conversation.

ENVIRONMENTAL ETHICS AND THE RECONSTRUCTION OF CULTURE

The conceptual implications of taking language seriously, for intellectuals generally as well as for ecophilosophers, are complicated, beyond the strict confines of this paper. But let me mention two. One is that we must recover something that philosophers have looked

down upon, at least since the time of Aristotle—namely, rhetoric.[65]
The linguistic turn implies that no rigid line of demarcation can be
maintained between rhetoric and philosophy. Yet the ecophilosophical community remains indifferent if not hostile toward rhetoric, which helps explain, at least in part, why environmental ethics
has not helped society turn onto the path of sustainability. Clearly,
epistemic rhetoric, if no other, offers resources to the ecophilosophical community that increase its potential to effect social change.[66]
Insofar as environmental ethics is to contribute to the reconstruction of society, at least some among us must consider seriously the
means through which knowledge is constructed and legitimated.[67]
Regrettably, pragmatists like John Stuhr and James Campbell, who
carefully consider the milieu in which knowledge is generated, are
more the exception than the rule. The Deweyan notions that communities are the matrix of inquiry, and that rational public policy
is rational not because it is supported by the majority but because
it has been placed in the crucible of public criticism, are entirely
consistent with the idea of ecophilosophy as aiming at the reconstruction of society.

Dewey argues that "Democracy as a form of life cannot stand still.
It, too, if it is to live, must go forward to meet the changes that are
here and that are coming. If it does not go forward, if it tries to stand
still, it is already starting on the backward road that leads to extinction."[68] Dewey implies that, simply as members of a democratic
society, philosophers have an obligation to participate in the reconstruction of culture. Yet as Stuhr surmises, philosophers have largely
retreated into the academy. "Having recognized . . . that they have
no special access to Truth, Knowledge, Justice, Goodness, Beauty,
or Reality, they wrongly have retreated to merely academic sanctu-
aries and logically possible worlds with special professional vocabu-
laries, techniques, and issues. Even when they deal with public issues, they do it—ironically—largely only within this professional
context or conversation."[69] It follows that insofar as ecophilosophy
remains academic, that is, isolated within the discourse community
constituted by experts, it has nothing to offer to the reconstruction
of culture. But the linguistic turn itself, as epitomized by the idea
that we are self-interpreting language animals, challenges ecophi-

losophers to reconceptualize themselves as catalysts for a public conversation that might refashion a cornucopian, consumerist culture into a sustainable one.

Apart from the rhetorical dimensions of the ecophilosophical conversation, if we take language seriously, then some account of the evolution of language itself is required—also an enormously complicated issue.[70] So pervasive are the implications of the linguistic turn that, as Stephen Toulmin argues, even the very forms of argument are now comprehended as linguistically and temporally dependent. While analytic philosophy has hoped for field-invariant criteria by which to judge arguments (that is, "a single, universal set of criteria applicable in all fields of argument alike"), including those of environmental ethics, that hope has not been fulfilled.[71] Today, Toulmin contends, any credible account of argument is necessarily historical. "To think up new and better methods of arguing in any field is to make a major advance, not just in logic, but in the substantive field itself: great logical innovations are part and parcel of great scientific, moral, political, or legal innovations."[72]

Most environmental philosophers yet live with the belief that argument is timeless, that the three laws of thought define all rational discourse. But if we take the evolution of language seriously, things look somewhat different. The law of the excluded middle may, for example, govern conventional discourse, that is, the day in, day out conversation of commercial, scientific, or even philosophical communication. But what of situations where there is a change in meaning itself, where discourse communities, in response to changed circumstances, refashion the web of belief, as when feudalism gave way to capitalism, or when Aristotelian physics gave way to Newtonian physics, or when medieval scholasticism gave way to Enlightenment rationalism?

I am ranging, perhaps, too far afield, since my task is one of recontextualizing environmental ethics. To the end of illustrating how environmental ethics can contribute to the reconstruction of culture, let me consider two examples—land ethics and ecofeminism—in further detail.

Land ethics, in its original Leopoldian formulation, was a remarkable intellectual achievement. Leopold's own intellectual odyssey, where he moved from a progressive conservationist point of view, emphasizing the values of efficiency and utility, to a land ethicist point of view, emphasizing the values of integrity, stability, and beauty, is well known.[73] Clearly, the continued deterioration of the biosphere is evidence that land ethics is not a panacea. But it has made real differences. For land ethics has been a catalyst for change, contributing to the emergence of environmental ethics as a professional field, as well as leading to actual changes in ecological management.

While some philosophers yet accuse Leopold of committing the is-ought fallacy (closely akin to the scholastic concern with how many angels can dance on the head of a pin), others have gone on to develop detailed expositions of a land ethics orientation in its relation to ecological management and also to land policy. Laura Westra, for example, has written a remarkable book that managerially operationalizes the Leopoldian emphasis on integrity. Focusing on the Great Lakes Water Quality Agreement, which states as an explicit goal the restoration of integrity to the Great Lakes Basin Ecosystem, Westra unpacks the concept of integrity in a way that shows that such an idea exists only at the interface of ecology with ethics. "The anthropocentric-nonanthropocentric distinction," she claims, "no longer operates at" the ecosystem level. "Humans are part of the biota and their life-support system is thus primary."[74] In another book with a similar approach, Lynton Caldwell, author of the National Environmental Policy Act, and Kristin Shrader-Frechette develop a land ethics point of view for land policy. They argue that land ethics challenges the convention that the land is nothing more than an inert resource for economic appropriation. Caldwell and Shrader-Frechette are concerned with actually changing both land policy and judicial interpretations of existing laws. But to do this, they also recognize that "a critical mass of the population," as they term it, "must demand a new order."[75] Clearly, their aim, as with Westra, is to engage us in conversation; the Westras, Caldwells, and Shrader-Frechettes of the world are getting down to the business of the reconstruction of culture, dealing with issues that too often have been considered beneath the dignity of philosophers, issues such as hands-on decision making by resource managers and the actual configuration of public policy.

Beyond the ecophilosophical community, land ethics has galvanized the ecological community. Leopoldian land ethics pivots on the notion that human beings are plain members and citizens of the land community. Such an idea challenges any absolute distinction between culture and nature, any metaphysical dividing line between human beings and the rest of creation: In effect, it denies the possibility of an objective study of the nature-culture interface. In Leopold's own time, ecologists were attempting to establish themselves as "hard scientists," like physicists, involved in the quantitative study of material systems, particularly through energetics. This stance encouraged claims to objectivity, that is, let ecologists off the ethical hook: What was, was, and what is, is, since ecologists only study what is "out there," apart from human intentions.

That way of thinking has become increasingly untenable, as a wide variety of ecologists themselves make clear. Robert McIntosh argues that "Ecology was, and is, a science which does not fit readily into the familiar mold of science erected on the model of classical physics, and it deals with phenomena which frequently touch very close to the quick of human sensibilities, including aesthetics, morality, ethics, and, even worse in some minds, economics."[76] Frank Golley, a senior systems ecologist at the University of Georgia, argues that there is no clear demarcation between the ecological study of nature and the study of environmental ethics; nor is it clear, Golley continues, "where biological ecology ends and human ecology begins. . . . Clearly, the ecosystem [concept] . . . has provided a basis for moving beyond strictly scientific questions to deeper questions of how humans should live with each other and the environment."[77] Timothy Allen and Thomas Hoekstra, also ecologists, extend the implications of Leopoldian ethics even further, contending that the crucial issues for ecological science have more to do with "the subjective end of doing science" than with field research, statistical analysis, and computer modeling per se. In their opinion, the human species has ushered in a new age of planetary disequilibrium that threatens to break us on the wheel of our own misdeeds.[78] The crucial issue for ecology, as they see it, entails achieving an epistemic consensus on an ecosocial paradigm that enables the construction of a sustainable culture.

Ecofeminism, on my reading, is a second example of environmental ethics that leads toward the reconstruction of culture. In some ways, ecofeminism seems less consequential than land ethics. Yet ecofeminism possibly portends greater cultural changes than land ethics per se, since all human beings are socially situated in gender roles. In contrast, Leopoldian land ethics, which extol the stability, integrity, and beauty of an ecosystem, are increasingly remote from the experience of the vast majority of First World people. The typical American is, after all, a city dweller who has likely seen few wild animals save in a zoo, doesn't know Bambi from a real deer, and on hearing the word *mustang* thinks of a sporty car manufactured by Ford Motor Company. The truth is that most "environmentalists" are city dwellers who have little or no affinity with a land community. In contrast, every human being can, with some effort perhaps, come to a self-conscious awareness of his or her own gendered experience.

No doubt, ecofeminism faces a tougher sell than land ethics, since land ethicists can mount appeals to so-called hard facts, such as integrity and stability (even if ecologists know they are not hard), while ecofeminists, who claim that environmental crisis is a consequence of patriarchy, appear to be ideological rather than objective in their analysis. Yet here again, we stumble over the hoary reality that there are no human positions outside the language of particular groups in particular places and times. Ecofeminists look closely at certain groups, such as the historians who have written Western history, the philosophers who have codified legitimating rationales for Justice, Truth, and Beauty, and the scientists who have uncovered the hidden laws of nature, and conclude that such groups are, among other things, dominated by men. That men write histories in which social relations play no role, philosophies that repudiate emotion, and scientific accounts of nature as inert, lifeless matter set in mechanical motion is, according to the ecofeminists, no surprise. Rather, it is a reflection of socially constructed realities. But on the ecofeminist account, gender roles are not hammered out of eternal verities but are subject to strong evaluation. Ariel Salleh catches this idea in her remark that if environmental ethicists "are to forge a politics based on a radically new appreciation of the potentials of all beings, then men's openness to the views of women is an essential part of the program."[79] And this is all the more true in considering the dialogue between deep ecologists and ecofeminists. Karen Warren contends that "Whatever the important similarities between deep ecology and ecofeminism (or, specifically, my version of ecofeminism)—and indeed, there are many— . . . the word feminist does add something significant to the conception of environmental ethics. . . . [Any] environmental ethic (including deep ecology) that fails to make explicit the different kinds of interconnections among the domination of nature and the domination of women will be, from a feminist (and ecofeminist) perspective such as mine, inadequate."[80]

Let me conclude by returning to Bryan Norton's conjecture that environmental ethicists likely have no place in departments of philosophy, and that we can expect they will increasingly be found within schools of environmental sciences, public planning, and public policy. Norton may be right; yet I am inclined to think that the desertion of the philosophical ranks will not happen soon, if ever. Of course, groups of philosophers have, historically considered, gone off in new directions under new names, as when natural philosophy ceased being philosophy and became physics, or during the early decades of this century when psychology emerged from philosophy. In such cases, it's not so much that the interesting questions have been answered, so that further philosophical inquiry is irrelevant, but rather that narrowly defined subject matters and rigorous methods of inquiry are settled upon, thereby creating a distinctive framework for dealing with certain kinds of phenomena, like classical physics' mathematical studies of matter in motion, or behavioral psychology's studies of the role of the environment in determining human behavior. But the very diversity of environmental ethics leads me to believe that no paradigm is going to emerge anytime soon. So environmental ethicists won't be going off en masse.

But Norton doesn't claim that they will. Rather, he speculates that over time we will increasingly find individual environmental ethicists outside philosophy departments. Yet I'm not so sure that this is likely. For one reason, the kind of background that inclines people to take up ethical (or even metaethical) questions is not typically found outside philosophy departments.[81] The kinds of educational experience that lead individuals to seriously take up cultural recon-

struction also inclines them to be socially, which is to say, intellectually (insofar as knowledge is social) unfit for residence in professional schools. The sad truth is that little more than lip service is
given to ethics in colleges of business, in engineering schools, in
medical colleges, and so on. Rather than strong evaluations, ethicists in professional schools are almost invariably concerned with
inculcating basic principles for an ethical practice within an already
established profession, such as medicine or business. The basic
framework or assumptions of the practice go uncriticized. There is
no concern with the reconstruction of culture.

Still, I cannot deny out of hand Norton's contention, since in some
ways environmental ethicists are not part of the philosophical mainstream. For one reason, our questions are not metaquestions (such
as questions of the form of explanation) but questions concerning
substantive issues that reflect the unsettled circumstances of contemporary life. And although we write in ways that often do not invite
others into our conversation (to extend Stuhr's observation to environmental ethics), neither do we write for the philosophical mainstream. Of course, insofar as we aim at the reconstruction of culture, our audience is necessarily not our fellow philosophers. Yet
even here, in considering the relation of environmental ethicists to
the philosophical mainstream, I find at least some reasons to think
that the gap is beginning to close.

Consider the collection titled *The Quality of Life,* edited by
Martha Nussbaum and Amartya Sen.[82] In one sense, its language of
public goods, welfare, and well-being, its technical discussions of
welfare economics and utility, and so on mark it as a mainstream
collection, apparently unconcerned with the sorts of issues that environmental ethicists take up. And yet I detect a convergence. Ignor-
ing the differences of vocabulary, the philosophical mainstream is
beginning to take up issues near to the heart of environmental ethics. When a Hilary Putnam cites Dewey and Peirce, claims that the
hallowed fact-value distinction is no longer useful, and argues that
we are beings "that cannot have a view of the world that does not
reflect our interests and values," and that "some views of the world
. . . [are] better than others," I begin to think that the mainstream
is reclaiming ground lost to environmental ethicists. At the least, the

mainstream is beginning to flow in the direction indicated by Taylor. And as Putnam suggests, the price paid for giving up a "metaphysical picture of objectivity" is small, if it leads the mainstream to assist in the reconstruction of culture. Neither environmental ethicists nor the philosophical mainstream, to embellish Putnam's conclusion, need to give "up the idea that there are what Dewey called 'objective resolutions of problematical situations'—objective resolutions to problems which are situated, that is, in a place, at a time, as opposed to an 'absolute' answer to 'perspective independent' questions. . . . That is objectivity enough."[83]

Notes

1. Eric Havelock's *Preface to Plato* (Cambridge: Harvard University Press, 1964) offers reasons why this is the case. Andrea Nye's *Words of Power: A Feminist Reading of the History of Logic* (New York: Routledge, 1990) is also useful.

2. See Eugene Hargrove, "After Fifteen Years," *Environmental Ethics* 15, no. 4 (1993): 291–92; and Kenneth M. Sayr, "An Alternative View of Environmental Ethics," *Environmental Ethics* 13, no. 3 (1991): 195–213. Hargrove, editor of *Environmental Ethics,* observes that environmental ethics "continues to be too 'practical' for mainstream philosophers and too 'theoretical' for environmentalists, policy makers, and the general public." ("After Fifteen Years," 292).

3. E. O. Wilson, *The Diversity of Life* (Cambridge: Harvard University Press, 1992), 32.

4. See E. O. Wilson, *Biophilia* (Cambridge: Harvard University Press, 1984), *Diversity of Life,* and "Conservation: The Next Hundred Years," in *Conservation for the Twenty-First Century,* ed. David Western and Mary C. Pearl (New York: Oxford University Press, 1992), 1–7.

5. A recent and unprecedented report by the Royal Society of England and the National Academy of Science warns that the window of opportunity for timely action is drawing to a close. See John Maddox, "National Academy/Royal Society: Warning on Population Growth," *Nature* 355 (1992): 759.

6. Bryan Norton and Eugene Hargrove, "Where Do We Go from Here?" in *Ethics and Environmental Policy: Theory Meets Practice,* ed. Frederick Ferré and Peter Hartel (Athens: University of Georgia Press, 1994), 239.

7. Norton and Hargrove, "Where Do We Go," 241.

8. There are many areas of disagreement also. For example, I am not as sanguine as Norton about the possibilities for philosophers to contribute to efforts at clarifying standards of evidence. So-called standards of evi-

dence, as in determining what the basic facts are, are more often than not the nub of contention. For example, what are old growth forests, and how are they to be ecologically described and finally valued?

9. John J. Stuhr, preface, in *Philosophy and the Reconstruction of Culture: Pragmatic Essays after Dewey,* ed. John J. Stuhr (Albany: State University of New York Press, 1993), x.

10. See Charles Taylor, "Explanation and Practical Reason," in *The Quality of Life,* ed. Martha Nussbaum and Amartya Sen (Oxford: Oxford University Press, 1993), 208–31.

11. Alasdair MacIntyre, *After Virtue: A Study in Moral Theory,* 2d ed. (Notre Dame: University of Notre Dame Press, 1984), 6.

12. See Arne Naess, *Ecology, Community, and Lifestyle,* ed. and trans. David Rothenberg (Cambridge: Cambridge University Press, 1989); and Bill Devall and George Sessions, *Deep Ecology: Living as if Nature Really Mattered* (Salt Lake City: Gibbs M. Smith, 1985).

13. See Richard Primack, *Essentials of Conservation Biology* (Sunderland: Sinauer, 1993).

14. See Peter Reed and David Rothenberg, eds., *Wisdom in the Open Air: The Norwegian Roots of Deep Ecology* (Minneapolis: University of Minnesota Press, 1992). Deep ecology does converge on the so-called deep ecological platform.

15. See Aldo Leopold, *A Sand County Almanac: With Essays on Conservation from Round River* (Oxford: Oxford University Press, 1949; San Francisco: Sierra Club Books, 1970); J. Baird Callicott, *In Defense of the Land Ethic: Essays in Environmental Philosophy* (Albany: State University of New York Press, 1989); and Eugene Hargrove, *Foundations of Environmental Ethics* (Englewood Cliffs: Prentice-Hall, 1989).

16. See, for example, Edwin P. Pister, "A Pilgrim's Progress from Group A to Group B," in *Companion to Sand County Almanac: Critical and Interpretive Essays,* ed. J. Baird Callicott (Madison: University of Wisconsin Press, 1991).

17. See Susan Griffin, *Woman and Nature: The Roaring Inside Her* (New York: Harper & Row, 1978); Ariel Salleh, "The Ecofeminism/Deep Ecology Debate: A Reply to Patriarchal Reason," *Environmental Ethics* 14, no. 3 (1992): 195–216; Karen J. Warren, "The Power and Promise of Ecological Feminism," *Environmental Ethics* 12, no. 2 (1990): 125–46; Carol Bigwood, *Earth Muse: Feminism, Nature, and Art* (Philadelphia: Temple University Press, 1993); and Rosemary Radford Ruether, *Gaia and God: An Ecofeminist Theology of Earth Healing* (San Francisco: Harper, 1992).

18. See Paul W. Taylor, *Respect for Nature: A Theory of Environmental Ethics* (Princeton: Princeton University Press, 1986); Naess, *Ecology, Community, and Lifestyle;* and K. S. Shrader-Frechette, *Risk and Rationality: Philosophical Foundations for Populist Reforms* (Berkeley: University of California Press, 1991).

19. See Yrjö Sepänmaa, *The Beauty of Environment: A General Model for Environmental Aesthetics* (Helsinki: Suomalaninen Tiedeakatemia, 1986); Leopold, *Sand County Almanac;* Hargrove, *Foundations of Environmental Ethics;* and Erazim V. Kohák, *The Embers and the Stars: A Philosophical Inquiry into the Moral Sense of Nature* (Chicago: University of Chicago Press, 1984).

20. See Vine Deloria, *God Is Red* (New York: Dell, 1973); Calvin Luther Martin, *In the Spirit of the Earth: Rethinking History and Time* (Baltimore: Johns Hopkins, 1992); and Jim Cheney, "Postmodern Environmental Ethics: Ethics as Bioregional Narrative," *Environmental Ethics* 11, no. 2 (1989): 117–34.

21. Lynn White Jr. "The Historical Roots of Our Ecologic Crisis," *Science* 155 (1967): 1203–7.

22. See Francis A. Schaeffer, *Pollution and the Death of Man: The Christian View of Ecology* (Wheaton: Tyndale House, 1970); Thomas Berry, *The Dream of the Earth* (San Francisco: Sierra Club Books, 1988); and more generally, Max Oelschlaeger, *Caring for Creation: An Ecumenical Approach to the Environmental Crisis* (New Haven: Yale University Press, 1994).

23. Ramachandra Guha, "Radical American Environmentalism and Wilderness Preservation: A Third World Critique," *Environmental Ethics* 11, no. 1 (1989): 71–83.

24. See Vandana Shiva, *Staying Alive: Women, Ecology, and Development* (London: Zed Books, 1989).

25. Wilson, *Diversity of Life.* Also see Max Oelschlaeger, *The Idea of Wilderness: From Prehistory to the Age of Ecology* (New Haven: Yale University Press, 1991).

26. See Susan Power Bratton, *Christianity, Wilderness, and Wildlife: The Original Desert Solitaire* (Scranton: University of Scranton Press, 1993).

27. See Max Oelschlaeger, ed., *Postmodern Environmental Ethics* (Albany: State University of New York Press, 1995), which collects fifteen essays converging on a postmodern center.

28. See Mark Sagoff, *The Economy of the Earth: Philosophy, Law, and the Environment* (New York: Cambridge University Press, 1988); and Murray Bookchin, *Remaking Society: Pathways to a Green Future* (Boston: South End Press, 1990).

29. See J. Baird Callicott, "The Case Against Moral Pluralism," *Environmental Ethics* 12, no. 2 (1990): 99–124; and J. Baird Callicott, "Moral Monism in Environmental Ethics Defended," *Journal of Philosophical Research* 19, no. 1 (1994): 51–60.

30. See Christopher D. Stone, "Moral Pluralism and the Course of Environmental Ethics," *Environmental Ethics* 10, no. 2 (1988): 139–54.

31. See Max Oelschlaeger, "Introduction," *Postmodern Environmental Ethics.*

32. Will Wright, *Wild Knowledge: Science, Language, and Social Life in a Fragile Environment* (Minneapolis: University of Minnesota Press, 1992), 114.

33. Yet fish also respond to their milieu, as in the positioning of a nest in water with the right temperature and acidity, or holding behind a rock that buffers the current.

34. See especially Derek Bickerton, *Language and Species* (Chicago: University of Chicago Press, 1990).

35. Although the frame of social constructionism is now a commonplace among historians of science, many philosophers continue to resist the idea. Peter J. Bowler, *The Norton History of the Environmental Sciences* (New York: Norton, 1993) is particularly useful, showing how Darwin's theory of evolution has undergone repeated reinterpretation, interpretations that can be contextualized in terms of class, gender, and nationality.

36. While the English-speaking philosophical world has resisted this line of thinking, historians, sociologists, and even ecologists have developed the thesis at length. See Donald Worster, *Nature's Economy: A History of Ecological Ideas* (Cambridge: Cambridge University Press, 1985); Peter Berger and Thomas J. Luckmann, *The Social Construction of Reality: A Treatise in the Sociology of Knowledge* (Garden City: Doubleday, 1966); and Timothy F. H. Allen and Thomas W. Hoekstra, *Toward a Unified Ecology* (New York: Columbia University Press, 1992).

37. See Charles Taylor, *Sources of the Self* (Cambridge: Harvard University Press, 1989), *Human Agency and Language: Philosophical Papers 1* (Cambridge: Cambridge University Press, 1985), and *Philosophy and the Human Sciences: Philosophical Papers 2* (Cambridge: Cambridge University Press, 1985).

38. Hans-Georg Gadamer, *Truth and Method* (New York: Crossroad, 1988), 491, 498. Work originally published as *Warheit und methode,* 1960.

39. See, for example, Julia Kristeva, *Language the Unknown: An Invitation into Linguistics,* trans. Anne M. Menke (New York: Columbia University Press, 1989).

40. See John Firor, *The Changing Atmosphere* (New Haven: Yale University Press, 1990), concerning the inadequacies of the engineering approach; and Sagoff, *Economy of the Earth,* on the inadequacies of a market approach.

41. On the roles of Descartes and Judeo-Christianity in ecocrisis, see (among many) Carolyn Merchant, *The Death of Nature: Woman, Ecology, and the Scientific Revolution* (New York: Harper & Row, 1980); Worster, *Nature's Economy;* White, "Historical Roots"; and Pete A. Y. Gunter, "The Disembodied Parasite and Other Tragedies; or: Modern Western Philosophy and How to Get Out of It," in *The Wilderness Condition: Essays on Environment and Civilization,* ed. Max Oelschlaeger (San Francisco: Sierra Club Books, 1992).

42. Taylor, *Sources*, 384.

43. Taylor, *Philosophy*, 280.

44. The formula, it should be emphasized, is a conceptual model. While intuitively accurate, its analytical utility is limited.

45. Taylor, *Philosophy*, 280.

46. Taylor, *Philosophy*, 304.

47. Taylor, *Philosophy*, 304. See Sagoff's brilliant *Economy of the Earth* for a trenchant analysis of these issues.

48. Taylor, *Philosophy*, 304.

49. Taylor, *Philosophy*, 304.

50. Taylor, *Sources*, 384.

51. See Taylor, pt. 3, "Philosophy of Language," in *Human Agency*.

52. See Kristeva, *Language the Unknown;* and Hilary Lawson, *Reflexivity: The Post-Modern Predicament* (LaSalle: Open Court, 1985).

53. Taylor, *Human Agency*, 248.

54. Taylor, *Human Agency*, 18.

55. Taylor, *Human Agency*, 17.

56. Taylor, *Human Agency*, 35,

57. Taylor, *Human Agency*, 37.

58. Taylor, *Human Agency*, 45.

59. Bowler, *Norton History*, 324.

60. James A. Diefenbeck's *A Celebration of Subjective Thought* (Carbondale: Southern Illinois University Press, 1984) remains unexcelled in its grasp of this fundamental. Also see José Ortega y Gasset, *The Origin of Philosophy*, trans. Toby Talbot (New York: Norton, 1967).

61. See Worster, *Nature's Economy*.

62. See José Ortega y Gasset, *History as a System and Other Essays in the Philosophy of History* (New York: Norton, 1961).

63. Taylor, *Sources*, 9.

64. See P. W. Sleeper, "The Pragmatics of Deconstruction and the End of Metaphysics," in Stuhr, *Philosophy and Reconstruction*.

65. Not all philosophers have ignored rhetoric. See Richard Peter McKeon, *Rhetoric: Essays in Invention and Discovery* (Woodbridge: Ox Bow Press, 1987).

66. See Michael Bruner and Max Oelschlaeger, "Rhetoric, Environmentalism, and Environmental Ethics," *Environmental Ethics* 16, no. 4 (1994): 377–96

67. See Bruce Lincoln, *Discourse and the Construction of Society: Comparative Studies of Myth, Ritual, and Classification* (Oxford: Oxford University Press, 1989).

68. John Dewey, *The Later Works, 1925–1953*, vol. 11, ed. Jo Ann Boydston (Carbondale: Southern Illinois University Press, 1986), 182.

69. John J. Stuhr, "Democracy as a Way of Life," in Stuhr, *Philosophy and Reconstruction*, 40.

70. See J. N. Hattiangadi, *How Is Language Possible? Philosophical Reflections on the Evolution of Language and Knowledge* (LaSalle: Open Court, 1987); and Bickerton, *Language and Species.*

71. Stephen Edelston Toulmin, *The Uses of Argument* (Cambridge: Cambridge University Press, 1958), 39.

72. Toulmin, *Uses of Argument,* 256.

73. Curt Meine's intellectual biography, *Aldo Leopold: His Life and Work* (Madison: University of Wisconsin Press, 1988), is considered definitive.

74. Laura Westra, *An Environmental Proposal for Ethics: The Principle of Integrity* (Totowa, N.J.: Rowman and Littlefield, 1993), xvi.

75. See Lynton Keith Caldwell and Kristin Shrader-Frechette, *Policy for Land: Law and Ethics* (Totowa, N.J.: Rowman and Littlefield, 1993).

76. Robert P. McIntosh, *The Background of Ecology: Concept and Theory* (Cambridge: Cambridge University Press, 1985), 1.

77. Frank Golley, *A History of the Ecosystem Concept in Ecology: More than the Sum of the Parts* (New Haven: Yale University Press, 1993), 205.

78. Allen and Hoekstra, *Toward a Unified Ecology,* 272.

79. Salleh, "Ecofeminism/Deep Ecology Debate," 199.

80. Warren, "Power and Promise," 145.

81. It is inconceivable to me that I would be doing what I do apart from the philosophical life I knew during my years at Southern Illinois University. The seminars I joined with Professor Leys, who insisted that philosophical inquiry was meaningful in the context of public policy, Professor Eames, who relentlessly argued for the reconstructive dimensions of American pragmatism, and Professor Diefenbeck, who introduced me to the importance of the temporal aspects of human being, shaped my future.

82. Martha Nussbaum and Amartya Sen, eds., *The Quality of Life* (Oxford: Oxford University Press, 1993).

83. Hilary Putnam, "Objectivity and the Science-Ethics Distinction," in Nussbaum and Sen, *Quality of Life,* 156.

5

What a Wonderful World!

Richard M. Zaner

What wonderfully strange and interesting times we live in, you and I. Even more if you, like I, enjoy collecting the exotic. To illustrate: Recently, Walter Gilbert, a Nobel laureate in genetics, proclaimed with rare enthusiasm that the human genome now being unraveled, mapped, and sequenced in projects sponsored by the National Institutes of Health's Human Genome Initiative and in many laboratories around the world promises to "put together a sequence that represents . . . the underlying human structure . . . our common humanity." Soon, he is convinced, an individual will be able "to pull a CD out of one's pocket and say, 'Here is a human being; it's me'!"[1]

If this is really true, I thought, that will be as stupendous and consequential as anything in human history! Think about it: There "I" am, right on that CD, and you, there on that other one. And none of the other, now passé notions filed away with so many others in that dusty room of human history should bother us any longer with their curious and incomprehensible, often unpronounceable notions—just stick that CD into a computer, and bingo! Up "I" pop!

Then I came across an article by one of the older and highly respected hands in bioethics, Albert Jonsen, where he pinpoints what he thinks is the pivotal question at the heart of the genome project.

"What constitutes the separateness that makes it possible to designate 'this person' and distinguish between 'this' and 'that' person?"[2] He's worried about what we hear all the time when the new genetics is discussed: How, in the bureaucratic world we inhabit, can we hope to keep information about ourselves from the prying eyes of people who seem so intent on getting to such information? Not only insurance companies, employers, or government agencies but nowadays just anybody with modest computer skills and nothing better to do can poke their digitized noses wherever they please! Privacy, Jonsen says, that's the problem! Appeals to confidentiality, informed consent, and disclosure only underscore its key place. Specifically, the "right of privacy" he takes to be the moral basis of the new genetics, and at the core of privacy is the idea of "moral personhood": Each of us has "a moral right to privacy because privacy is an acknowledgment of the moral personhood of each individual."[3]

"Moral personhood" is fundamental, for it constitutes "the core of my 'individual substance.'"[4] Which brings him to a remarkable claim: "My genome constitutes me," he asserts, for "at the core of my individual substance" is a "repeated molecular structure that is mine alone," even though "much of that structure is the same in other individuals who have been generated by my ancestors and by my siblings."[5]

So, the way Jonsen works it out is to claim that the prospect of testing and screening turning into meddling makes privacy the prominent concern. As a "moral right," it affirms an individual's "moral personhood," which invokes the idea of "individual substance" whose meaning or definition is "in" a genome that is not just any genome but, somehow, at once both "me" and "mine." Expressed the other way around: A molecular structure that is "mine" alone (but shared with numerous others in my genetic kindred) constitutes "me," since it makes me this "individual substance" that is privileged as a moral right (of privacy), since the individual is endowed with personhood (is "me")—which, finally, is the only true barrier to those nosy hackers with nothing better to do than surf the Web in search of what they have no right to.

Since presumably the same must be said about any individual with its own genome—whether fetus, embryo, or zygote, and whether the individual is retarded, comatose, or whatever—then precisely the same story has to be told about each of these individuals, a proposal that seems at best quite odd. Unless, that is, such claims are supposed to hold only for individuals like Jonsen or you or me—although this is not actually stated, it should be observed that it would be rare indeed for such theoreticians to exclude themselves from the class of "moral persons." Be that as it may, what might be asked about this increasingly popular view is whether it does, in fact, deliver what it promises: "me." Am "I" "my" genome? Am "I" somehow "in" that genome that, thus far unaccountably, nevertheless is said to constitute "me"?

Who am I? Well, it is alleged, I am "my" genes. Am I? Are you? Is the one who says such a thing also, in the very saying of it, only giving voice to those genes? Do they talk, or do I? Is what, at the nub of such things, separates thee from me found solely in the differences in the genome each of us respectively "is" or is somehow "in?" If so, of course, then all the perennial, passionate pursuits so many driven philosophers and theologians have embarked on must be swept away: The answer, being in the genes, cannot then be in those quaint metaphysical quests that drove the likes of Plato or Hegel, Kierkegaard or Kant!

Something like full circle is then achieved, for in the days around the time of DNA's discovery—what *Life* magazine, in 1961, announced on its cover as the "secret of life," and which Kurt Vonnegut cut a literary jib about in his classic *Cat's Cradle*—it was thought that the new genetics was indeed, as Gilbert says, the "holy grail."[6]

WILL WONDERS NEVER CEASE?

We have been fairly inundated over the past few years with announcements coming directly from, or closely associated with, the genome project—for instance, that cloning of human cells, embryos, even individuals is ongoing.[7] Which raises other intriguing questions: If a clone has not almost the same but by definition the very same molecular structure—the same DNA, genes, chromosomes, the works—what are we to think of Jonsen's or Gilbert's notions? If my clone and I have the same genome, what would we have—me, so to speak, "here" and "over there" or what? But twisting things a bit, if I am both "here" and "there," is this the same "I"? Can we say of Gilbert's CD, "Here is a human being; it's me!"? Since being on a CD means that any number of identical individuals can in principle be produced, of which of these can it be said "it's me"? What should we make of this? Am I my replicable genome or not?

These questions are far from idle. When Jerry Hall and colleagues[8] at George Washington University Medical School's in vitro fertilization (IVF) clinic reported in late 1993 their success with a more efficient embryological technique to assist infertile women achieve pregnancy, *Time, Newsweek,* and other media worldwide promptly announced that "human cloning" was here—reactions that were quite as fascinating as the research itself. Fascinating also were the controversies that rapidly appeared among those in the odd but charming field of bioethics.

These reactions were a hint of what is surely going to be much more to come in the encounter between two old adversaries battling it out once again. For his part, John Robertson, warmed by the prospects of "blastomere separation," promptly embraced it as "ethically acceptable."[9] In a critical note accompanying Robertson's article, Richard McCormick expressed surprise at the "breathtaking . . . speed with which [Robertson] subordinates every consideration to its usefulness in overcoming infertility."[10] Overcoming infertility is what Hall's experimental protocol was all about, although that was effectively obfuscated by the ensuing media barrage insisting that "cloning" of human embryos had really and truly been achieved— to the consternation of critics and the delight of others. Cloning, of course, has been known for some time in animal and plant genetics. Reports about it, for some reason a good deal more newsworthy than infertility, have typically conjured images of chimeras, fantastic oddities, even monster dinosaurs cavorting about in some bizarre Jurassic Park ready to devour, crush, or otherwise leave carnage in their calamitous and altogether clamorous wake.

The idea underlying Hall's technique[11] was that new individuals with identical genetic makeups can be mass-produced by copying the DNA from the embryos of a dead (or live) creature, whether dinosaur, sheep, or mere mice or cattle—the latter having already been reported in the early 1980s. An embryo at a very early stage of development (before cells have begun to specialize) was separated into as many as eight cells.[12] DNA extracted from each cell was copied and transferred into unfertilized eggs, which were then grown into individual embryos, each of which was implanted in the uterus of a surrogate mother, giving rise to eight identical offspring: "clones." Although Hall's team denied that they had "cloned" human embryos—it was, Hall reported, only a more efficient embryological technique for IVF and, it was hoped, for resolving infertility problems—Hall admitted that they showed the possibility of doing in the laboratory what humans at times do naturally: "test-tube" twins. However, using nonviable embryos, Hall felt that no ethical codes or norms had been violated—that would have been true, he implied, only if viable embryos were used.[13]

In response to questions during the public outcry, Hall reported that he had "no plans" to continue the research. Even so, the procedure was clearly a crucial first step on the way to the stunning prospect of animal (and even human) cloning, which we may be sure is being avidly pursued elsewhere.[14] Indeed in 1994, it was estimated that "the actual birth of children as a result of embryo splitting might well occur in the next two to five years."[15]

Now, I find all this somewhat peculiar: people getting terribly worked up about "cloning," especially if it is people who are being cloned. Why would that be praiseworthy or disturbing? That is, so what? If the "issue" is human, what's the difference?

THE PUBLIC REACTION: CAN SCIENTISTS BE TRUSTED?

Robert Pollack confidentially asserted in a *New York Times* op-ed piece that Hall's experiment "has brought us one step closer to Aldous Huxley's anti-utopian vision of mass-produced people."[16] Critics who like to play the "what-if" game then had a field day:

What if: a pregnancy were achieved and the identical twin embryo had been frozen? The couple later decides their child is so good they want another just like it: The frozen embryo could be thawed and implanted, and if successful, could produce identical twins of different ages!

What if: the first child develops a fatal illness treatable only by transplant? The best chance is to use its identical twin, who would have to be sacrificed in the process!

What if: a wife requests she be implanted with the twin embryo her mother-in-law had requested be frozen many years ago? The mother-in-law agrees, and the wife then presents her husband a gift—his own twin as his son![17]

Such scenarios were regarded by most embryologists as "highly fantastic." Still, Robertson consoled, the likely uses of the technique "are neither so harmful nor so novel" as to justify a moratorium; in fact, it should be added "to the armamentarium of infertility treatments."[18] To which McCormick derisively replied, "If one has no ethical misgivings about cloning by blastomere separation, then John A. Robertson's essay should be a corrective."[19]

Many others were deeply unsettled by the news. Jeremy Rifkin promised to man barricades at every laboratory against these "sinister plots." A leading Islamic thinker, Munawar Anees, condemned it as "the arrogance of Western science," arguing that "the human body is God's property, not man's laboratory."[20] Speaking for the pope, Rocco Buttiglione damned cloning as "unscrupulous" and "perverse," for "each child has the right to be born into a human family out of conjugal love between a man and a woman . . . [and] cannot be 'produced' in a laboratory."[21] Gino Concetti wrote in the Vatican newspaper that such research is a "horror story" that "humiliates" and "offends" the sanctity of life—which must be left to the wisdom of the natural estate instituted and sustained by God.[22]

Where Will It End?

Though perhaps only a momentary blip on the always dense screen of public sound bites, the uproar had a remarkable result: It was reported that Hall and his colleagues, voices "choking with emotion," recanted in an almost medieval way and proclaimed "deep reverence" for human life.

Scattered through the many books, articles, conferences, and endless committees trying earnestly to formulate policies is a fundamental rift between two views, each with its own assumptions, reasons, and conclusions. On the one hand are those who praise the enhanced range of practical options for combating infertility and genetic diseases on the immediate horizon. All that is needed, they argue, is a modest revision of the usual morality of autonomy, beneficence, and nonmaleficence, for who would deny the potential of relief from the horrors of Alzheimer's, Tay-Sachs, or other diseases or from infertility?

On the other hand, scholars such as McCormick, Kurt Bayertz,[23] or Hans Jonas[24] are far less optimistic. Jonas emphasized years ago that the prospect of genetic control "raises ethical questions of a wholly new kind" for which we are ill-prepared. "Since no less than the very nature and image of man are at issue, prudence becomes itself our first ethical duty, and hypothetical reasoning our first responsibility."[25] Tinkering with traditional ethical norms is hardly sufficient to address the profound ethical, existential, even metaphysical issues inherent to the new genetics. For that, we must radically question genetic science and technology; indeed, the very foundations of moral life must be rethought.[26] Along with Bayertz, David Heyd concurs.[27]

Battle lines tend to be drawn very quickly, for our times are ripe for severe disputes, often erupting in literal violence. What are these all about? How and why do they arise in our society? What are the stakes? Even a casual glance at the professional or public literature discloses not one but a plethora of problems. For example, a July 1995 issue of *Time* magazine reported in its cover story the zealously pursued ventures occurring daily in laboratories here and abroad: "Scientists peer into the brain looking for that evanescent thing called consciousness," the cover cleverly announced, and the story confidently anticipates "answers" soon.[28] Paul Churchland thinks we already have them: Everything distinctively human is to be found in the brain.[29] If so, and if the nature of intelligence can and will be laid open, should we then try to create "Grade A Individuals,"[30] so to speak, "kids to order," whether privileged deciders of policy or merely dumb drones designed for the duller chores of life? And would this inevitably include the ever-popular forcible sterilization of "feebleminded" people? Since patenting of "new life forms" has been legally endorsed for the past decade, and since such made-to-order human cells, embryos, and even individuals are clearly both "new" and "life-forms," are these next for patenting? Is that a violation of morality, as Isidro Acosta, president of the Guaymi General Congress, alleged? On learning that scientists from the Centers for Disease Control (CDC) were listed on a patent application as the inventors of a Guaymi woman's cell line, he declared: "It's fundamentally immoral, contrary to the Guaymi view of nature and our place in it."[31]

BREEDING PEOPLE: AN ASSAULT OF CHIMERAS?

Alongside much conceptual, not to say emotional, confusion is a marked ambivalence toward biomedical technologies—we are at once bewildered and hopeful, enchanted and panicky. But when researchers are asked, often as not they tell us how "useful" is their work and their products. Is that true, or is it true only for those who understand and can actually use—and who pay for—the research and the technologies?

These disputes are not new, as was evident at the beginning of the IVF debate decades ago. Interpreting infertility as a "disease," thus falling within the purview of medicine, IVF swiftly became a growth industry for the new "medical treatment"[32]—but what is it supposed to treat? Paul Ramsey early on had doubts about the whole affair: IVF is but "manufacture by biological technology, not medicine."[33] Others, too, were dubious. For instance, Otto Tiefel, arguing strongly against this so-called treatment, noted that infertility is not a disease but rather an expression of parental wishes—which, he then insisted, cannot be conceived as a proper form of medical treatment but instead threatens to sink us into ethical relativism. The fact that parents may feel deeply about such matters as the wish to have babies does not in the least make such feelings proper objects for medical attention.[34]

The same turbulent dispute over IVF was also present in genetics. In her 1977 study, for instance, June Goodfield was vexed about three concerns she thought implicit to genetics: a slow erosion of what makes us uniquely human, an assault on personal autonomy and integrity, and a loss of control over the conduct and direction of human affairs.[35] Shortly afterward, the physician-researcher Gerald Weissmann lamented that such critics are simply ignorant of science and its technological payoffs. He harshly rejected her anxieties as plays on popular superstitions that merely indulge the always eager harbingers of doom and gloom: Her first worry is simply an expression of the fear of creating human beings by cabalistic rites (Golems); the second merely restates the chimera myth; and the third confuses *Brave New World* with *The Double Helix*.[36]

For that matter, Weissmann wrote, the question of ends has already been settled: "if [the scientist] performs his task professionally by doing well, he is doing good."[37] We can therefore concentrate on the "magnificent" means made available in the "toyshops of technology and the purses of our government"[38]—with a myriad of new drugs, anesthesias, surgical procedures, diagnostic wonders, and the like pouring out daily.

The single ethical stricture that governs biomedical science is, Weissmann believes, "thou shalt not fudge the data."[39] Otherwise, scientific and medical morality are the same as society's: We "get not only the government, but the science, [we] deserve."[40] The "utilitarian values" of the biomedical enterprise are a "moral guarantee" that scientific interventions into human life are "intrinsically benign"— even though, he admits, some problems have occurred whether society wanted it or not: the Hiroshima bomb, Auschwitz laboratories, and the psychiatry of the Gulag archipelago.[41] He didn't mention, however, questionable radiation experiments, some of which were public knowledge at the time he wrote, as were the "unethical" experiments documented by Henry Beecher in 1966[42] and the more than two hundred by Henry Pappworth in 1968[43]—not to mention the long-standing venture at Tuskegee.

MEDICINE: THE "SINGULAR ART"?

Biomedical technologies have long had a peculiar fascination in our society—we are at once enchanted and fearful about them. Why is this? Consider Engelhardt's words: "Medicine is the most revolutionary of human technologies. It does not sculpt statues or paint paintings: it restructures man and man's life. . . . [It] is not merely a science, not merely a technology . . . [but is the] singular art . . . of remaking man, not in the image of nature, but in his own image."[44]

In a word, those toyshops make available powerful means to

make "our human nature conform to our chosen goals."[45] Hence, the more powerful medicine becomes, "the more able it is to remake man," and therefore the more necessary it is to "understand what medicine should do with its competence."[46] The critical question is, he says (echoing Hans Jonas's earlier words): Who decides which goals should be pursued? We should add: How are those who eventually decide themselves to be selected?

Following the initial creation of transgenic mice in 1980 by Frank Ruddle at Yale and the cloning of specially bred cattle by Texas A&M geneticists, it clearly became plausible to design and plan for the genetic manipulation and control of human life, individual and collective: if transgenic mice or cattle, why not transgenic humans? So pressing are such questions, Kurt Bayertz urged in agreement with Jonas, that a new discipline, "genethics," is now imperative, as there is little in our traditional moral understanding or legal codes that is adequate to understand or even to articulate the full ramifications of the new genetics.[47] Nor is he alone, as even a modest scan of the burgeoning literature in genetics and alternative reproductive techniques makes plain.

For instance, highly effective psychoactive drugs have made it plausible for some time to conceive, design blueprints for, and practice wholly novel forms of behavior control and "mind" control over individuals and entire populations, thus giving quite new content to perennial issues such as "self-awareness" and "freedom versus determinism" and making humanity itself a profound moral issue— perhaps making treasured notions such as "autonomy" the stuff of nostalgia. Beyond this, death is now being interpreted as a genetic error in the body's somatic cells—a "disease" to be forestalled or even prevented—with current blueprints already afoot to bring our mortality under control, making death and the extension of life span serious and heady issues.

That these are by no means fanciful notions may be judged from the writings of two Nobel laureates in the field. In his 1978 Gifford Lectures, brain specialist Sir John Eccles, who has long been centrally concerned with the physiology of self and self-consciousness,[48] triumphantly declared that "planned genetic manipulation" will supersede the otherwise chancy "natural process of biological mutation" and urged that new genetic techniques be used to "enslave" biological (including human) evolution—making animal and human species "more useful for exploitation."[49] Eccles here picked up on a proposal that has played a central role in Western societies at least since the mid-nineteenth century: that controlled human breeding should be undertaken, in particular by restricting the reproductive capacities of what many nineteenth-century writers regarded as the dregs of humanity—the feebleminded, syphilitic, weak, disadvantaged, and poor, all of whom had hitherto been allowed, even encouraged, to reproduce ad nauseam, and who seriously threaten the quality and integrity of humanity.[50]

Then, the Australian geneticist Sir Macfarlane Burnett argued that disease, physical injury, malnutrition, and every "critical matter" in human life are "wholly dependent" on our genes. "Here, if anywhere," he asserted, "a modern philosopher will be most likely to find his approach to the problem of evil in the world. We may find in the end that war and evil, pain and disease, aging and death were inevitable as soon as a working pattern of life . . . had been devised."[51]

It was thus hardly surprising that psychologist Kenneth B. Clark would argue in 1973 that if we want to combat human violence, we must allow behavioral sciences to use pharmacological substances: These sciences "are now the critical [ones]; they will determine the answer to the ultimate moral question of human survival."[52] In order to "stabilize and make dominant . . . [the] moral propensities" needed to control hostility and violence, he unblushingly proposed a target then that would doubtless win considerable favor today: experiments on "compulsive criminals" to determine "precise forms of intervention and moral control of human behavior"[53]—which he thought morally justified.

All of which gives those horror stories and slippery slopes of which many of us have become so fond quite a bit more bite than they may otherwise be thought to have had. Medicine and biomedical science provide powerful means for ensuring that some people conform, at least to someone's sense of norms. As Eccles said, for the first time in human history, evolution can and should be controlled. This means, Burnett was quick to emphasize, that most if not all the perennial puzzles that have long plagued philosophers and theologians have now been—or soon will be—answered by the new genetics: death, disease, violence, and evil and presumably life, peace, and justice as well. Proposals like Clark's—which conform well with the long-enduring idea of eugenic prevention and breeding, to harness if not nullify stupidity, violence, and other disagreeable traits—still make good sense to many people, indeed fit rather well today with the prevailing winds of much public and scientific opinion.

Such ideas are, of course, deeply rooted in our history. The core views of biomedical scientists such as Muller, Lederberg, Eccles, Gilbert, and others were already implicit to Francis Bacon's clarion call for a "new science." He expressed the cardinal point of his "general admonition to all" in the Great Instauration: the deep affinity between theory and practice. To subdue and alleviate the "necessities and miseries of humanity," he claimed "a line and race of inventions" (technologies) is needed. For that battle, "those twin objects, human knowledge and human power," must come together "for the benefit and use of life."[54] Still, Bacon insisted, "charity and benevolence" are needed to govern our uses of knowledge and inventions, since theory in his sense says nothing about that. But from whence do we learn what "charity and benevolence" are, much less how to incorporate them in our lives?

The hard issue within medical research, in Engelhardt's words, is to discover "proportion and measure so that its Promethean endeavor can be undertaken without the hubris which invites tragedy. . . . Man has become more technically adept than he is wise, and must now look for the wisdom to use that knowledge he possesses."[55] But is there any such wisdom, and where might it be found? It may be well to recall T. S. Elliot's incisive questions: Where is the knowledge we have lost in information, where the wisdom we have lost in knowledge? Keen barbs, these, which Jonas later echoed: "[We are] constantly confronted with issues whose positive choice requires supreme wisdom—an impossible situation for man in general, because he does not possess that wisdom, and in particular for contemporary man, who denies the very existence of its object: viz., objective value and truth. We need wisdom most when we believe in it least."[56]

From Galen to Darwin: Modern-Day Eugenics

A driving force already evident in Bacon's writings is the need to combat the "miseries and necessities" endemic to the human condition (famine, epidemic, pestilence, etc.)—quite obviously also at work in the writings of Clark and Weissmann and later in Hall's experiment, as well as in much of the Human Genome Initiative.

Bacon's call for a "race of inventions" to alleviate human misery is not, to be sure, altogether novel. Jonas notes, for instance, the "awestruck homage to man's powers" in classical times—a celebration of humanity's "violent and violating irruption into the cosmic order," although it had "a subdued and even anxious quality" about it. Despite a "restless cleverness" in human building, the encompassing character of nature and natural things is left unchanged and undiminished. "They last, while his schemes have their short-lived way."[57] Bayertz recalls, too, one of the earliest known "eugenic Utopias": Plato's *Republic,* with its concern for "deliberately breeding human beings."[58] Moreover, as I've suggested elsewhere,[59] this theme seems to have been a guiding motif in medicine at least since the appearance of dietetics and clearly since Galen[60]—for whom health had become a "responsibility and disease a matter for possible moral reflection," and for whom medicine promised to "elevate man beyond the possibilities of purely moral teaching."[61] Thus, the idea of improving the human lot is quite as ancient as the effort to diagnose and heal.

Bayertz emphasizes that until very recently such eugenic conceptions, essentially extrapolations to human beings from plant and animal breeding, were merely playful musings with little lasting effect. Soon, however, it became a widely embraced movement[62] inspired in many ways by Darwin's biological understanding of human "miseries and necessities." Key to the success of Darwin's theory and later of social Darwinism was the pervasive mood of degeneration through much of the nineteenth century. The central notion behind this was that, while the survival of the fit is the driving force behind the evolution of plants and animals, it does not function in the same way in civilized human societies, wherein the feeble in body and mind are not eliminated in the struggle to survive. To the contrary, they are actively supported and even encouraged to reproduce at will, as Darwin insisted in 1871: "With savages, the weak in body or mind are soon eliminated; and those that survive commonly exhibit a vigorous state of health. We civilized men, on the other hand, do our utmost to check the process of elimination; we build asylums for the imbecile, the maimed, and the sick; we institute poor-laws; and our medical men exert their utmost skill to save the life of every one to the last moment."[63]

Since "the weak members of civilized societies [are encouraged to] propagate their kind," which is "highly injurious to the race of man" because it directly leads to the degeneration of "man himself,"[64] such individuals must be prevented from reproducing—as in fact they were, here and elsewhere, for decades. As Bayertz points out, "if modern civilization strips natural selection of its powers, and if this causally leads to degeneration, then natural selection must be replaced by consciously controlled artificial selection . . . on the one hand, [by] excluding genetically 'inferior' individuals from reproduction . . . and, on the other hand, by giving individuals with desirable characteristics the opportunity to have as many off-spring as possible."[65]

Detailing this fascinating movement, later taken over by the National Socialists in Germany, is beyond the scope here.[66] Of immediate concern, rather, are certain of the underlying assumptions that gave life to those early (and later) eugenicists and continue today, often more subtly, as one of the more prominent features of the genome project.

PANDORA'S BOX OR UTOPIAN CORNUCOPIA?

For more than three decades, a highly animated and far-reaching dispute has been going on over the prospects and implications of the new genetics—highlighted by the recent success at blastomere separation and exacerbated when James Watson led the fight for federal funding of the Human Genome Initiative, which Gilbert termed the "holy grail" of human biology.[67]

Most of the project's reports fascinate, because they supposedly focus on flawed genes whose abnormal functioning (or normal malfunctioning) results or will result in a disease. What used to be called "negative eugenics"—the effort to diagnose and treat the more than five thousand such diseases—has captivated physicians and the lay public alike: the ability to know, truly, why certain debilitating conditions occur, and with that knowledge, the promise of at some time doing something about it.

If that were all there were to it, there would be little reason for anything more than arcane celebrations, since to date, despite the many discoveries, no tested therapies have yet emerged. But much more is at stake than mapping, sequencing, diagnosing, and eventually treating genetic disorders. Underlying much of the professional and public discourse is the already noted dispute, each side of which has its own, almost apocalyptic vision. Typically, discussions of eugenics involve one of two contradictory images—a fateful sense of impending disaster to be avoided and resisted at all costs, or an idyllic dream of a future to be embraced and energetically brought about.

As for the latter, one can readily detect its vision of a time when not merely the currently known three thousand or so but every such disease and disorder will be known down to its most minute, submolecular detail, along with the means to change its otherwise inexorable course. What we will presumably learn from all this, in Gilbert's words, is everything essential about humanity, in a form capable of encryption on convenient CDs.[68] The underlying promissory note is the awesome prospect of actually and definitively knowing with scientific precision what we are, where and when we appeared, what can be hoped for, even, I suppose, why we are born. The announcements stir such dramatic media responses because the genome project promises finally to resolve the ancient puzzle of who, where, when, why, and what we human beings are: The answer doesn't blow in the wind, it's in our genes. If so, who could possibly object to genetic research?

On the other hand, there is a central theme running throughout the long history of eugenics, from the early hints in the Hippocratic corpus and Plato's *Republic* to the time when the genetic code was first cracked: in Bayertz's words, the "orientation of eugenic policies towards the practice of [human] breeding."[69] From the earliest inklings that what was learned from animal and plant breeding could be transferred to human populations, the dominating themes are, on the one hand, to correct the defects people suffer, and on the other, to search for ways to improve human life so that the ironic propensity of civilized humanity to degeneracy can be stopped in its tracks. While the driving force of genetics is often said to be negative eugenics (diagnosing and treating diseases), positive eugenics has clearly been an underlying, motivating force from the beginning. These deep-lying motifs within Western society, medicine in particular, have at the same time regularly met with equally passionate opposition, usually in the form of religious and moral objections accompanied by a profound sense of doom if nature is given over carte blanche to human scientific manipulations.

What gives these frequent objections their power to move us, sometimes in surprising ways? Do they merely mean that scientists just can't be trusted? The respected scholar C. S. Lewis flatly states that the promised power of the new genetics is in fact "the power of earlier generations over later ones." However, since there are no guarantees about their wisdom or lack of it, there is a perfectly understandable fear that stems from recognizing that such power is only "possessed by some men which they may, or may not, allow [others] to profit by."[70] In a different vein, in an editorial in the November 1993 issue of *Time* whose cover story was the Hall experiment, Barbara Ehrenreich expressed serious reservations, suggesting that she agreed with Lewis,[71] though her concern took a different direction: What we should fear is not twenty-first-century technology so much as putting these potent technologies into the hands of twentieth-century capitalists—whose funds, after all, pay the way for these adventures.

In a word, we seem strung on the horns of an irascible, perhaps irresolvable dilemma—either to embrace the science of genetics and its apparently invariable companion, the eugenic "breeding of people" (for which cloning is a key component), or to reject the very idea of genetics, there being no way to prevent a slippery slide from negative to positive eugenics.

Here is the one side: Celebrating genetic knowledge, Eccles and others urge taking control of human evolution—which means, Ehrenreich and Lewis remind us, control by those who have the know-how, and often control over, the magic of the marketplace to pay for the "holy grail" of genetics. And the other side: Leon Kass decries it as a violation of "the nature of man himself . . . making himself simply another of the man-made things"[72] and urges strenuous opposition to this "new holy war against human nature";[73] but this is little more, Weissmann and others aver, than illicit playing on folk superstitions.

Not unexpectedly, of course, the next step down the slippery slope has already been taken—blastomere separation of human embryos—and the inevitable dispute is again heating up, with Robertson extolling the prospect of cloned children being born "in the next two to five years," and McCormick acidly rejecting the idea that "anything that is useful . . . is ethically acceptable."[74] With subsequent steps seemingly inevitable, is there any way out of these straits?

AM I MY GENOME? IS IT ME?

In no small way, I think, these developments, especially cloning, powerfully evoke the deepest, most intimate questions, which in turn are fueled by the notion that genetics definitively does away with what Gilbert Ryle once derisively termed the "ghost in the machine"—soul, spirit, mind, self, or any of the many other terms by which we name ourselves. Is Churchland right, that advances in neurology and artificial intelligence force adoption of psychological materialism, and that human psychological life is ultimately physical, therefore reducible to the biological computer that is the brain? Reviewing Churchland's book, Robert Wright argues that he is wrong, for if that view is correct, what do we make of consciousness and awareness of self? Are these, so to speak, related to the brain merely in the way a shadow is related to the body that casts it, or the rainbow to the light-reflecting droplets that create it—the filmiest, flimsiest sort of epiphenomenon? Wright asks, "if consciousness doesn't do anything—then why does consciousness exist?"[75] Why would subjective experience—which, after all, is what gives life its meaning—ever arise in the first place—or for that matter, we might wonder, from whence the very words we maddeningly insist on using to name ourselves? Are these questions merely naive, failures to respect the tremendous complexity and evolutionary power behind and in the neural system?[76]

What about Jonsen's proposal, that I am my genome?[77] "My genome constitutes me" can hardly be the last word, since it takes for granted what can on no account be taken for granted in the terms of the proposal itself: Who is this "I" that asserts the claim, and what possible sense can we give to the alleged "belonging" asserted in the "my"? In what sense does the genome in question "belong"—much less to "me"? Or is it "me"? Is it nothing more than a linguistic trick to say that someone makes the assertion, a someone who, however, remains utterly outside the theory asserted? What is fundamental, even if deeply problematic, is not the idea of "individual substance" but rather how it can possibly be that such a substance (if such there be at all) could possibly be the most concrete of all, "mine" and even "me." The real poser is not the abstraction "this" person or "this" self (which worries Jonsen) but to the contrary, that very specific me-myself who is nothing other than Al Jonsen himself—not "that" person or "that" self but you-yourself—and on that basis, how we can then distinguish me from you, him, her, us, or them?[78]

The flaw here is, in part at least, what William James termed the "psychologist's fallacy": The "great snare of the psychologist is the confusion of his own standpoint with that of the mental fact about which he is making his report."[79] Just that confusion is evident in Churchland's main argument, as it is in Jonsen's, for both adopt the stance of an observer—only then to forget they've done so—an observer who, usually for theoretical reasons, posits that certain contents are an immanent part of the sensory or mental life of some observed subject—but who then forgets that "me" who is both observer and observed.

As Wright says against Churchland: "Other people can in principle observe my gustatory Pathways. . . . But they can't observe my subjective sensation of taste." True, it may be that the brain or the genes are causally efficacious: Without them, a person could not experience things in the world or himself or herself. But the analysis of those causal conditions by no means tells us anything at all about what is in fact experienced by an individual. Whether illusory, epiphenomenal, or something else, the character of human experience is a legitimate topic of concern for its own sake, and the idea that it is nothing but the brain or the genes begs that question. In different terms, at the root is a plain reductio ad absurdum: as the geneticists Richard Lewontin[80] and Ruth Hubbard[81] urge, the illicit thesis of genetic determinism.

IS THERE A MORAL TO THIS TALE?

I'm quite aware that my admiration of James may not be shared by all; that my sense of the incoherence of views that rest on a sort of "this is nothing but that"[82] may not be shared; that the allegation of genetic determinism can and doubtless will be disputed. Suppose, in a word, that I'm wrong; what then? Well, I must say, pretty much what I've been urging all along anyway. What Eccles, Weissmann, Gilbert, and others involved with the genome project tend to forget or to pass over is that, as Jonas urged years ago, "The biological control of man, especially genetic control, raises ethical questions of a wholly new kind for which neither previous praxis nor previous thought has prepared us. Since no less than the very nature and image of man are at issue, prudence becomes itself our first ethical duty, and hypothetical reasoning our first responsibility."[83]

Understandable as it surely is, the rush to find yet another magic bullet—among the more powerful motive forces in medicine since penicillin's discovery—to find a cure-all that promises relief and release from the dread and loss associated with disease, damage, and other dark things (ultimately, death) about our human condition—this rush seems to me to be itself cause for serious moral concern. Since we simply do not know or know so little about our genetic constitution and even less, it seems, about the very matters because of which genetics seems so glowing—intelligence, emotion, playfulness, the gamut of what we do and are—if knowledge is imperative, then it must surely follow that what Jonas terms "hypothetical reasoning" (or perhaps better, the ability of imaginative envisioning, or "possibilizing")[84] is our prime ethical responsibility. If action is deemed necessary to counteract the devastation of heritable diseases, then surely "prudence itself" is equally imperative, an ethical responsibility of the first order just because we do not and perhaps cannot know in advance what the long-term (and many short-term) aftermaths of genetic interventions will be. It is thus an ethical responsibility of the first order that we be *mindful* of what we think and do (and even propose to do), as it is also morally requisite that we be clearly aware of what we risk if we denigrate or think not at all of what genetics has uniquely forced into question: with profound irony, what, who, how, and why human beings *are* at all, and thus whence we go from here.

All things considered, the push for or against cloning may only divert attention from concerns and issues we must face in any case. Considering that most of the reduction in disease and the death rate have been due less to medicine or science than to better sanitation, sewage, water supply, and other aspects of healthy living conditions, perhaps the best way to ensure that people are healthy is to focus on cleaning up our devastated environment from decades of toxic pollution and radioactive releases. The best way to help people become smarter and more civilized, if not cultured, is not to rely on the fugitive promise of some magic genetic bullet but to learn to educate far better than we have—a task that must in any event be done. The best way to square off with violence is to help people gain personal self-respect and respect for others through ensuring decent jobs, housing, and access to needed health and other services. In Barbara Rothman's sharp words, "Our problems lie in darker corners, in poverty and the poor nutrition and inadequate health care and increasing homelessness that accompany poverty in America"—not to mention the "costs to our understanding of ourselves as people."[85] For the real problems in our "darker corners," there are no quick fixes to substitute for the needed, hard work of thoughtful and imaginative moral reflection—again, a task that must in any event be undertaken, all the more so if those dark corners remain obscure.

Vigorous exploration of our genetic estate is unquestionably important—but only as part of the discipline needed to understand our humanity, our common world, and our future. Too, the talk of "rights" that has so focused recent social and political discourse has its place in any moral cosmos—but only within a broader, more embracing texture of connections and relations with others. In the end, the fascination with our genetic estate cannot substitute for a clear perception of the reality, the all-too-often dismal reality and urgent needs of our moral and social estate.

NOTES

Since I first presented this lecture, much has happened both in genetics and especially in animal cloning: Ian Wilmott's cloning of Dolly (and from some reports, Molly and Polly); then in July 1998, the announcement of the successful cloning of mice (and clones from clones). Despite these dramatic developments and the expected widespread public responses, my basic arguments seem to me unaffected (indeed, if anything, supported even more) and my somewhat ironic observations still appropriate. In any event, except for the addition of footnotes noting later developments, the current version is substantially the same as was presented in 1995. A significant part of this lecture was originally published in "Surprise! You're Just Like Me! Reflections on Cloning, Eugenics, and Other Utopias," in James M. Humber and Robert F. Almeder, eds., *Biomedical Ethics Reviews: Human Cloning* (Totowa, N.J.: Humana Press, 1998), 103–51, and has been reprinted with permission of the publisher.

1. Walter Gilbert, "A Vision of the Grail," in Daniel J. Kevles and Leroy Hood, eds., *The Code of Codes: Scientific and Social Issues in the Human Genome Project* (Cambridge: Harvard University Press, 1992), 95.

2. Albert R. Jonsen, "Genetic Testing, Individual Rights, and the Common Good," in Courtney S. Campbell and B. Andrew Lustig, eds., *Duties to Others,* Theology and Medicine, vol. 4. (Dordrecht: Kluwer Academic, 1994), 283.

3. Jonsen, "Genetic Testing," 283.

4. Jonsen, "Genetic Testing," 284.

5. Jonsen, "Genetic Testing," 284.

6. See especially Sir John C. Eccles, *Facing Reality,* Heidelberg Science Library (Heidelberg: Springer-Verlag, 1970) and his numerous references, particularly in chapters 1 and 4.

7. Subsequent developments have been quite dramatic and have had highly significant scientific implications—e.g., the more recent demonstration of mouse cloning from cloud cells. I reflected on some of these in "Surprise! You're Just Like Me!"

8. J. L. Hall et al., "Experimental Cloning of Human Polyploid Embryos Using an Artificial Zona Pellucida," American Fertility Society with the Canadian Fertility and Andrology Society, program supplement, 1993 Abstracts of the Scientific Oral and Poster Sessions, S1.

9. See, for instance, John A. Robertson, "The Question of Human Cloning," *Hastings Center Report* 24, no. 2 (March–April, 1994): 6–14.

10. Richard A. McCormick, SJ, "Blastomere Separation: Some Concerns," *Hastings Center Report* 24, no. 2 (March–April, 1994): 14.

11. It should be noted that this technique is quite different from that pioneered by Wilmott and later used by the University of Hawaii team led by Ryuozo Yanagimachi when they cloned mice (and used the clones for

another generation of clones)—see Yanagimachi's letter to the editor, *Nature* 394 (July 1998), 369.

12. Part of the hypothesis of Hall's research was to determine how many cell divisions yielded maximum potential for growth (see note 13).

13. Hall et al., "Experimental Cloning." Demonstrating that sodium alginate (a seaweed derivative) can substitute for the embryo's membrane, the researchers split the undifferentiated cells, or blastomeres, placed them in different cells, and then allowed them to grow into separate but identical embryos. Studying forty-eight blastomeres from seventeen polyspermic embryos (i.e., fertilized by more than one sperm and therefore nonviable, as they survive only a few days), they learned that the two-cell stage seemed more conducive to further development than did separation at four- or eight-cell stages. But they did not go on to look into that, since it would require using viable embryos—which they thought would be "unethical." That they used nonviable embryos supposedly made the ethics of the procedure unproblematic.

14. As has proved to be the case, of course; e.g., Wilmott's announcement came in 1997, and Yanagimachi's in the following year (1998).

15. Robertson, "Question of Human Cloning," 7.

16. Robert Pollack, "Cloning Humans," *New York Times,* November 17, 1993, p. A15.

17. With Wilmott's announcement, the game continued with even more fantastic scenarios—and at the same time, some fascinating prospects were opened up: using his technique to produce cloned sheep whose blood contains one or more much-needed human drugs and proteins, for instance.

18. Robertson, "Question of Human Cloning," 7, 9, 14.

19. McCormick, "Blastomere Separation," 14.

20. Munawar Ahmad Anees, "Human Clones and God's Trust: An Islamic View," *NPQ: New Perspectives Quarterly* 11, no. 1 (winter 1994): 23–24.

21. Rocco Buttiglione, "Immoral Clones: A Vatican View," *NPQ: New Perspectives Quarterly* 11, no. 1 (winter 1994): 20.

22. Father Gino Concetti, editorial, *L'Osservatore Romano* (1993), reprinted in *NPQ: New Perspectives Quarterly* 11, no. 1 (winter 1994): 21.

23. Kurt Bayertz, *GenEthics: Technological Intervention in Human Reproduction as a Philosophical Problem,* trans. S. L. Kirby (Cambridge: Cambridge University Press, 1994). Originally published in German as *GenEthik* (Hamburg: Rowohlt Taschenbuch Verlag GmbH, 1987). As Bayertz noted, the "fascination surrounding the possibilities offered by science and technology is confronted by great uneasiness concerning the technological revolution of human reproduction and possible abuse of this technology" (p. 12).

24. Hans Jonas, *Philosophical Essays: From Ancient Creed to Technological Man* (Englewood Cliffs: Prentice-Hall, 1974).

25. Jonas, *Philosophical Essays*, 141.

26. Jonas undertook this investigation in his last work. See Hans Jonas, *The Imperative of Responsibility: In Search of an Ethics for the Technological Age* (Chicago: University of Chicago Press, 1984).

27. David Heyd, *Genethics: Moral Issues in the Creation of People* (Berkeley: University of California Press, 1992).

28. Michael D. Lemonick, "Glimpses of the Mind," *Time*, July 17, 1995, 44–52.

29. Paul M. Churchland, *The Engine of Reason, the Seat of the Soul* (Cambridge: MIT Press, 1995).

30. Daniel J. Kevles, "Out of Eugenics: The Historical Politics of the Human Genome," in Kevles and Hood, *Code of Codes*, 9–12.

31. See Andrew Kimbrell, "Life for Sale," *Utne Reader*, July–August 1995, 26.

32. See R. G. Edwards, "Fertilization of Human Eggs In Vitro: Morals, Ethics, and the Law," *Quarterly Review of Biology* 40 (1974): 3–26; and Leon Kass, "Babies by Means of In Vitro Fertilization: Unethical Experiments on the Unborn?" *New England Journal of Medicine* 285 (1971): 1174–79.

33. Paul Ramsey, "Shall We 'Reproduce'? II: Rejoinders and Future Forecast," *Journal of the American Medical Association* 220 (1972): 1481.

34. Otto Tiefel, "Human In Vitro Fertilization: A Conservative View," *Journal of the American Medical Association* 247 (1979): 3235–42. See my response to Tiefel, "A Criticism of Moral Conservatism's View of In Vitro Fertilization and Embryo Transfer," *Perspectives in Biology and Medicine* 27, no. 2 (winter 1984): 200–212.

35. June Goodfield, *Playing God* (New York: Random House, 1977).

36. Gerald A. Weissmann, "The Need to Know: Utilitarian and Esthetic Values of Biomedical Science," in W. B. Bondeson, H. T. Engelhardt Jr., S. F. Spicker, and J. White, eds., *New Medical Knowledge in the Biomedical Sciences* (Dordrecht: Reidel), 108.

37. Weissmann, "Need to Know," 106.

38. Weissmann, "Need to Know," 106.

39. Weissmann, "Need to Know," 106.

40. Weissmann, "Need to Know," 110.

41. Parenthetically, it might also be noted that researchers themselves often blow the whistle on ethical violations—Beecher's article was a major factor in establishing the national commission that led to the first requirement of informed consent for federally funded research using vulnerable human subjects.

42. Henry K. Beecher, "Ethics and Clinical Research," *New England Journal of Medicine* 74 (1966): 1354–60.

43. M. H. Pappworth, *Human Guinea Pigs: Experimentation on Man* (Boston: Beacon Press, 1968).

44. H. T. Engelhardt Jr., "The Philosophy of Medicine: A New Endeavor," *Texas Reports on Biology and Medicine* 31 (1973): 443–52.

45. H. T. Engelhardt Jr., "Why New Technology Is More Problematic than Old Technology," in Bondeson et al., *New Medical Knowledge,* 179–83.

46. Engelhardt, "Philosophy of Medicine," 445.

47. Bayertz, *GenEthics.*

48. Eccles, *Facing Reality.*

49. Sir John Eccles, *The Human Mystery: The Gifford Lectures, 1977–78* (Berlin: Springer-Verlag International, 1979), 120.

50. See sources cited by Bayertz, *GenEthics,* 27–37.

51. Sir Macfarlane Burnett, *Endurance of Life: The Implications of Genetics for Human Life* (London: Cambridge University Press, 1978), 2.

52. Kenneth B. Clark, "Psychotechnology and the Pathos of Power," in F. W. Matson, ed., *Within/Without: Behaviorism and Humanism* (Monterey: Brooks/Cole, 1973), 94, 95.

53. Clark, "Psychotechnology," 96, 98.

54. Cited in Hans Jonas, "The Practical Uses of Theory," *Social Research* 26, no. 2 (summer 1959): 127–28.

55. Engelhardt, "Philosophy of Medicine," 451–52.

56. Jonas, *Philosophical Essays,* 18.

57. Jonas, *Philosophical Essays,* 5.

58. Bayertz, *GenEthics,* 23.

59. Richard M. Zaner, *Ethics and the Clinical Encounter,* Englewood Cliffs: Prentice-Hall, 1988), 199–201.

60. See Ludwig Edelstein, *Ancient Medicine* (Baltimore: Johns Hopkins University Press, 1967).

61. Oswei Tempkin, *Galenism: Rise and Decline of a Medical Philosophy* (Ithaca: Cornell University Press, 1973), 85.

62. Bayertz, *GenEthics,* 40–46.

63. Charles Darwin, *The Descent of Man and Selection in Relation to Sex,* rev. ed. (1874; reprint, Chicago: Rand McNally, 1974), 130–31; cited in Bayertz, *GenEthics,* 41.

64. Cited in Bayertz, *GenEthics,* 42.

65. Bayertz, *GenEthics,* 44.

66. See George J. Annas and Michael A. Grodin, *The Nazi Doctors and the Nuremberg Code: Human Rights in Human Experimentation* (New York: Oxford University Press), 1992.

67. Gilbert, "Vision of the Grail."

68. Gilbert, "Vision of the Grail."

69. Bayertz, *GenEthics,* 65.

70. C. S. Lewis, *The Abolition of Man* (New York: Macmillan, 1968), 69.

71. Barbara Ehrenreich, "The Economics of Cloning," *Time,* November 22, 1993, 86.

72. Leon Kass, "New Beginnings in Life," in M. P. Hamilton, ed., *The New Genetics and Future of Man* (Grand Rapids: William B. Eerdmans, 1972), 54.

73. Kass, "New Beginnings," 20.

74. McCormick, "Blastomere Separation," 14; Robertson, "Question of Cloning," 7.

75. Robert Wright, "It's All in Our Heads," *New York Times Book Review* (Sunday), July 9, 1995, p. 16.

76. All of which evokes Suzanne Langer's argument in 1942; see *Philosophy in a New Key* (New York: Mentor Books, New American Library, 1942), 42, 43.

77. Jonsen, "Genetic Testing," 284.

78. See Richard M. Zaner, *The Context of Self: A Phenomenological Inquiry Using Medicine as a Clue* (Athens: Ohio University Press, 1981).

79. William James, *The Principles of Psychology,* vol. 1 (New York: Henry Holt, 1890), 196.

80. See R. C. Lewontin, *Biology as Ideology: The Doctrine of DNA* (New York: Harper Perennial, 1991).

81. See Ruth Hubbard, with Elijah Wald, *Exploding the Gene Myth* (Boston: Beacon Press, 1992).

82. Termed by Gabriel Marcel the fallacy of the *rien que*—to say something is nothing but something else—is already to create an impossible problem: if true, whence the very idea of the something that is supposed to be "nothing but"?

83. Jonas, *Philosophical Essays,* 141.

84. Zaner, *Context of Self,* 165–80.

85. Barbara Rothman, "Not All That Glitters Is Gold," special supplement, *Hastings Center Report* 22, no. 4 (July–August 1992), S14.

6

Bang! Bang! You're Dead?
Rethinking Brain Death and Organ
Transplantation in Japan and China

Carl B. Becker

Southern Illinois University is duly famous in Asia as well as America for its contributions to philosophy. The Library of Living Philosophers, founded by Paul Schilpp, is highly regarded and frequently consulted as a unique resource in the field. The Dewey Center has become somewhat of a mecca for foreign philosophers as well as educators studying American thought. SIU graduates teach not only in Japan, where SIU has a branch campus, but in major universities in Hong Kong, Singapore, and Taiwan. I am proud of my own affiliation with SIU, treasuring fond memories of my years of teaching philosophy in Carbondale and of the supportive colleagues and families who made life here so meaningful.

Not least of the contributions of the SIU Philosophy Department is the legacy of the late Wayne Leys and this lecture series to the study of practical ethics. When I teach philosophy, whether in the ancient capital of Japan or here in southern Illinois, my main message to students is the same as my message here today: As Wayne Leys also believed, philosophy is not an ivory tower pastime but an indispensable part of daily life. We face moral and ethical problems every time we go shopping, every time we set the thermostats in our homes and cars, and especially when we plan for our retirement and final passing from this world.

In today's talk, I want to focus on those last issues, the questions of how we respect the bodies and wishes of dying people. Now in many respects, the debate about brain death in America is considered closed. Anybody with enough money can contract for someone else's body parts, just like buying used car parts from a junkyard, and few people in this society display moral qualms about this procedure. But is it really as simple as one-two-three, bang-bang, and we know who's dead?

Today, I propose that we review this situation from the perspective of some foreign cultures that are just now in the throes of thinking through issues of brain death and organ transplantation. By looking at the cases of Japan and China, I suggest that we will find a number of ethically problematic issues that turn out to pertain to our own thinking about life and death as well.

The Perspective of the Medical Profession

First, let's review some of the basic background to the whole discussion of brain death and organ transplantation. Normally, when people die, first their breathing stops, and then their hearts stop. If they don't receive artificial respiration or CPR (cardiopulmonary resuscitation, like a heart massage) within a few minutes, the blood stops flowing to their brains. Traditionally, if even CPR fails to revive a heartbeat, and if even mouth-to-mouth resuscitation fails to get patients to breathe on their own, they are pronounced dead. In other words, breathing and heartbeat have long been the criteria of human death.

Of course, not all human cells die so quickly. If you remember the eyes of fish caught the day before, you'll recall that their eyes are still clear and viable, even though the fish themselves are dead. Hair follicles and nail cells continue to produce hair and nails for many days after a person dies, just like a flower that continues to bloom or go to seed after it is cut. But we tend to believe that what's important about personhood, about someone *being a person*, is not whether their fingernails continue to grow or not but rather whether they can communicate or interact with the rest of the world *as a human being.*

Modern medical technology has radically transformed the traditional view of cardiopulmonary death that I have just outlined. Today, when Americans with enough money stop breathing, their throats are cut open, and they are connected to respirators, machines that will mechanically continue their breathing almost indefinitely. If a well-to-do American's heart stops beating, doctors may connect the person to a pacemaker or similar machine that electrically stimulates the heart to keep beating. In some cases, rich people are even connected to mechanical hearts that completely bypass their own failed hearts and perform all the functions of keeping their blood pulsing through their veins. In a few years, electromechanical hearts small enough to fit in the human body may become affordable and reliable enough to replace living human hearts. Today, the most reliable artificial hearts, like dialysis machines, are so large that they require patients to rest beside them, and receiving another person's living heart remains the operation of choice for wealthy terminal cardiac patients.

This new medical technology gives rise to many questions, not least of which concerns the gap between the wealthy who can afford to buy longer lives and the poor who cannot. But the two bigger issues that require moral decisions of every one of us are the questions of treatment termination and organ donation.

The Moral Question of When to Terminate Treatment

Imagine you have the funds or insurance to live connected to machines that will keep you breathing and pulsing almost forever. Then sooner or later, the question arises: How long do you really want to go on living (and paying for living) in that state? Or do you want to draw the line somewhere, and say, for example, that when your mind stops functioning, and you can no longer communicate with the rest of the world, you'd rather not have your body prolonged any longer?

Once the doctors have gone to all the time and trouble of attaching you to respirators and artificial heart pumps, they are not going to risk facing charges of manslaughter for turning off those life-support systems. But other patients may be in need of the same life-support systems. If there is no chance of your reviving, it seems there ought to be some cutoff point where we say, "sorry, but it's no use any more, let's give these machines to someone with a fighting chance of recovery."

This is one reason that many states and countries now recognize what are called "living wills" or "advanced directives." Living wills and advanced directives legally document personal desires for terminal care: for example, either that you wish all your life-support systems to be terminated in the case that you are unconscious and your doctors agree that there is no real chance of your regaining consciousness, *or* that you do not wish to be put on respirators and artificial life-support systems in the first place. When such documents are properly signed and witnessed, they protect your doctors from charges of homicide and protect you and your family from prolonging your body in an unconscious (some people would say undignified) state. In this day of high-tech and high-cost medical technology, each of us must contemplate the ways we want to spend our last days and document our desires in advance.

But what about the many people who fail to document their desires before a traffic accident puts them in a terminal coma, and their hospital puts them on a whole range of life-support systems? Even when unable to know the wishes of the patient, we cannot keep every patient on life-support systems forever. In many states and countries, brain-death laws give another alternative. They say that when a patient connected to life-support systems has no detectable brain activity for a period of six or twelve hours, then the patient should be considered "brain dead." Their chances of reviving from the brain-dead state are one in many thousands, so the law allows the medical profession to detach life-support systems from people with no measurable brain activity for a specified period.

Of course, this changes the meaning of the word *death*. Death used to mean "the end of breathing and heartbeat," but in this case, since breathing and heartbeats are artificially extendable, death comes to mean "the end of detectable brain activity." Most doctors believe brain activity can be measured by shining a flashlight in the pupils of the patients' eyes and hitting their knees with a hammer.

If patients' pupils fail to contract and they exhibit no knee-jerk re-
action, we have prima facie evidence that the brain is not doing its
job. Other doctors suggest that EEGs (measuring surface electrical
changes), NMR or CT scans (like X-ray pictures of the brain), or
angiograms (measuring the flow of blood to the brain) are desirable
or necessary adjuncts to check whether the brain is capable of functioning. The important point is that all of these new definitions presuppose without proof that consciousness is equal to, or dependent
on, brain processes—in other words, that if you have no brain processes, you cannot experience anything. This is more a philosophical point of faith than a medical fact, and we shall have reason to
return to this issue a little later.

MORAL QUESTIONS SURROUNDING ORGAN TRANSPLANTATION

There is another reason that doctors are highly interested in pro-
nouncing people brain dead: the use of their bodies for organ transplantation. As we noted above, some organs, such as eyes, bones,
and kidneys, can be taken from corpses and used even days after the
donors have died. So for example, if you want to help a blind or
nearly blind person, you can donate your eyes by registering with
your local eye bank. After you are dead, even by traditional definitions, and about to be embalmed or cremated, your eyes may be
removed and your corneas may be transplanted to help someone else
see "through your eyes."

On the other hand, many organs cannot be used after blood stops
flowing through them. The heart, liver, lungs, pancreas, and others
require continuous perfusion of fresh blood to function properly. Of
course, a recipient's immune system will try hard to reject such foreign organs, so transplant recipients must take immunosuppressant drugs such as cyclosporine, most of them for the rest of their
lives. What really made such transplants viable was not just the development of immunosuppressant drugs but the legal possibility of
removing organs from a body while the heart is still beating and
blood is still coursing through the organs. "Brain death" provides
an ideal condition for transplantation, because people are pronounced "dead" while their organs are still not only fresh but actively functioning.

So, hot on the heels of brain-death legislation in many states and countries came legislation enabling doctors to take out the beating hearts and lungs of brain-dead patients and to transplant them into waiting recipients. This created a plethora of problems, not the least being how to prioritize the recipients. If a hundred people all await the same heart, and there is only one donor available, how do we choose one of them and say, "you get it," and tell the other ninety-nine, "sorry, you folks die"? America has largely allowed market price mechanisms to resolve this problem; organs tend to go to the richest, best connected, and most famous, like the Mickey Mantles on the waiting list. Other countries have drawn up criteria including age, health, responsibility, education, and social contribution of the individuals waiting for organs.

From a purely logical and philosophical point of view, it is appropriate to distinguish between (a) the definition of death, or the point at which human bodies are no longer to be treated as persons; (b) the permissible use of body parts from dead bodies; and (c) the prevention of abuses of (a) and (b), in which desire to use human body parts would motivate either hastening persons' deaths for the use of their organs or selling and marketing of body parts in unethical ways. From a more realistic social standpoint, however, permission to use cadaveric organs is tantamount to opening the doors to marketing of body parts on the black market, if not more publicly (as seen in recent Internet advertisements for body parts). The situation is analogous to that of legalized gambling and broken homes.

There is no *logically necessary* connection between the legalization of gambling on the one hand and the increase of divorce, bankruptcy, suicide, and broken homes on the other. However, social statistics demonstrate that the two phenomena go hand in hand, and indeed, many states prudently choose to restrict gambling precisely because of the human tragedies it is known to entail. Analogously, some states and countries hesitated to legalize brain-death criteria partly out of the fear of creating the very black markets in body parts that are now surfacing around the developing world.

The ethical problems introduced by brain-dead organ transplantation were heralded but widely ignored in an important article by the philosopher Hans Jonas, writing from the University of Chicago in the mid-1970s.[1] Opposing the 1968 Harvard Report on Brain Death, which was fast becoming the basis for most American law-making on the subject, Jonas argued that our visceral fears of vivisection were experiential data indicating an intuitive glimpse of truth more than mere "irrationality." Jonas pointed out that there is no evidence to prove that people termed *brain dead* really could not feel or experience anything, and he was among the earlier prophetic voices to express the concern that utility and profiteering would come to govern our treatment of the dead and nearly dead. In fact, most of Jonas's fears have now been realized, even in the United States.

Japan and China have long resisted the Western trend of organ transplantation from brain-dead patients, based on a quasi-Confucian tradition of respect for the integrity of ancestors' bodies. While their general publics continue to harbor grave doubts about such practices, their medical and political elites are hastening towards the road of organ harvesting and organ marketing, largely for economic reasons. Let's now take a look at the situations of Japan and China, to see what their problems can tell us about our own.

JAPANESE BRAIN DEATH TIED TO ORGAN TRANSPLANTATION

Prior to 1997, Japan had no brain-death laws. In 1968, Dr. Juro Wada at Sapporo Medical University failed in an illegal heart-transplant procedure, killing both donor and recipient. Wada was acquitted for lack of testimony—an indication of the difficulty of whistle-blowing in Japanese society.[2] Despite the lack of brain-death laws, thousands of kidneys were transplanted from live donors, many of whom were judged brain dead, in the 1980s and 1990s, resulting in at least a dozen lawsuits by the mid-1990s.[3] At the same time, Japanese were proposing to pay Philippine kidney donors $30,000 per kidney.[4] Dr. Kazuo Ota (of Tokyo Women's Medical School), head of the Japan Society for Transplantation, confessed to having personally performed "at least" thirteen liver transplants using old, diseased livers rejected for age or hepatitis by the American transplant network UNOS.[5] Although Japan's Liberal Democratic Party (LDP) prime ministers formed ad hoc committees to oversee such matters, these committees are notoriously paternalistic and unconcerned with public opinion.[6] While opinion polls show that over 50 percent of Japanese people are acquiescent to brain-death criteria, some of these polls include the telltale but practically unimaginable proviso "if everyone else in the family agrees," while other questions indicate that less than 12 percent of respondents even know the meaning of the brain death to which they are acquiescing.[7]

In the process of discussing the possibilities for brain death in Japan, Japan's preeminent philosopher, Takeshi Umehara, has argued that doctors should take the lead in establishing a voluntary organ-donating society (he would call it the "Bodhisattva Society") to give their organs when they were dead or nearly dead. This would raise public faith in both the medical profession and the practice of organ donation and possibly obviate the need for brain-death determination. Ironically, doctors have been reluctant to volunteer their organs on the condition of brain death, implying their underlying fears either about the state of brain death itself or about the process of its determination.[8]

The driving force behind Japan's brain-death laws has never been popular opinion. On the contrary, it tends to be the Japanese Medical Association (JMA), especially foreign-educated surgeons, hospital CEOs, and the highly conservative LDP politicians whom they back, such as Taro Nakayama. When the government convened "open forums" in several locations around Japan, ostensibly to get a sense of public opinion on brain death, they in fact devolved into medical professionals' explaining the procedures planned, bulldozing the doubts and objections of their audiences.

With the strong support of the JMA and the LDP, Japan's brain-death law passed the lower house of the Diet on April 24, 1997, and the upper house on the eve of its adjournment, October 16, 1997. A compromise hammered out in late-night political negotiations, the bill contains a number of problematically ambiguous phrasings that we need not examine individually here. More striking are its two major features: that brain death is inextricably intertwined with organ transplantation, and that two bodies in absolutely identical physical states may receive opposite diagnoses.

THE JAPANESE DOUBLE STANDARD

In brief, the law defines the following criteria for brain death: that the body meets standard brain-death criteria for six hours, that a valid organ donor card for the patient has been confirmed, that there are no objections to organ transplantation by family members, and that the hospital is qualified to conduct such transplantation. In other words, it enjoins, "First, see if the patient is clinically brain dead. If she is brain dead, then try to locate a valid organ donor card for her, and ask her relatives what they think. If you can find her valid donor card, and if her relatives agree to harvesting her organs, then she is legally dead. If her relatives do not want her body cut, or if you cannot find a valid donor card for her, then she is not dead."[9] In other words, although two people may be in the very same medical condition ("brain death"), one can be legally pronounced dead if his relatives want him dead and a valid donor card can be found, while another must be maintained by machines because a card cannot be found, or because some relative doesn't want to acknowledge her death yet, or because the hospital is not prepared to conduct such an organ transplant.

Compare this Japanese stance with that of brain-death laws everywhere else in the world. Most brain-death laws are discrete from laws governing transplantation. They are designed to free terminal patients from tubes and respirators, allowing a more natural death— the Japanese law does not. Other brain-death laws free doctors from liability for terminating brain-dead patients and free hospital resources for use by other patients—the Japanese law does not. Other brain-death laws reduce costs to society and to insurance companies—the Japanese law does not. Other brain-death laws accord with the popular will that brain-dead patients need not be prolonged— the Japanese law is not grounded upon any popular understanding. It refuses to recognize as brain dead anyone but organ donors. What is the motivation here?

Prima facie, the Japanese law lets patients's families *choose* whether they believe that the patients are dead, based on feeling rather than on medical criteria. Yet families cannot choose to allow their tube-and-respirator-supported relatives to die naturally unless they agree to organ donation. Seen from the economics of hospital management, this is a blatant attempt to derive as much income as possible from the patients' families and insurance. Keeping a patient alive mechanically costs great sums every day. In other countries, when people are found to be brain dead, they are taken off life-support systems, and the hospital "loses" that source of income. In Japan, however, they cannot be taken off life-support systems, so the hospital never loses that income. The only time the machines can be stopped is when everyone concerned agrees to organ donation, which produces even more money for the hospital.

So, full of contradictions, this Japanese brain-death law is welcomed by Japanese hospitals and ridiculed by other countries. It does not respect Japanese people's desire to die naturally nor Japanese people's desire to reduce the tax burden for indefinite prolongation of brain-dead patients. It opens the door to legal organ transplantation from warm, pulsing cadavers. External second opinions and whistle-blowing are still unthinkable in the Japanese hospital context, but this law provides no safeguards against the Japanese fears that donors may be prematurely pronounced brain dead. It does, however, grandfather protection for those Japanese doctors who procured kidneys from consenting brain-dead patients before the brain-death law had been passed.

In sum, Japanese doctors' (and politicians') desires to maximize hospital incomes brought them to a simple dilemma. Many want to conduct transplantation partly for the high fees that it will bring (not purely for the patients that it will save, as shown by the many cases of transplants they already conduct with old, contaminated organs that have almost no chance of success). But if they were to follow worldwide brain-death criteria, then they would have to remove thousands of mechanically sustained Japanese patients from life-support systems, potentially losing precious income.

Their political solution was to allow termination of life support only when hospitals would gain even greater income through transplantation. This has not satisfied the Japanese minority who wanted brain-death criteria to enable death with dignity. Nor has it pleased the majority who still fear unscrupulous transplantation.[10] It has only placed Japanese doctors in a win-win situation, regardless of the rights or the will of the people. It guarantees that public insurance funds for life support will continue to pour into hospitals' coffers unless even greater income is procurable for transplantation.

ETHICAL PROBLEMS IN JAPAN SINCE LEGALIZATION OF BRAIN DEATH

In the first three years since Japan's passage of brain-death and organ-transplantation legislation, only six cases of transplantation occurred. The heavy media coverage afforded them raised questions about the anonymity of donors and about the privacy of donors and recipients alike. This emphasizes the dilemmas inherent in the situation: of privacy versus disclosure, of terminal care versus organ donation, of secret selection of recipients versus public funding.

Present Japanese procedures wallow in uncertainties about disclosure and privacy. Even before families had given their consent, Japan's mass media descended upon some of the hospitals where potential donors were expected, placing tremendous unspoken pressure on families to consent and further highlighting their demands for greater privacy. At the same time, claims that the brain-death determination itself was mistaken or premature and that potential donors received different treatment than they would have if they had not been donors add to the calls for greater public disclosure that already haunt the paternalist, protectivist, privatist Japanese medical profession.

A second dilemma is found in the question of whether patients who are also potential donors receive the fullest degree of terminal support and resuscitation that they could. In one transplant case, a potential donor was carried around Tokyo in an ambulance without treatment for some eighty minutes before being taken to Keio Hospital, although there were hospitals available within ten or fifteen minutes, and even Keio should have been reachable in far less time. Such cases suggest that the carrying of a donor card may in fact shortchange one's own treatment and hospitalization options for the sake of potential organ recipients. Some cases present a visible conflict between one medical team trying to preserve the life of the dying donor and another team awaiting harvest of the donor's organs for their recipient; in other cases, this same conflict lurks in the hearts of the same medical team who are called upon to make decisions that may prolong the life of one person at the expense of another.

Along with issues of privacy and priority of care remain questions about how recipients are chosen. The long and growing list of patients waiting for organ transplants is not made public, nor are the process and criteria by which some are told that they have been chosen to live and others that they are doomed to die. In some countries, such decisions are largely left to economic forces, with the organs going to the financially well-heeled; in many countries, criteria of age, education, health maintenance, and even potential contributions to society may affect selection of organ recipients. In Japan, no standards have been publicly explained or even suggested. Organs are flown at great public expense to recipients in distant hospitals; nor is any rationale given why geographically closer patients with probably higher survival rates are not chosen.

This is particularly of concern in the context that all such operations and associated expenses—from flying organs by Lear jet to distant hospitals, to the police escorts given the cars carrying the organs and recipients—are covered by taxes, in the name of science. No system has yet been made public to decide how many cases will be covered outright by tax monies or to set a cap on such federal funding. At present, Japan is the only country in the world to use taxpayers' national health insurance funds to foot the exorbitant medical bills of the elite handful who are secretly chosen to receive organs from brain-dead donors.

It is particularly odd that the public, which is paying for these rare and expensive operations, is given no account of how their monies are being allocated or apportioned. The Japanese health insurance system already operates at a deficit, spending more than it procures from mandatory contributions. Originally designed to provide public health coverage for the kinds of diseases, injuries, and child birthing that average citizens face in daily life, it has been increasingly bankrupted by rare and expensive operations for which everyone in the country must pay but from which few stand to benefit. The exorbitant cost of organ transplantations, in the face of the unconscionable inequity of everyone paying for something to which virtually no one has access, again raises the need for public ethical debate—but this has not been forthcoming.

The double standard of the Japanese brain-death law was a product of economic incentives in the JMA and the conservative LDP. Ethically, it disregards the will of the people by denying termination of life support when desired and by urging transplantation from those who by their own admission do not even understand the meaning of brain death.

For many years Japanese nationals used intermediaries with connections to the underworld to locate paid kidney donors in other countries. One ring of *yakuza* gangsters operating through connections at a major medical center in Boston was uncovered by journalists and broken up by police more than a decade ago. More recently, Japanese kidney patients travelled to Taiwan and Singapore to purchase organs obtained—without consent—from executed prisoners. This practice was roundly condemned by the World Medical Association and prohibited in 1994.[11] Yet in Japan, economics only rarely results in donors' premature deaths from organ harvesting or in recipients' deaths from nonviable organ transplants.

Organ Transplantation Without Brain Death in China

The situation in China is much more alarming. In the 1990s, the largest source of cadaveric organs by far was mainland China. Since the issue is potentially political, we should take pains to document the Chinese situation rather carefully before discussing its ethical ramifications.

Communist China has no laws about brain death, so technically the transplantation of most organs is legally impossible. The Chinese lack of brain-death criteria—not to mention their lack of the technology required to keep brain-dead persons' bodies functioning—means that traffic accident victims (the major source of donors in the West) cannot donate most of their vital organs. There is no donor card system, nor is the hospital and ambulance system in China geared to deal with unanticipated traffic accident victims.

However, China has the world's largest market for "fresh" organs (those viable for only a few minutes apart from their donors' bodies, as opposed to quick-frozen ones), derived almost entirely from the bodies of sentenced "criminals." In other words, the major way organs can be obtained is from those already condemned to die, in facilities that will not be required to attest that the patients were brain dead when their organs were removed. A Western surgeon who worked in China reported that over 90 percent of transplanted organs came from prisoners,[12] while Hong Kong surveys found that 75 percent of patients knew they had received prisoners' kidneys.[13]

CHINESE LAW ON "UTILIZATION OF CORPSES"

Immediately following the discovery of cyclosporine (the immunosuppressant that facilitated organ transplants) in 1983,[14] China announced its first "strike hard" campaign allowing the death penalty for common criminals;[15] in 1984, it announced the follow-up law, "Rules Concerning the Utilization of Corpses or Organs from Corpses from Executed Criminals," specifying that organs can be used from any prisoner who consents to organ donation. It is preposterous, of course, that a shackled, solitary, or tortured prisoner could give meaningful, free consent—or free refusal. Once a prisoner is executed, it is the state's word against anyone else's. Human Rights Watch has documented that prisoners are rarely even informed that their organs will be transplanted.[16] The Rules also say that "use of corpses or organs of executed prisoners must be kept strictly secret, and attention paid to avoiding negative repercussions."[17]

While the masses of Chinese were still Confucian enough to reject organ reception as well as donation, elite members of the communist party began receiving organs from executed prisoners. The number of common criminal executions increased, their timing often scheduled for the convenience of senior party officials or well-connected families.[18] In a country where hardly anyone will donate their bodies for science, this underscores that most of China's organ donors are executed prisoners.[19]

Another reason for China's high secrecy is that legally speaking, China does *not* recognize brain death. Since many organs must be transplanted before the heart stops beating, this means that many prisoners have their organs removed before they are legally dead.[20] Even official Chinese law texts describe how to botch executions deliberately to keep organs alive longer, and they describe cases of removing organs *before* the official executions.[21] In other words, vital organs are removed from living prisoners to be directly transplanted into waiting recipients.[22]

For example, a young lady teaching middle school in Jiangxi in the 1970s was found guilty of possessing politically incorrect manuscripts written by a colleague. Her blood type was determined, she was condemned and shot in the head twice, but even *before* she died, her kidneys were removed and transplanted to the son of the military officer who arranged the operation.[23]

Thousands of prisoners are executed every year in order to provide fresh organs for transplantation in the times and places where they are most needed. Most prisoners are shot through the back of their heads (except when their corneas are needed, in which case they are shot through the heart).[24] If the situation requires, they are drugged, given an IV, and occasionally even put on a respirator so their hearts will keep beating until they are brought adjacent to the organ recipients. Then the doctors cut the functioning organs out of the heart-beating prisoners and transplant them to the waiting patients—often either high-paying foreigners or members of the communist elite. Since the donor has been classified as a criminal, an enemy of the state, there is no concern for the pain or death that this causes the prisoner. In this situation, doctors cooperate with executioners not only to "save" life but to take it away.[25]

Invited to China to oversee transplants, American physicians have been assured that the proper types of donors can be arranged in the proper locations to suit their convenience, as is often the case for wealthy recipients coming from Hong Kong or Southeast Asia.[26] Unlike the rest of the world, where recipients wait for months for the chance of compatible organs, China's touted ability to schedule compatible organ transplants "on demand" points to the conclusion that the transplant business motivates the timing of the execution of prisoners, if not the conviction of healthy suspects.

China's Procedures for Imposing Capital Punishment

The problem is not simply that China sells executed criminals' organs. The use of prisoners' organs has to be understood in the context of the entire process of the Chinese "justice" system: apprehension, imprisonment, prosecution, and execution.

Prisoners can be apprehended on hearsay, detained for months without being allowed contact or without being told of the charges against them, pressured into confessions, and only told of their death sentences hours before their executions. They have no right to real

defense lawyers; neither they nor their lawyers are allowed to inter-
rogate their accusing witnesses or to examine the evidence or briefs
used against them. Their judge is normally a communist cadre who
not infrequently is related (by blood or money) to the patient who
expects to receive the kidneys or liver of the suspect. Convicts have
the "right" to appeal, but higher courts do not normally hold hearings, merely rubber-stamping the authority of the lower courts;
appeals to still higher courts are technically "permitted" but often
scheduled after their executions.[27]

Torture, food- and sleep-deprivation, and other methods are frequently used to extract confessions.[28] The "justice" system is so
unbelievably draconian and contradictory to justice that it may
warrant briefly quoting an Amnesty International Report to the
Senate Foreign Hearings Committee:

> Criminal Procedure Law allows the police to hold suspects
> for at least four and a half months before a decision is taken
> on whether or not to prosecute them. During this period, the
> police are able to interrogate the suspect but the suspect has
> no right of access to a lawyer or to meet with a judge. There
> have been numerous reports of the use of torture and physi-
> cal intimidation to extract confessions during such interroga-
> tions. In *China—The Death Penalty,* Amnesty International
> documented cases in which official admissions were made that
> the death sentence had been handed down on the basis of con-
> fessions extorted through police mistreatment.
>
> Defense lawyers are seriously handicapped by established
> judicial practices. They have access only to a part of the file
> concerning the defendant, they cannot confront witnesses and
> are effectively barred from challenging the validity of the
> charges. Some lawyers have been subjected to demotion, de-
> tention and even physical violence as a consequence of attempt-
> ing to mount an adequate defense in criminal cases.[29]

Condemned prisoners are allowed to write their wills—sometimes
with their hands tied to their chairs—but the authorities have the
official power to censor or confiscate them, particularly if they disagree with the views of the state.[30]

Even within the Chinese legal system, it is widely recognized that capital punishment is frequently conducted upon innocent suspects. But executions are thought to have a salutary effect on the public who witness them, and mistakes are rarely admitted publicly or only many years after the fact; attempts at restitution are the exception rather than the rule.[31]

A Continuing History of Horror

The practice of taking organs from prisoners may date back to the 1970s, but it mushroomed in the 1990s. In 1990, *Newsweek* magazine's photo exposé of China's capital punishment led the Chinese government to deny that the materials were genuine and simultaneously to pass edicts concerning journalistic coverage of execution sites.[32] This was to become a common pattern: Every time observers report human rights abuses in China, China denies the content of the reports while legally tightening its secrecy surrounding the very practices that it denies exist.

In the early 1990s, prominent physicians from the leading cities of Beijing, Shanghai, and Guangzhou reported that most of their transplanted organs were obtained from shot prisoners, and that their doctors assisted in organ removal at the execution sites or immediately thereafter.[33] BBC television specials from 1990 to 1992 reported that virtually all of China's kidney transplants came from executed prisoners;[34] in October of 1994, the BBC's broadcast of locations and participants of organ transplant operations in China led Taiwan to ban the use of criminals' organs for transplantation.

The evidence indicated that this state execution machine was driven increasingly by economic motives rather than motives of criminal justice or law enforcement. In 1996, a new "strike hard" death penalty campaign was instituted, and documented death sentences rose from some 3,000 in 1995 to over 6,100 in 1996, three times more than the criminal executions of the entire rest of the world put together, including African and Islamic police states.[35] (This is probably but a fraction of the total, for China does not wish to admit the full number.) The death sentence can be imposed for approximately seventy crimes, including hooliganism, pornography, bribery, political deviance, and reselling tax receipts.[36] Of course, the levying of the death penalty is very selective; not every hooligan or deviant is killed.[37] In 1996, two Shanghai men were executed for stealing badminton rackets and ballpoint pens from powerful officials, and a Sichuan farmer, for selling a stone Buddha head he had found. Dozens of Tibetans and hundreds of Xinjiang separatists have been executed annually.[38]

However, even legal specialists in China itself acknowledge that these death penalties do not deter crime—rather, they are directly related to the demand for organ sales.[39] Both the timing and the choice of which prisoners are to be sentenced is as much influenced by their organ donation as by their crimes. In other words, whether a young protester is let off with a warning or shot and harvested for organs depends more on the person's blood type and the state of organ demand in that region than on the public danger of the person's crime.

In June 1997, pursuant to alarming reports issued by Amnesty International, ABC began the research that was to lead to a Polk Award for Journalism: its October broadcast of "Blood Money," in which it documented Dr. Dai Yong's offer to procure kidneys for American clients from executed Chinese prisoners, for a fee of $30,000 for the organ and a $5,000 commission.

Shortly thereafter, on February 20, 1998, the FBI arrested Hainan prosecutor Wang Chengyong and Chinese national Fu Xingqi (in New York working as a "laundryman"!) for contracting in a New York hotel room with an undercover agent to sell organs, including lungs from nonsmokers and skin from "young" Chinese. Mary Jo White's Southern District Court of New York placed Marcia Isaacson in charge of the prosecution, specifying that the two Chinese faced up to five years in prison and a quarter-million-dollar fine. At a joint hearing in June 1998 of the House International Relations Committee and the House Government Reform and Oversight Committee on Organ Harvesting in Communist China, Assistant Secretary of State John Shattuck testified before Chairman Ben Gilman (R-New York) about the seriousness and pervasiveness of these practices and the need to pressure China to curtail them. However, in the following year, not only did the Clinton administration fail to raise seriously the issue with the Chinese government but the two Chinese organ sellers mysteriously escaped America without pros-

ecution. It is difficult to understand how both the federal courts and
the FBI could allow such criminal suspects to leave the country unless
there was concern that the trial itself would have proven an embarrassment to American politicians.

Nor has the Chinese use of prisoners' organs decreased in light
of these arrests and congressional hearings. Since that time, Chinese
doctors even advertised their procedures in Malaysian Lions' Clubs,
offering "discount rates" for affiliated members and encouraging
their recipients to come in January or May when executions are
commonest.[40]

ECONOMICS DISTORTS THE ROLE OF DOCTORS

In the 1990s, thousands of wealthy clients from Hong Kong,
Singapore, Thailand, Malaysia, Korea, Japan, and surrounding
countries went to China to receive lung, heart, kidney, and liver
transplants. The cost of a transplant runs anywhere from the "special discount price" of $10,000 to $45,000—sometimes less than a
third of what it might cost in the West—but the value of that same
foreign currency within China is more than three times what it would
be worth outside of China.[41]

Moreover, in the 1990s, Chinese hospitals have fallen on economic hard times and often resort to selling medicine and overcharg-
ing patients to avoid bankruptcy.[42] So a single prisoner's organ transplantation to a foreign recipient can keep a hospital economically
solvent, even after appropriate payoffs to concerned officials. Like
many Chinese hospitals operated by the People's Liberation Army,
the Nanfang Hospital in Guangzhou advertises that one-third of its
thirteen hundred beds are set aside for foreign guests, generating two
million dollars in foreign income annually.[43]

These fees far exceed the costs billed to local residents, violating
1991 World Health Organization (WHO) guidelines specifying that
payment for transplants should be limited to justifiable fees for services rendered. Foreign patients are advised to bring "gifts" for the
hospital personnel, who in turn send gifts to the judges and police
involved in executions, hoping to ensure the future supply of organs.[44] This may help to explain the apparent caprice in the Chinese
court convictions: that petty criminals can be executed if they have

the right organs and blood type at the right time and place, whereas much more heinous criminals may work in prison if they are old or alcoholic or their organs are otherwise in low demand.[45]

Following Taiwan's ban on the use of Chinese organs, the Korean government announced (on April 16, 1998) measures to curtail the booming organ market in Korea, in which Chinese kidneys were sold for $25,000 to $38,000, of which 10–20 percent goes to the broker. In Japan, travel posters outside major Tokyo hospitals read "Tired of kidney treatments? Visit China in Golden Week!" referring to the first week of May when a series of Japanese holidays neatly coincide with the annual Chinese May Day "clean-up" executions, and there is a large supply of fresh kidneys available for Japanese "tourists."

Of course, all sales of body parts are prohibited by international law. Charging more than the minimally required surgical and processing fees violates WHO guidelines. Involving doctors in the execution of criminals violates the United Nations' "Principles of Medical Ethics," which reads in part: "It is a contravention of medical ethics for health personnel, particularly physicians, to be involved in any professional relationship with prisoners or detainees the purpose of which is not solely to evaluate, protect or improve their physical and mental health."[46]

So on a range of counts, the Chinese transplantation practice runs afoul not merely of common morality but of internationally recognized conventions.

INTERNATIONAL INDIGNATION

The above litany of human rights abuses is doubly of concern because of their link to the sale of Chinese citizens' body parts for foreign cash. This leads us to consider the response of the international community to this situation. Lord Thomas of Gresford's indignation in the House of Lords (December 18, 1996) is representative and worth excerpting:

> There is a temptation for many people to ask whether we have anything to do with China; why should we interfere? Do we not have enough on our plate? To people who have that self-doubt are added the mercantile voices, "Don't do anything to upset

China; don't do anything to affect our competitive position in that country.". . . I am wholly persuaded to the contrary. China must understand that we shall publicise and continue to criticise violations of human rights wherever they may take place. Torture, as an instrument of oppression, is no less objectionable when it is practised in an undeveloped country than it is in an advanced democracy. Political views, political systems, are meaningless and immaterial. China must be called to account for a number of reasons. First, as some noble Lords have already said, it seeks to play a leading role in the affairs of the UN as one of the five permanent members of the Security Council; secondly, although . . . China is a state party to seven UN treaties, it has crucially failed to ratify the International Covenant on Civil and Political Rights. . . . Beyond that, China blocks criticism in the UN by procedural methods. Where a state seeks to strut the stage of world affairs, it cannot pick and choose those standards of international behaviour which it will obey and those which it will not. It cannot cloak itself in the robe of sovereignty to avoid international responsibilities.[47]

In recent years, many governments have become critical of China's unethical organ trade: Singapore has charged Chinese doctors with responsibility for the death of Singaporeans;[48] America has refused to return suspects to Hong Kong for fear that they may be summarily executed for organ harvest;[49] and German pharmaceutical companies have left China over this issue.[50] British, German, French, US, and UN delegations have repeatedly asked China for clarification of its practices and of the involvement of its physicians, without obtaining clear responses. Despite British House of Lords and American Senate Hearings condemning these practices,[51] America continues to grant China most-favored-nation status for economic reasons.[52]

We should grant China the right to non-Western views of crime and crime control.[53] Yet the ethical problems in China's death sentencing for organ transplantation are legion. The utter disregard for human rights of prisoners and their families, the vagaries of trial and sentencing procedures, the cruel and unusual methods of removing organs from heart-beating and sometimes conscious convicts, and the doctors' participation in the execution of prisoners all give serious pause. But our central criticism is that the economics of organ sales and transplants itself influences and motivates China's inordinately high rate of capital punishment for petty crimes.

ETHICAL ISSUES

The cases of Japan and, more starkly, of China call for the rethinking of a number of ethical positions. We do not propose to give complete answers to all of these doubts but rather voice them so that they may receive fuller and more proper consideration. Broadly speaking, these ethical issues can be divided into medical, juridical, intercultural, and fundamental values. Let us briefly treat each in turn.

Medical issues. We have already alluded to some of the medical questions in our previous discussion of the dilemmas raised by the Japanese introduction of organ transplantation: for example, privacy versus disclosure, optimal terminal care versus optimal organ procurement, the prioritization of recipients, and universal taxation for the gain of a privileged few.

However, the whole presumption of brain death itself deserves further scrutiny, as Hans Jonas argued years ago. The medical profession presupposes that when brain functions cannot be observed, the body is insensate and death is imminent. Medical evidence is increasingly challenging this unproven postulate of the medical profession. As long as a century ago, animal experiments demonstrated that pigeons and dogs with surgically disconnected brains still responded to pain. This would indicate that a body's sensations of pain need not depend on brain function.

More recently, some organ recipients have reported changes in personal tastes and character with the receipt of other's organs. Shaking Cartesian presumptions of the supremacy of the brain, this would support the long-standing Japanese belief that bodily memories may be carried not only in brain cells but also in other bodily organs. Japanese studies of LIS (locked-in syndrome) patients have found that some patients with brain activity so minimal as to suggest no audiovisual comprehension are in fact capable of understanding what is happening to them, although unable to communicate except through eye movement. By appropriate heating and cooling of heads and bodies, Nihon University doctors have successfully revived patients who demonstrated insignificant brain activity for more than a month, some of whom would have been thought brain dead and subject to organ donation by the laws of other countries. Elizabeth Kübler-Ross reported cases of people reviving after more than twelve hours of brain death, some of whom even remember what was happening to them during part of the time they were thought to be brain dead.[54] All of this circumstantial evidence sheds doubt on the widely unquestioned assumption that detectable brain activity is a prerequisite for human cognition—and hence bodily life.

In the context of transplantation, we are also forced to ask, does the fact that we are capable of conducting organ transplantation make it *right* to do so? Cleveland doctor Robert White's 1999 experiments leading to the successful transplantation of monkeys' heads imply that it is only a question of time before human head transplants will become medically possible.[55] This is no longer merely the stuff of science fiction or of philosophical theories about the nature of personal identity. Before long, we may acquire the technical ability to transplant the head of genius Stephen Hawking onto the healthy body of a decapitated criminal. But should we? Or are there limits beyond which the lure of "longer life" should not be dangled before mortals? What if this life extension comes at great cost to the public exchequer, or worse, to another human life? Perhaps the time has come to review our fundamental presumptions about the nature of experience and respect for persons.

"Juridical" issues. The Chinese situation casts China's juridical system and so-called human rights issues in stark relief. It is fairly clear that the "consent" of a tortured prisoner in a Chinese death row is meaningless. But this raises the larger issues of whether "consent" can be truly free if doctors press for it in a medical setting, even in the West. How much psychological or circumstantial pressure is sufficient to invalidate claims that consent is freely given? (Perhaps the myth of "uninfluenced" freedom must be laid to rest, but for the time being, it may be sufficient to reexamine the forces brought to bear on cases of consent.)

On a different level, can a country choose to commandeer the resources (or even bodies) of its people for what it deems a greater good? When do "states' rights" outweigh the rights of individual citizens? When do criminals forfeit their rights to participate as free citizens in a society? China's tradition of arguing that criminals, by their very behavior, have forsworn their humanity and therefore their rights to treatment as humans goes back at least twenty-three hundred years.[56]

For a variety of reasons, the majority of civilized nations have moved in the direction of abandoning capital punishment altogether. Without debating the whole question of the moral acceptability of capital punishment at this juncture, it may at least be appropriate to ask what kinds of special demands the threat of capital punishment makes on due process of law. Since capital punishment is arguably more irreversible than other forms of punishment, most forensic authorities agree that it should require additional safeguards and appeals procedures lest it be applied mistakenly. But what procedures suffice to assure that the state does not execute innocent suspects? Or in China's view, how can the costs of defending criminal suspects be balanced against the other costs of operating an effective police and justice system? Such ethical issues are also raised by the cases we have been considering.

Intercultural issues. The application of such theories on an international and an intercultural stage is beset with thornier ethical issues of a different order. China participates (and seeks to participate more forcefully) as a member of the United Nations Security Council and has ratified several UN treaties. Yet it complacently violates some of the treaties that it has publicly endorsed and still rejects the International Covenant on Civil and Political Rights. Should a country that refuses to play by the rules of the international community be allowed a significant voice in the direction of that community?

China argues that its internal affairs are its own business. But in cases ranging from the Holocaust to apartheid, the international community has used force and economic sanctions to demand that nations respect their citizens' rights. The world community has forcefully condemned rights abuses in Uganda, Cambodia, Bosnia, and East Timor, to name a few. The nature of international involvement deserves careful consideration, but the *scale* of the abuses is not at issue; sovereignty cannot be used as a rubric under which to defend mass executions of a citizenry, whether of insurrectionists in Tibet or of hooligans whose organs are salable in Guangzhou.

If parents abuse their child, then their neighbors—and the government—take steps to protect the child and to restrain the parents. Civilized countries have moved to eliminate sweatshops not only in their own lands but also in those of their trading partners. Most of us would think it unethical knowingly to buy stolen goods from a thief, particularly if our purchases would motivate further crimes. By analogy, should not China's neighbors refrain from patronizing China's illegal organ markets and perhaps influence her by connecting our trade agreements with agreements to respect the rights of her "children," her citizens? If we cannot demand that China's trials all be as public as those in the West, could we not at least ask that it provide full and clear information about the sources of organs offered and fees charged to foreigners for transplantation? Shall we use our foreign trade to affect the behaviors and activities of our trade partner, as we did to end apartheid in South Africa? Or do we draw an ethical difference between influencing South Africa, which seemed small and economically dispensable, and influencing China, which seems large and economically attractive to us? In short, will we put our money where our "rights talk" is or sell out to the cheapest provider of Wal-mart toys?

Fundamental values of human life. Ultimately, this discussion of organ transplantation concerns more than Japan's health care priorities and China's execution of criminal suspects. It relates to the much more fundamental question of what we will allow to be bought and sold—of whether we can ethically maintain humanity as more valuable than money, or whether we will reduce everything to the common denominator of cold cash: justice, human bodies, human lives. Medical technology is pushing us to reexamine our basic assumptions about capitalism and life itself: How can we hold "sacred" human lives and bodies above capitalist market forces? How can market economic forces be reconciled with the demands for human body parts? How can we locate values more important than time and money alone—in the quality of human relationships and experience, for example—and come to terms with our finitude instead of attempting to bargain even with our own deaths?

If market forces are allowed to become the ultimate arbiter of technology's direction, as some conservatives would propose, then a more ethical education of consumers should move technology in a better direction. However, it appears that most countries as well as corporations desire to acquire capital regardless of the real benefits or sufferings they confer on humankind in the process. In turn, corporations (and countries) hire media to brainwash vulnerable consumers by incessantly reiterating such lies as "acquisition is the greatest good" and "this product (or organ?) will make you better and happier than you are now; you are inferior as long as you lack it!" So, our problem becomes how to guide, if not govern, the masses of consumers who are vulnerable to such brainwashing, who lose their better judgments and deeper values in the onslaught of such ceaseless barrages.

My prejudices as a philosopher have been more or less apparent throughout this lecture. It is not my intent here to propose final solutions to all these ethical dilemmas as much as to urge our ongoing reexamination of them. Medical and forensic science alone cannot resolve the plethora of problems that their new technologies are dumping at our doorsteps. For this, it requires our own conscientious contemplation of what we know to be right, of what we desire for our world, our children, and our neighbors, and of what we are willing to pay or sacrifice to approach our ideals. This is the reason we need to be ethicists, as Wayne Leys would have liked me to remind you. I hope that our discussion today has given some grounds for action as well as for talk in the future, that we all can find ways to value and respect qualities of human life other than merely the price tag that is placed upon it.

NOTES

1. Hans Jonas, *Philosophical Essays: From Ancient Creed to Technological Man* (Chicago: University of Chicago Press, 1980), 132–40; and *The Imperative of Responsibility: In Search of an Ethics for the Technological Age.* Chicago: University of Chicago Press, 1984.

2. Jiro Nudeshima, "Obstacles to Brain Death and Organ Transplantation in Japan," *Lancet* 338 (October 26, 1991): 1063.

3. Katsunori Honda, "Expunge the Secrecy Surrounding 'Brain Dead' Transplantation and Medical Mistakes" (in Japanese), *Shin Iryou,* August 2000, 39–41.

4. Honda, "Expunge the Secrecy."

5. C. Ross, "Towards Acceptance of Organ Transplantation?" *Lancet* 346 (July 1, 1995), 41–42.

6. Nudeshima, "Obstacles," 1063.

7. Carl Becker, "When Are You Really Dead?" *Japan Times,* June 21, 1997, p. 18.

8. Takeshi Umehara, "Descartes, Brain Death, and Organ Transplants: A Japanese View," *NPQ: New Perspectives Quarterly,* 11, no. 1 (winter 1994): 25–30.

9. Steven Butler, "Dead When You Say You're Dead," *U.S. News and World Report,* June 30, 1997, 42.

10. Sheryl WuDunn, "In Japan, Use of Dead Has the Living Uneasy (Organs from the Brain-Dead Patient)" *New York Times,* May 11, 1997, p. A1.

11. Nancy Scheper-Hughes, "The New Cannibalism," *New Internationalist,* no. 300 (April 1998): 14–16.

12. Ronald D. Guttman, M.D., "On the Use of Organs from Executed Prisoners," *Transplantation Reviews* 6, no. 3 (July 1992): 189–93.

13. Ella Lee, "Prisoners' Organs for Sale," *South China Morning Post,* January 9, 2000, p. 3.

14. C. Ikels, "Kidney Failure and Transplantation in China," *Social Science and Medicine* 44, no. 9 (May 1997): 1271–83.

15. John P. Burns, "When Peking Fights Crime, News Is on the Wall," *New York Times,* January 28, 1986, p. A2.

16. Asia Watch Committee, Human Rights Watch, "China: Organ Procurement and Judicial Execution in China," *Human Rights Watch* 6, no. 9 (August 1994): 42.

17. See David Rothman, "Body Shop: China's Booming Trade in Organs for Transplant," *Sciences* 37, no. 6 (November 1997): 17–21.

18. John P. Burns, "Peking Focuses on Execution of Three Officials' Sons," *New York Times,* February 25, 1986, p. A11.

19. Barbara Basler, "Kidney Transplants in China Raise Concern about Source," *New York Times,* June 3, 1991, p. A1.

20. Paul Lewis, "China Executes Dissidents in Secret, Amnesty International Reports," *New York Times,* August 31, 1989, p. A3.

21. Asia Watch Committee, "China," 42.

22. "Dalu Sigiu Bei Gegu Qiguan Zhenxiang" (The Truth about Organs Taken from Condemned Prisoners in China), *Jiushi Niandai* (Nineties), February 1993, 24–27.

23. Lao Gui, "Baoshi Huangye de Nüfan" (Female Prisoners Die Violent Deaths in the Wilderness), *Zhongguo Zhi Chun* (China Spring), September 1992, 76–91.

24. Paul Lewis, "Method of Execution: A Stark Tradition," *New York Times,* June 22, 1989, pp. A6, A10; see also Lena H. Sun, "China's Execu-

tioners: A Punishing Schedule," and "China's Executed Convicts Unwitting Organ Donors," *Washington Post,* March 27, 1994, p. A1.

25. David P. Hamilton, "China Uses Prisoners for Transplants, Human Rights Watch Asia Report," *Wall Street Journal,* August 29, 1994, pp. A6, A7.

26. Rothman, "Body Shop," 17.

27. See Timothy A. Gelatt, *Criminal Justice with Chinese Characteristics: China's Criminal Process and Violations of Human Rights* (New York: Lawyers Committee for Human Rights, May 1993).

28. Harry Wu Hongda, "A Grim Organ Harvest in China's Prisons," *World Press Review* 42, no. 6 (June 1995): 22–23.

29. For Amnesty Reports, see the home page of Amnesty International (London): www.amnesty.org/ailib/aireport/ar98

30. Testimony of Zhang Xin, former judge of the Shenzhen Intermediate People's Court (Economic Judgments Enforcement Division), interviewed by Human Rights Watch Asia in August 1994. See also "'Outcast' Judge Sneaks Son Out," *South Chinay Morning Post,* August 21, 1994.

31. "Many 'Unjust, False and Erroneous' Verdicts Found among Cases Tried Between 1977 and 1978," *Renmin Sifa Xuanbian* (articles from *People's Justice Magazine*) (Beijing: Law Publishing House, February 1983), 116–18.

32. "Guanyu Yange Kongzhi Zai Sixing Zhixing Xianchang Jinxing Paishe He Caifang de Tongzhi" (Notification Concerning the Strict Control of Photographic and Journalistic Coverage at Sites Where Executions Are Being Carried Out), issued by China's Ministry of Public Security, Supreme People's Court, and Supreme People's Procuracy, Beijing, July 16, 1990.

33. "Deacon Chiu Recovers with $1 Million Kidney," *Hong Kong Standard,* May 17, 1991, and "Organs of Shot Prisoners Used," *South China Morning Post,* August 17, 1992.

34. "The Great Organ Bazaar," BBC documentary, June 23, 1992. See also Lam Siu-Keung, "Kidney Trading in Hong Kong," *Lancet* 338 (August 17, 1991): 453.

35. Dmitry Balburov, "China's Chechnya," *Moscow News,* May 22, 1997, p. 22.

36. Stacy Mosher, "Ultimate Response, Execution of Smugglers in China," *Far Eastern Economic Review* 155 (June 8, 1992): 9.

37. Donald C. Clarke, "The Execution of Civil Judgments in China," *China Quarterly* 141 (March 1995): 65.

38. Keith B. Richburg, "China Executes Hundreds in Crackdown," *Washington Post,* July 6, 1996, p. A1.

39. *Economist,* June 15, 1996, 4; "Three Embezzlers Executed in South China," *Beijing Review,* August 8, 1994, 6.

40. Thomas Fuller, "Execution for a Kidney," *International Herald Tribune,* June 15, 2000; Lee, "Prisoners' Organs for Sale," p. 3.

41. Rothman, "Body Shop," 17.

42. S. Hillier and X. Zheng, "Reforms of the Chinese Health Care System: The Jiangxi Study," *Social Science and Medicine* 41, no. 8 (October 1995): 1058.

43. Neil Peretz, "China—Medical Equipment in Guangdong," *National Trader Data Bank,* US Department of Commerce, December 1994, CD-ROM.

44. Fuller, "Execution for a Kidney"; and Senate Committee on Foreign Relations, *China: Illegal Trade in Human Body Parts,* 104th Cong., 1st sess., May 4, 1995, 104–26.

45. Clarke, "Execution," 65.

46. "Principles of Medical Ethics Relevant to the Role of Health Personnel, Particularly Physicians, in the Protection of Prisoners and Detainees Against Torture and Other Cruel, Inhuman or Degrading Treatment or Punishment," resolution 37/194, principle 3, adopted by the General Assembly of the United Nations, December 18, 1982.

47. Testimony of Lord Thomas of Gresford before the House of Lords, December 18, 1996, 7:44 P.M., cols. 1579–80. The entire debate of 18 December is available on the Web via the Lords Hansard home page: www.parliament.the-stationery-office.co.uk/cgi-bin/htm (Lords Hansard text for 18 December 1996 (161218-08).

48. Barbara Crossette, "Singapore Ties Seven Deaths to China Kidney Transplants," *New York Times,* February 7, 1988, pp. 9, 20.

49. David E. Rovella, "No Extradition to Hong Kong," *National Law Journal,* January 20, 1997, p. A6; and see Christopher Drew, "US Says Two Chinese Offered Organs from the Executed," *New York Times,* February 24, 1998, p. A1.

50. See "Fresenius Medical Care Divests Dialysis Center in China," press release, March 5, 1998. Fresenius announced its divestment based on reports of organs being sold on the black market in China to wealthy foreigners as "unacceptable to Fresenius Medical Care AG." See "German Firm Leaves China amid Convict Organ Claims," *Reuters,* March 6, 1998. "Kidneys-from-Prisoners Scandal Scares Off Germans," *South China Morning Post,* March 6, 1998. Asked about the economic losses that divestment might entail, Fresenius responded that it "cannot care about losses when there are ethical considerations." Edmund L. Andrews, "German Company to Leave China over Sales of Organs," *New York Times,* March 7, 1998, p. A5.

51. The Laogai Research Foundation is America's leading organization researching civil rights abuses in China's gulag prison (laogai) system. Its Web site provides full texts of testimonies to governmental bodies (www.laogai.org/tstmny), printed reports of testimony (www.laogai.org/

reports/index.html), and films, including those of the BBC (www.laogai.org/public.htm).

52. Assistant Secretary of State for Asian and Pacific Affairs Stanley Roth expressed his condemnation of Chinese executions for organ transplantation but admitted in a Foreign Relations Committee hearing on May 14, 1998, that "this is not an issue where we have made any progress since the summit" between presidents Clinton and Jiang in October 1997.

53. Ronald J. Troyer, ed., *Social Control in the People's Republic of China* (New York: Praeger, 1988).

54. Elizabeth Kübler-Ross, quoted in Joseph Head and S. L. Cranston, *Reincarnation: The Phoenix Fire Mystery* (New York: Warner Books, 1979), 452.

55. Alison Motluk, "Body Politics," *New Scientist* (London) 164, no. 2207 (October 9, 1999): 48–51. See also BBC News online: news.bbc.co.uk//hi/english/health/newsid_1263000/1263758.stm

56. See Carl Becker, "Language and Logic in Modern Japan," *Communication and Cognition* 24, no. 2 (1991): 160–63.

7

Insurrectionist Ethics: Advocacy, Moral Psychology, and Pragmatism

Leonard Harris

A philosophy that offers moral intuitions, reasoning strategies, motivations, and examples of just moral actions but falls short of requiring that we have a moral duty to support or engage in slave insurrections is defective. Moreover, a philosophy that does not make advocacy—that is, representing, defending, or promoting morally just causes—a seminal, meritorious feature of moral agency is defective.

I query whether pragmatism offers compelling intuitions, strategies, motivations, and examples for persons to be insurrectionists or to support slave insurrections.[1] I do so by first exploring the sort of morality practiced and advocated by model insurrectionists. In this way, I provide a sketch of the intuitions, strategies, and motivations common among insurrectionists. I then consider common features of pragmatic moral thinking. The argument is conjectural and incomplete; it is intended to raise vexing issues as much as it is intended as a more coherent inquiry.

David Walker, Maria Stewart, Henry D. Thoreau, and Lydia Child, I believe, practiced insurrectionist morality. I choose these authors as models because they lived during the formative years of classical pragmatism. The authors of classical pragmatism inherited a world shaped by racial slavery and lived in a completely racially segregated society. Insurrectionists fought to end both such worlds. My model insurrectionists lived during America's period of slavery and fought against a system that by any reasonable account was historically antiquated. Every Western and industrial nation, for example, had abolished slavery, racial as well as endogamous, prior to America's Civil War. If slavery was considered justified by appeal to some version of evolutionary ethics, America's racial slavery retarded evolution by stifling a valuable work force. If slavery was considered warranted because it was unknowingly used to enhance material production and thereby help secure longevity for a favored gene pool, or because it was a consequence of inevitable group conflict pitting a weaker group against a stronger one, then America's racial slavery lacked warrant. It was historically antiquated because the "white" gene pool became a hybrid; and it was hardly inevitable because the racial group categories of black and white were historically constructed.

David Walker (1785–1830), born in North Carolina, published and distributed the *Appeal to the Coloured Citizens of the World* in September 1829. Walker, a free black, owned a secondhand clothing shop near Brattle Street, in Boston. Walker was the Boston agent for the distribution of the *Freedom's Journal,* a New York–based weekly abolitionist newspaper. Walker's *Appeal* provided a secular and theological basis for insurrection by arguing that racial slavery was morally the worst form of slavery in history: It made race a marker separating humanity and promoted perpetual servitude for a people as a way of transferring assets from one population to another, preventing the possibility of manumission save through purchase and promoting the enslavement by Christians of Christians. In addition, he argued that the fact that the majority of white Americans were proslavery indicated the morally deficient character of Americans. The unfortunate outcome of American democracy was not a warrant for those that suffered death, beating, rape, and dismemberment. Biding their time in hopes of some future salvation was no solace for slaves. Walker and his work were banned in several states, although Walker as well as his book was instrumental in initiating slave escapes and insurrections. On June 28, 1830, Walker was found dead near his shop, the most likely cause being assassination by proslavery forces. Walker used instrumental reasoning techniques as well as foundational principles to advance abolitionists' arguments and objectives.

Maria W. Stewart (1803–1879) promoted Walker's form of morality with particular emphasis on the liberation of women. As Stewart proclaimed in an 1832 Boston lecture: "Why sit ye here and die? If we say we will go to a foreign land, the famine and the pestilence are there, and there we shall die. If we sit here, we shall die. Come let us plead our cause before the whites; if they save us alive, we shall live and, if they kill us, we shall but die."[2] Stewart expresses a sense of tragic possibility: death with either action. And she expresses a sense of the possible: freedom if blacks confront the very population that holds them in chains. Stewart also expresses righteous indignation not only at the condition of slavery but also at discrimination practiced for the benefit of white business women: "I have asked several individuals of my sex, who transact business for themselves . . . would they not be willing to grant them [Negro girls] an equal opportunity with others? Their reply has been, for their own part, they had no objection; but as it was not the custom, were they to take them into their employ, they would be in danger of losing the public patronage." No matter the character, skill, taste, or ingenuity of Negro girls, they could scarce "rise above the condition of servants. Ah! Why this cruel and unfeeling distinction?" It is a lack, for Stewart, of moral character and religious conviction and the presence of greed that motivates persons to accept and to perpetrate prevailing heinous conventions. A sense of identity, the *we* Stewart uses, entails herself and all persons subject to being enslaved or who were slaves. As a free black, Stewart faced the possibility of being forced into slavery. She expressed righteous indignation and a refusal to accept instrumental calculations of individual benefits at the expense of the lives of others.

Henry D. Thoreau (1817–1862), in two important works, "Slavery in Massachusetts" (1854) and "A Plea for Captain John Brown" (1859), expressed deep sensibilities concerning the plight of blacks.[3] His "Slavery in Massachusetts" argued against the fugitive slave acts. Numerous states, including Massachusetts, passed a series of laws that allowed whites to treat blacks as chattel even if they were in a state that did not sanction slavery. Thus, if black persons who had escaped slavery were found in a state that did not practice slavery, they could be captured and forcibly returned to their former owner. Blacks thus maintained the status of property even in free states; free blacks could become property if they traveled to states that outlawed free blacks and were deemed, through any number of contrivances, to be property. Moreover, in certain states, a child of a runaway slave might be deemed property of the parents' owner even if the child was born in a free state. Thoreau found such laws a violation of all good governance and human rights. "I would remind my country-men, that they are to be men first, and Americans only at a late and convenient hour. No matter how valuable law may be to protect your property, even to keep soul and body together, if it do[es] not keep you and humanity together."[4] And in his support for the insurrec-tion at Harper's Ferry led by John Brown, he praises Brown as "A man of rare common sense and directness of speech, as of action; a transcendentalist above all; a man of ideas and principles."[5]

Brown, a white abolitionist who attacked a federal arsenal, was considered notorious by much of white America for participating in the killing of white soldiers and attacking the principal supporter— the government—of slavery. Thoreau evinces a willingness to defy convention, popular preferences, and the instrumentality of law by sanctioning the use of civilian violence against reigning authority:

> The slave-ship is on her way, crowded with its dying victims . . . a small crew of slaveholders, countenanced by a large body of passengers, is smothering four millions under the hatches, and yet the politicians assert that the only proper way by which deliverance is to be obtained, is by the "quiet diffusion of the sentiments of humanity," without any "outbreak." As if the sentiments of humanity were ever found unaccompanied by its deeds, and you could disperse them, all finished to order, the pure article, as easily as water with a watering-pot, and so lay the dust. What is that I hear cast overboard? The bodies of the dead that have found deliverance. That is the way we are 'dif-fusing' humanity, and its sentiments with it.[6]

The absolutely murderous sentiments and acts of barbarity com-monly practiced by American slavers to maximize profit and create subservience among blacks were not the sort of character traits Thoreau believed were sufficiently condemned by discourse. Moreover, romantic notions of persons as subject to change without force would leave generations of victims to suffer.

Lydia Child (1802–1880), the noted abolitionist and suffragette, was hailed by the famous antislavery agitator William Lloyd Garrison as "the first woman in the republic."[7] The Radical Republican senator Charles Sumner credited her with inspiring his career as an advocate of racial equality; Samuel Jackson, an African American correspondent for the *Liberator,* proposed enshrining her alongside John Brown; suffragist Elizabeth Cady Stanton cited Child's encyclopedic *History of the Condition of Women* (1835) as an invaluable resource for feminists in their battle against patriarchy. Child's 1824 novel *Hobomok* included interracial marriage as a positive good. In so doing, she incensed liberal and conservative whites, despite her well-established reputation as an author and a journalist. In 1833, her literary reputation and her livelihood were sacrificed by publishing *An Appeal in Favor of That Class of Americans Called Africans*— continuing the approach to advocacy of Walker's *Appeal*—a sweeping indictment of slavery and racism that called for an end to all forms of discrimination, including antimiscegenation laws. After the Civil War, Child crusaded for black suffrage and land redistribution and designed a school reader for emancipated slaves; she campaigned against the dispossession and genocide of Native Americans, publicized the plight of the white urban poor, championed equal rights for women, and worked to promote religious tolerance and respect for non-Christian faiths. Child's life is indicative of what it is to engage in advocacy. Child knew that living by her principles would involve material losses, decline in social status, confrontation with established authority and opinion, and disadvantages to her family. When her sense of self-worth and respect as a principled person were measured and weighed against losses to others and to herself, surely there were reasons to avoid principles and actions for which there was little public support. Child, however, was dedicated to downtrodden and outcast groups that, like all the insurrectionists mentioned above, were groups understood as ontological entities and collectives of kinds (for example, Negroes, slaves, whites, women, and Native Americans).

Representative heuristics "involves the application of relatively simple resemblance or 'goodness of fit' criteria to problems of categorization. In making a judgment, people assess the degree to which the salient features of the object are representative of, or similar to, the features presumed to be characteristic of the category."[8] The use of representative heuristics is replete with inferential problems. There is a tendency to view outcomes as if they represented their origins (if a Chinese American is found guilty of a crime, for example, it's not unusual for persons to suppose that China itself is implicated); or to judge each individual instance as if it represents a category (thinking that each rose, for example, is an exemplar of all roses); or to judge antecedents as representatives of consequences (for example, if America caused the action and is assumed to be a moral nation, then the consequence of the action is assumed to bear the marks of a moral outcome).[9]

There are also forms of stereotyping associated with representative heuristics. Some of the classical ways that representative heuristics is used in relation to racial and ethnic stereotyping include metonymic displacement, metaphysical condensation, fetishistic categorizing, and dehistoricizing allegories that strip the racial or ethnic category from being understood as a historically changing group. Representative heuristics is often a way of reifying the subject.

One fallacy and common feature of representative heuristics deserving special attention is that more often than not we believe that acts and beliefs are "dispersed" within the category. That is, we have a tendency to believe that individual bad moral acts are members of the class of bad moral acts, and that if such acts are performed by a group member, other members are highly likely to so perform; each act is not only added to the aggregate number of bad moral acts in the moral universe but substantively influences that universe, that is, the universe is worse off, and each act influences that universe in a way that makes more such acts possible. Conversely, good acts add to the moral universe and will influence others (possibly because a good act adds to the aggregate and thus makes the good moral universe stronger, or in some amorphous world of consciousness, others will learn and be influenced by good acts).

We know that representative heuristics are faulty logical reasoning methods but that cognition is impossible without them, and they may not be, collectively, ineffective reasoning methods for the species. The naturalization of epistemology, at least the naturalization of this feature of how we understand reality, makes the idea of living "behind" reasoning impossible. In addition, the use of representative heuristic forms of cognition are not necessarily the source of ideations justifying or motivating oppression, although they can be major contributing factors. That is, it is not that the sheer existence of a necessary feature of what makes cognition possible is invariably a cause of oppression—a claim not even held by Derrida in *L'écriture et la différence*.[10] Rather, representative heuristics helps inform what sorts of categories we live through and how those categories inform our lived experience.

Insurrectionists were often against the imposition of conceptions of block universes, absolutes, and arid abstractions and against treating abstract social entities as stable categories. This is possible—self-identity as both transvaluing and representative of a kind—if the category that one understands oneself to be representing is a category that one is seeking to ultimately destroy. The deeply divided classes for Marx, the poor for Martin Luther King Jr., and the slaves for Walker are groups destined to go out of existence. For Alain Locke, limiting and provincial identities of segregated communities should, and would, succumb to a broader identity of humanity; a broader identity that would be mediated by local identities with much less meaning and stability than existed in human history. Walker, Marx, King, and Locke, however, saw themselves as representing groups that they hoped would go out of existence. Whether insurrectionists see themselves as representing a group that would eventually disappear, or whether they see themselves as representing the broad interest of humanity that should be used to end fractured or essentialized local groups, insurrectionists envision a world overcoming the very bounded local identities, categories, and kinds that they represent. In this sense, it is arguable that insurrectionists may very well stand against block universes, absolutes, arid abstractions, and stable categories. Yet, they promoted interests of narrowly defined categories, such as slaves, women, and natives. The world of limitation is replaced by a world with broader and more inclusive categories, for example, humanity, men and women, blacks and whites, and so on. But these categories are not without the same sort of problems associated with any category invested with ontological status to some degree.

Pragmatists have frequently cautioned against the use of representative heuristics, particularly the use of general categories as if they were ontological entities, such as class or nation. Pragmatists contend that arid abstractions, treated as if they were real beings, are misleading. We should use categories as heuristic tools to help us think about problems and not about stable essences. What Alain Locke termed our "invariable tendency to make categories into entities," or what William James held was treating abstractions as a block universe, is to be viewed with suspicion. Pragmatist social psychology holds that "we" categories are suspect, even if a necessary or integral feature of cognition.

There are numerous ways that one might define oneself. Livingston, for example, might be right in believing that James's conception of the subject is extremely radical and revolutionary because it offers a way of seeing the subject as always in formation.[11] Moreover, for Livingston, James's view of the subject requires that we move beyond traditional Western conceptions of the subject as either "real"—having objectively defined and limited traits—or "natural"—having traits solely shaped by limited historical experience. Moreover, Livingston may have a strong defense for a Jamesian subject, because he argues that pragmatists are indebted to the ideals of proprietary capitalism—particularly ideals of small communities and self-motivated, experimenting entrepreneurs.

Would a Jamesian subject feel compelled, against popular sentiment, to promote, organize, or encourage slave revolts and insurrections? Would such a subject organize slave escapes, knowing that they would need to kill Jim and Jane Crow slave-catchers and sellers of children, as well as cause the unintentional death of innocent bystanders? These are not the same sort of questions as "should Americans have participated in World War I or II," because insurrectionist actions are against established community consent (quite possibly democratically formed) and against established authority. Nor are they the same sort of questions as "should workers have participated in or supported the Chicago Haymarket riots," which erupted in an effort to promote an eight-hour working day. Although James in 1888 considered the riots senseless and anarchist, the rioters were not attempting to destroy a system of governance. Moreover, riots, organized and spontaneous, are important and influential features helping to create social change.[12]

Are the normative resources so deeply ingrained in classical pragmatism adequate? Is the category of *humanity* understood in a way that would justify radical action on behalf of the downtrodden, even if the consequences were likely to be harmful to the actors and others?

Contemporary forms of slavery, whether in Mauritania or southern Sudan, demand contemporary insurrectionists. In addition, they often require rejecting a commitment to one's own community and citizenship in favor of commitment to unknown persons. In America's racial slavery, slaves were seen as members of a separate human type and outside of the moral community established by whites. Commitment to such persons by whites was a commitment to people outside their community; so, too, for blacks who, in the early days of American slavery, frequently saw one another not as "black" but as strangers. It was not until the 1850s, for example, that blacks held "Negro only" conventions, and this was only after years of debate concerning whether it was justifiable to hold conventions organized by blacks for the purpose of establishing black organizations to promote racial uplift. Such organizations or meetings were considered anathema to the objective of ending slavery, racial segregation, and a race-conscious society. What resources are available in pragmatism that compels individuals to reject their own community, citizenship, and national allegiance to risk their lives for the well-being of strangers?

It will do no good to point to the accomplishments of Jane Addams and the Hull House any more than it will be convincing to point to the Paris Commune or the First International as adequate examples of how pragmatist or communist practice can be enriching. Where, for example, are the pragmatist insurgents against contemporary slavery or the indentured servitude of Philippine nurses in California? I know where the monks, nuns, liberation theologists, Buddhist altruists, and communists are located on the world historical stage as agents of insurrection—but it is not clear that pragmatists are on the world historical stage as insurrectionists *as a function of their pragmatism.* There are certainly persons who cite pragmatism as one philosophy central to their philosophic orientation. Cornel West, for example, is a self-described prophetic pragmatist. However, his insurrectionist morality is clearly a function of his radical socialism, left-Christian sensibilities, and African American traditions of resistance against slavery, racism, and exploitation. Certainly, John Dewey, Alain Locke, and Jane Addams held deep commitments to uplifting the downtrodden. My query is whether there exist features of pragmatism that require, as necessary conditions to be a pragmatist, support for participation in insurrection.

Possibly, Theodore Draper is right in his story of the American Revolution—the revolutionaries never intended to create a democracy.[13] Their intentions, quite like those of most advocates seeking greater spheres of power, authority, and the imposition of their wills against prevailing traditional, religious, and political practices, were not realized. As agents in violation of prevailing customs and laws, they failed to shape social consequences to match their intentions. Voting, for example, involving the participation of the citizenry unfettered by exclusions according to station was hardly intended. Women, nonwhites, and men of low station, such as indentured servants, were normally considered persons that should not be allowed to vote because of some inherent defect. Possibly, Theda Skocpol has a defensible view: Revolutionary theories purporting to predict outcomes based on scientific analysis of social conflict systemically fail in their predictions.[14] Her institutionalist, comparative-historical approach, rather than a Marxist class analysis, a rational choice approach, an interactionalist sociology, or an interpretative narrative, may very well prove a more effective account of revolution. Institutionalist accounts look at how rules and regulations shape behavior independent of the reasoning actions and behaviors of agents. Institutional rules and practices often generate results that have more to do with expectations and disappointments than models of change usually allow.

One reason an institutional account may prove more effective than its rivals is because it insists on an incongruity between explanations and predictions, intentions and outcomes. Yet, Skocpol is not blind to the radical changes in ways of living shaped by strong advocates and actors. There is at least accord between many competing explanations of revolution to some degree on the singular point of importance to my argument: Concrete predictions of revolutionary outcomes are rarely in accord with the intentions of revolutionaries, yet fundamental alteration of social structures does not occur without the concerted effort of individuals who see themselves as representative of a group intentionally trying to create a new world. There simply are no modern revolutions that did not include, if not decisively, at least in terms of important discourses, class conflict; no modern revolutions without conflicts over what rules should be followed; no modern revolutions in which intelligent plans and reasonable predictions were not nearly all wrong. Moreover, there are no revolutions or insurrections without representative heuristics, that is, without women who see themselves as representing "women" as an objective category; without persons who see themselves as representing the interests of the poor; without workers who see themselves as the embodiment of meritorious traits; without environmentalists who see themselves as pressing for the best interests of all sentient beings by pressing for the interests of environmentalists.

What are the pragmatist sources for justifying insurrection, given that the outcomes of insurrectionist action or support for such actions are not predictable, that the vast majority of insurrectionist actions and movements fail to liberate, and that contributions to liberating a population by insurrection or support for insurrection range from useless to tremendous? Instrumental and functional reasoning can be of limited value for predicting future events.

Insurrectionists normally believe that the outcome of their actions will lead to eventual success. Walker held the romantic belief that individuals and groups responsible for unjust acts would eventually be punished—if not while they were alive, at least in the next life.

Socialists normally believe that if not human nature then humanity's embedded sense of justice will incline people to favor greater income and ownership equity rather than less equity. Yet, income and ownership disparities have only increased over human history. Evolutionists and Marxists characteristically hold that antiquated forms of production will be replaced either because of a biologically driven tendency for populations to seek more effective and efficient control over reproduction or because conflicts tend to be resolved in favor of dialectically driven solutions. However, it is arguable that hope for ending the misery of existing generations is highly unlikely.

If an individual has no duty, from a pragmatist standpoint, to alleviate the existing misery of strangers, will that absence of action negatively influence that individual's flourishing and moral development? Assuming we have duties that are not contingent on the successful outcome of action nor on effective predictions of what will become successful, what duties are there from a pragmatist standpoint to overthrow slavery? No Americans had good reason to believe that their heroic acts to destroy slavery would, as an isolated set of acts, produce the desired results for themselves or for persons they loved. Nor had they any historical evidence to suggest that highly risky social acts would substantively encourage others to fight for abolition or result in successful outcomes.

The unpredictability of outcomes does not stand as a sufficient reason to defeat the justification that oppressed individuals or groups can offer for pursuing instrumentally useful paths. There is no human progress without the discord of social conflict, insurrections, and revolutions.[15] These are instrumental social actions. The outcomes are uncertain. Even if one is committed to an evolutionary view of change, there is no history of evolution without the history of insurrections, revolts, and revolutions. The uses of intelligence, dramatic rehearsal, dialogue, and discourse are hardly the sole modes through which institutions fundamentally change. As one author saw Dewey's views about revolution, "His theory could ride the crest of change but could not explain how such change might be initiated."[16] Moreover, even in Dewey's *Reconstruction in Philosophy*, there is no escaping the value of instrumental reasoning, although Dewey has numerous other reasoning techniques he promotes: "If ideas, meanings, conceptions, notions, theories, systems are instrumental to an active reorganization of the given environment, then the test of their validity and value lies in their accomplishing this work. If they succeed in this office, they are reliable, sound, valid, good, true. . . . Confirmation, corroboration, verification lie in works, consequences."[17] As I have argued, however, consequences and their predictions are not good criteria for justifying insurrection.

The range of sentiments that can work as means for defensible ends is hardly limited to the ones most appealing to Dewey, such as dialogue. Murder, pillage, and destroying the property of democratically supported governments have on occasion produced favorable consequences for some individuals and groups. The material and mental well-being of interested populations may also gain from such actions. To deny this would be like denying that evolution exists without conflict, parasites, or unanticipated consequences of intentional and unintentional action.

In Walkerian terms, what sort of slave, Christian, or republican is it that does not strike a blow for abolition? Slaves in nearly every society used a wide array of strategies to survive and resist. These strategies included, but were not limited to, infanticide, suicide, self-mutilation, poisonings of masters and their children, flight, marooning, arson, and revolt. What method is considered preferable is irrelevant to my argument. That the use of some methods of absolute destruction of slaveholders and the bonds of servitude, however, should be given meritorious ranking is a crucial feature of insurrectionist moral criteria. Moreover, advocacy representing, defending, or promoting in some form the liberation of self and other from bondage is a good that warrants special honorific status. Change may be best understood as irreversible, cumulative, and gradual. Change is not "one" phenomenon. It is a multitude of accidental, intentional, and unpredictable results. It does not happen, however, outside the context of insurrection—persons who want a different world and are willing to be insurrectionists of one form or another.

Advocates and advocacy, regardless of the goal or method used, are necessarily authoritarian but not necessarily dictatorial—advocacy presupposes that the advocate or what is being advocated should determine reality and that the advocates have a fundamentally advantageous viewpoint. Advocating is always expressed in an authoritative voice; advocates want their ideals to shape or become reality. Moreover, character traits of aggressiveness, self-assurance, sell-confidence, tenacity, irreverence, passion, and enmity are evinced and applauded by insurrectionists. Lydia Child and Maria Stewart were in no way passive in promoting women's suffrage, abolition, and racial equality. Nor did they believe that traits associated with aggressive behavior were traits best left to men. Such traits as benevolence, piety, temperance, compassion, self-assurance, and self-confidence were character virtues. That is, insurrectionists prescribed character traits that included traits associated with aggressive behavior for the downtrodden.[18]

John Diggins and Cornel West, for radically different reasons, recognize a serious lack in classical pragmatism: There seems no way to require advocacy and authoritarian moral voices.[19] West argues for a sense of the prophetic, particularly a Christian-inspired visionary leadership with an optimistic approach to the future as an authoritarian voice. It is the prophetic, rather than an evasion of philosophy as belief in that which cannot be established through the aegis of reason, that West considers important for our web of beliefs. Diggins, a critic of pragmatism in this regard, argues that pragmatism lacks the resources to justify the need for democratic institutional authority.

Is it the case that pragmatists see the self as necessarily lacking if it is bereft of such traits as aggression, self-assurance, self-confidence, tenacity, and irreverence? Are self-deprecators not just instrumentally and functionally disadvantaged but in some sense morally lacking? It is certainly the case that self-deprecators could live more fulfilling lives if they had a greater sense of self-worth. But what principle or conception of fulfilling lives is there in pragmatism that says we are compelled to act in ways that prevent people from living self-deprecating lives? Walker describes the wretchedness of the slave in terms that make one feel that such a condition violates basic human nature. Normal life for Walker should include the possibility of accumulating assets, transferring assets to one's progeny, loving one's mate, and freely selling the product of one's labor. Are these endogenous to a pragmatist conception of the self such that if others lack such desires or the means to carry them out, pragmatists are duty bound to seek their liberation? If self-deprecators do use the method of intelligence and remain self-deprecators, are we duty bound to nonetheless change the conditions under which they labor, for example, change the conditions of poverty from which voluntary slaves do not seek to escape?

Evaluating processes, means, ends, and reflective considerations—the basic features of Dewey's method of intelligence—is no surety against someone's being a racist. Racism is not inherently a set of propositions that are internally contradictory.[20] It is arguable that the method of intelligence so frequently applauded by Dewey as a reasoning strategy, joined with the objective of socially engineering progress and increasing democratic participation, was useless during the era of America's racial slavery. The persons empowered to engage in social engineering favored slavery; persons invested with the education capable of appreciating the subtleties of Dewey's method were often proslavery; and Americans practiced one of the highest levels of democratic participation in human history, and the majority were in favor of slavery. As Orlando Paterson argues, societies that favor democratic freedom have been societies that characteristically practiced slavery.[21] Lives of millions were destroyed as abolitionists engaged in debates and protest. Abolitionists that promoted or helped persons escape the horrible trade could more often than not count actual lives saved—all such persons acted against extant law and popular authority. That is, the immediate lives of the enslaved were not changed by dialogue, debate, democratic voting, or petitions—such actions helped to eventually end slavery and certainly helped abate the misery that slaves might have suffered if not for the tempering norms influencing slaveholders and their friends. The point is that pregnant women, children, old men, and young men were lynched, beaten, raped, threatened, and coerced while the world of relatively civil abolitionist discourse and protest occurred.

In America's advanced capitalist society, democracy works without centralized planning to effectively exclude and exploit while allowing open political participation. Corporations and rich families can accumulate vast sums of capital and enormous profits. Many personal life choices are open to them. Those who own little to nothing have their choices and employment options, by contrast, severely restricted. The city and the country, if Rabin's *Soft City* is at all near to being an appropriate picture, are spaces in which there are hundreds of overlapping locations of authority and no single entity capable of planning, implementing, or controlling social experiments or policies.[22]

Of what use is a "method of intelligence" in a postmodern society where very few persons are motivated by a desire to socially engineer society to enhance everyone's well-being? Of what use is the method of intelligence in a society where the misery of noncitizens is considered of little consequence, although the profit of citizens is contingent on expropriating the wealth of noncitizens? Without the self that James, Dewey, Locke, and Addams seem to presuppose—a self that is already motivated to desire the well-being of others—is there any reason to suppose that the method of intelligence would incline anyone to be motivated to seek the abolition of slavery through insurrection or seek the end of servitude, if it required a commitment to an ontological or an heuristic category (i.e., moral commitment to a group of strangers)?

Commitment to humanity is always a commitment to some group of humans first and always requires the use of representative heuristics. That is, it requires us to do just what good reasoning methods tell us to avoid—treat groups as if they were real ontological entities. Moreover, commitment to improving the condition of humanity requires that persons share meager resources with strangers and take personal risk they could well avoid. What, then, are the intuitive motivations, guidances, and criteria for pragmatists that require them, as pragmatists, to advocate insurrection, to help destroy realms of viciousness, the trade in land mines, proliferation of nuclear weapons, tremendous expropriation of wealth from less-developed countries to wealthy Western nations, the sale and use of life-destroying drugs among adults and children, forced prostitution, and the selling of stolen babies and body parts?

If the advice a pragmatist would give to persons in a society of racial slavery did not include insurrection and honor for those engaged in insurrection—if no more than as a form of self-defense—

then pragmatism's penchant for prudence and dialogue is sufficient to suggest that pragmatism is woefully inadequate. Moreover, if there are no resources in pragmatism to motivate and encourage persons to be insurrectionists, it is defective. The metaphorical reincarnation of Walkerian character traits are appealing—tenacity, irreverence, aggressiveness, self-assurance, self-confidence, tenacity, enmity, and passion—because they help make possible the sort of advocacy and authoritarian voices that demand liberation of the enslaved. The moral sensibilities of insurrectionists, including a willingness to lend support or act when consequences are likely to be unfavorable in the immediate future, disadvantageous for individual actors, and contrary to popular beliefs and practices, are important sources of motivation for insurrectionists. An insurrectionist would desire the destruction of oppression and would have a willingness to work through the enmity of irreconcilable differences. Advocates for change use authoritarian voices often representing abstract social entities, entities excluded from dominant moral communities.

Achieving the possibility of honor for communities or for members of communities is contingent on facing the reality of advocacy and authority enlivened by insurrectionist moral sensibilities and character traits. Moreover, the reality of representative heuristics should not be understood as inherently unfortunate features of cognition, always associated with misguided, arid abstractions. Rather, a philosophy such as Walker's that makes representing, defending, and promoting the well-being of a community because that community's human rights have been violated is preferable to one that makes such commitments suspect.

NOTES

Portions of this paper were used in "Revolutionary Pragmatism," the Dotter Lecture, Pennsylvania State University, March 1966.

1. For an example of the vast variety of slave revolts, see Joseph C. Carroll, *Slave Insurrections in the United States, 1800–1865* (New York: Negro University Press, 1938).

2. Maria Stewart, "Lecture Delivered at the Franklin Hall, Boston, September 21, 1832," in *Philosophy Born of Struggle,* ed. Leonard Harris (Dubuque: Kendall Hunt, 1999), 34.

3. Henry D. Thoreau, *Civil Disobedience and Other Essays*, (New York: Dover, 1993).

4. Thoreau, *Civil Disobedience*, 26.

5. Thoreau, *Civil Disobedience*, 33.

6. Thoreau, *Civil Disobedience*, 39.

7. *A Lydia Maria Child Reader*, ed. Carolyn L. Karcher (Durham: Duke University Press, 1997), p. 1. Also see *The First Woman in the Republic* (Durham: Duke University Press, 1994), ed. Carolyn L. Karcher.

8. Richard Nisbett, Lee Ross, Daniel Kahneman, and Amos Tversky, "Judgmental Heuristics and Knowledge Structures," in *Naturalizing Epistemology*, ed. Hilary Kornblith (Cambridge: MIT Press, 1985), p. 195. Also see Richard E. Nisbett and Lee Ross, *Human Inference* (Englewood Cliffs: Prentice-Hall, 1980).

9. See discussion of the judgment of the degree to which outcomes are representative of their origin, judgments of the degree to which instances are representative of categories, and judgments of the degree to which antecedents are representative of consequences, in Daniel Kahneman, Paul Slovic, and Amos Tversky, eds., *Judgment under Uncertainty* (Cambridge: Cambridge University Press, 1982).

10. Jacques Derrida, *L'écriture et la différence* (Paris: Editions du Seuil, 1967).

11. James Livingston, *Pragmatism and the Political Economy of Cultural Revolution, 1850–1940* (Chapel Hill: University of North Carolina Press, 1994).

12. See John P. Diggins, "Pragmatism: A Philosophy for Adults Only," *Partisan Review* 66, no. 21 (spring 1999), 255–61.

13. See Theodore Draper, *The Struggle for Power* (New York: Times Books/Random House, 1996).

14. See Theda Skocpol, *States and Social Revolution* (Cambridge: Cambridge University Press, 1979), and *Social Revolutions in the Modern World* (Cambridge: Cambridge University Press, 1994).

15. For an argument against the idea of evolutionary social change without revolution, see my "Response to a Conversation: Richard Rorty," *Sapina: A Bulletin of the Society for African Philosophy in North America* 8, no. 3 (1995), 14–15.

16. Richard Crockatt, "John Dewey and Modern Revolutions," in *Real*, vol. 7, ed. H. Grabes, H. Diller, and H. Isemhagen (Denmark: Gunter Narr Verlag Tubingen, 1990), 218.

17. John Dewey, *Reconstruction in Philosophy* (1948; Boston: Beacon Press, 1963), 128.

18. See Elizabeth Fox-Genovese, *Within the Plantation Household: Black and White Women of the Old South* (Chapel Hill: University of North Carolina Press, 1988).

19. John P. Diggins, *The Promise of Pragmatism* (Chicago: University of Chicago Press, 1994); Cornel West, *The American Evasion of Philosophy* (Madison: University of Wisconsin Press, 1989).

20. See David Goldberg, "Racism and Rationality: The Need for a New Critique," *Philosophy of Social Science* 20, no. 3 (summer 1990), 317–50, for an argument that racism need not violate the canons of formal logic and that it might rely on available facts as advocated by normal science. There are normative reasons to be against racism, but I doubt that any reasoning method invariably leads to such norms.

21. Orlando Paterson, *Freedom* (New York: Basic Books, 1991).

22. Jonathan Raban, *Soft City* (London: Hamilton, 1974); also see Leonard Harris, "Postmodernism and Racism: An Unholy Alliance," in *Racism, the City and the State,* ed. Michael Cross and Michael Keith (London: Routledge, 1993), 31–44.

Index

John Howie, a professor emeritus of philosophy at Southern Illinois University Carbondale, received his Ph.D. degree from Boston University. He is the author of *Perspectives for Moral Decisions*, the editor of *Ethical Principles for Social Policy* and *Ethical Principles and Practice*, and the coeditor of *Contemporary Studies in Philosophical Idealism*, *Ethical Issues in Contemporary Society*, and *The Wisdom of William Ernest Hocking*.